AUTHOR	CLASS
RIDEN, P.	A01

TITLE

Record sources for local history

Record Sources for Local History

Record Sources for Local History

Philip Riden

B. T. Batsford Ltd · London

© Philip Riden 1987
First published 1987

Typeset by Progress Typesetting Ltd
and printed in Great Britain by
Billings Ltd Worcester

Published by B. T. Batsford Ltd
4 Fitzhardinge Street, London W1H OAH

British Library Cataloguing in Publication Data
Riden, Philip

Record sources for local history.
1. England—History, Local—Information services
2. England—History, Local—Bibliography
I. Title
942'.007   DA1

ISBN 0 7134 4726 5

CONTENTS

PREFACE

The idea for this book came to me as I was moving along the shelves of the Round Room at the Chancery Lane branch of the Public Record Office, looking for topographical indexes in which to search for the name of 'Chesterfield', on the history of which I was then working. It occurred to me that many other people must do much the same sort of thing, both there and at Kew, and that a guide to classes of the public records which can be searched reasonably expeditiously and profitably for local studies might be useful. This is hardly the function of the PRO's own *Guide*, although some of the excellent series of leaflets on particular topics are aimed at the local historian, nor did any of the existing textbooks seem to provide as much detailed advice as they might for those visiting the PRO for the first time. A book of this kind should probably also describe material in local record offices, I felt, although this ground has been covered before on several occasions.

The end-result of this scheme, happily accepted by the publishers of my earlier introductory handbook for local historians, is presented here. It is improbable that every relevant class of document, whether in a local office or a national repository, has been included but I have tried to cover as many as possible within the space available, concentrating on those which have not attracted much attention hitherto and dealing more briefly with better known topics. I have also tried to be explicitly practical, identifying published finding-aids and adding a few comments from personal experience as to the usefulness of some of the material.

Inevitably, a book like this must draw heavily on the advice and assistance of colleagues with a wider knowledge than I of parts of the lengthy period covered here. I am greatly indebted to Dr Anthony Johnson for his comments on the two early modern chapters and to Dr John Blair for help with the middle ages. Dr Clive Knowles not only generously spared time to read and discuss the medieval chapter but also suggested changes to Chapter 1 which improved the overall structure of the book. Amongst library colleagues, Tom Dawkes and Brian James have both been extremely helpful in locating bibliographical references; both Mr James and Dr Gwynfor Jones have also clarified a number of points concerning Welsh material. The book could not have been written at all without the customary generous and courteous assistance of staff at the PRO, especially David Crook at Chancery Lane, while for local material I am indebted, as on so many previous occasions, to the perceptive comments of an experienced county archivist, Dudley Fowkes (Staffordshire), and also those of Christopher and Margaret Whittick (East Sussex). Several government departments and other public bodies have kindly responded to specific enquiries about their records.

My greatest debt is both conventional and slightly unusual. When I undertook to write this book I was unmarried and customarily worked a seven-day week. Following an unexpected piece of good fortune I reduced this to five. Various consequences have ensued, including the need to seek the publishers' indulgence in allowing additional time to complete the book. Above all, however, Elizabeth has had to experience one of the less attractive sides of marriage to a university teacher as pressure has built up on both of us as the book approached completion. I am therefore more than usually indebted to her for support and encouragement.

PHILIP RIDEN
Cardiff, April 1986

Chapter One
RECORDS AND RECORD OFFICES

This is not another general guide to sources for local history, nor an introduction to the subject for beginners. Up-to-date books of both kinds already exist and need not be duplicated.[1] Rather it is intended as a guide to one particular area of source material, setting out what is available, where it is likely to be found and what finding-aids exist to assist its exploitation.

The title clearly requires some definition, since it is not intended to refer merely to documents normally found in a local record office. Had I confined my attention solely to material of this kind the book could have claimed little novelty or usefulness. But records in local custody represent only a small part of the United Kingdom's uniquely rich archival heritage, while one of the most important features of the administrative structure which has evolved since the early middle ages and created such wealth is the close connection between central government and the localities. At no time since 1066 have local communities been entirely free from central control, even if the nature and degree of regulation have varied over the centuries. The archival consequences of this are obvious: any study of a community, at whatever date, must make use of documents created both centrally and locally. Since this book is intended for users, rather than custodians, of records, its scope thus extends beyond the contents of a county record office or similar repository. 'Record sources' included here are, broadly, those which relate to the history of a local community, whether originally created locally or centrally and irrespective of where they are now preserved. The word 'record' itself has been used in the sense normal in modern archival practice to mean material, whether manuscript, printed or reproduced by some other means, created through administrative as well as judicial activity, including both private and public administration.[2]

Inevitably these definitions require further qualification, since the 'history of a local community' can embrace a remarkably wide range of topics. In particular, many records of value to local historians are of equal interest to genealogists, some of whom may find this book of use. Genealogy, however, even when disguised as 'family history', is not the same as local history and its practitioners consult sources some of which will only occasionally be of wider application. This kind of material has not been included here and thus, for example, I have made no mention of the use of service records for tracing the careers of sailors, soldiers or airmen. Similarly, if one wishes to pursue a local resident who happens also to have been, say, a leading politician, civil servant or colonial administrator, it will be necessary to use the records of such departments as the Cabinet Office, Foreign Office or Colonial Office which in general contain nothing of local interest.

There is also the question of geographical scope. Today, the United Kingdom comprises four main elements – England, Wales, Scotland and Northern Ireland. The last two have been excluded entirely, since in each case a different administrative and judicial history have produced quite separate archives. For the same reason the Isle of Man and Channel Islands are omitted. That leaves 'England and Wales' or, as it was generally known until recently, 'England'. Although Wales has been wholly subject to the dominion of the English crown since the reign of Edward I, the country retained a separate administrative structure until the mid-sixteenth century. The Act of Union of 1536, followed by a second statute in 1543, established a system of local government identical to that in England, the only institutional difference being the existence in twelve of the thirteen Welsh counties of a court of Great Sessions in place of assize sittings (p. 71). When these courts were abolished in 1830 there was little, if anything, to distinguish Welsh administration from English. But the situation soon changed: as early as 1844 the management of main roads in South Wales was placed on a different footing from the rest of the country (p. 139), while in 1889 separate provision was made for secondary education in Wales (p. 143). The establishment of an autonomous Welsh Department of the Board of Education in 1907 was followed by the appointment of separate National Insurance Commissioners (1911), which led directly to the setting-up of the Welsh Board of Health in 1920, coincidentally the year in which the Anglican Church in Wales was disestablished. Since then, especially since 1964, when the first Secretary of State for Wales was appointed, there have been distinct differences between Welsh and English administration.

The archival legacy of administrative devolution, coming after three centuries of almost complete integration, are complex. In some cases, Welsh records are identical in form to those in England but generally less well preserved. In others, there are significant variations. However, while local record keeping in Wales has evolved on somewhat different lines from England (p. 17), records relating to Wales in central custody are mostly at the Public Record Office, whereas the records of Scotland have always been kept in Edinburgh. Similarly, the parliament at Westminster has generally legislated for England and Wales together, whereas, even since 1707, Scotland has tended to be provided for separately. For these reasons, Wales has been included here, with variations from English conditions explained as necessary.

The other omission is London. The institutional differences between the capital and even the largest of the provincial cities are so great, at all periods, that to have included London records would have greatly lengthened the book, since so many statements applicable to the rest of the country would have required qualification.

Most of the discussion so far has been concerned with records created in the course of public administration and it will be clear from the contents page that much of the book is about documents of this kind. In fact, a closer examination of the subheadings within each chapter shows that the records of the Church of England are also included, although dealt with comparatively briefly, not least because so much has already been written on the subject. But what of the the records of landownership, business, politics, other religious organisations and voluntary bodies of all kinds?

The reason why such documents appear only incidentally is that, very often, it is difficult to add to what will be self-evident to most readers, or to what has been said elsewhere. In the case of family and estate muniments, investigators will either already know what sort of documents make up such collections, or can obtain the information from my previous book, which also suggests how one can go about locating the records of a particular estate.[3] If enquiries at a local record office prove fruitless, the next step will often be to consult the Historical Manuscripts Commission, which, in conjunction with the National Register of Archives housed at its offices, is usually the best source of information as to the whereabouts of private papers of any kind.[4] Large quantities of estate records are, of course, to be found in the PRO, for various reasons, and these are mentioned in the appropriate section of each chapter here.

Local historians interested in trade, industry or communications will likewise appreciate that businesses create records, although they should understand that such documents are far less well preserved than muniments of title or other estate papers. Nor is it necessary to state the obvious by suggesting that enquiries should normally begin at the local record office for the area in which the company in which one is interested operated. I have also explained elsewhere the need to think of alternative sources, rather than business records, from which one can write business history, not least the personal papers of partners or directors, which may again be located with the help of the HMC. In addition, the Commission has recently compiled an index of company names from NRA lists, which should help considerably in locating migrant records.[5] Other sources are preserved amongst the records of central government, as a result either of the increasing regulation to which most kinds of private enterprise have been subject over the last century or so, or the nationalisation of large sectors of industry after 1945. Records of this kind are discussed in Chapter 6 (pp. 172-4), while Chapter 5 (p. 159) has a short section outlining material arising from 'municipal trading' in the nineteenth century, the origin in part of the modern fuel utilities and local bus undertakings.

A third type of record which falls outside the main plan of this guide are those created by religious denominations other than the Church of England, except for material resulting from contacts between such organisations and the state. Enquiries at record offices concerning nonconformist and Roman Catholic archives may be fruitless, since some of the free churches have a policy of centralising their records while the Roman Catholic church retains its own material in each diocese. The best advice that can be offered is probably to check what, if anything, survives in the hands of a particular denomination locally or in the appropriate record office and then to consult W.B. Stephens's thorough discussion of this topic, which gives details of specialist repositories.[6]

The position in Wales in this case is particularly depressing, given the importance of protestant nonconformity in that country's recent history. As chapels have closed most records seem to have been destroyed and the holdings of both local offices and the National Library are very limited. The NLW has secured recognition as the official repository for records of the Presbyterian Church of Wales (formerly the Calvinistic Methodists) but this example has not been followed by other denominations. The main collection of Welsh Quaker archives, mostly relating to the south-east of the country, is in the Glamorgan Record Office, while the two Roman Catholic sees, Menevia, covering north and west Wales, whose bishop is seated at Wrexham, and Cardiff, the seat of an archbishop who has both metropolitan and diocesan jurisdiction, retain their own records. The archives of the Church in Wales, since 1920 an independent province within the Anglican communion, are discussed in later chapters alongside those of the Church of England.

Investigators interested in local trade unions, friendly societies or similar voluntary organisations which flourished in many nineteenth-century communities may also be disappointed with the outcome of local searches. Most repositories have some trade union material, either the records of local branches of a national organisation deposited after the closure of the branch or, less commonly, the archives of a local union now merged into a larger body. Some local trades council archives have also been deposited. Much, however, has clearly been lost, as branches of unions in declining industries have been wound up and no thought given to the preservation of records. The two main central collections of trade union and employer association records are at Warwick University and Nuffield College, Oxford.[7] Proportionately less survives from the vast number of friendly societies, savings banks, co-operative societies and the like which have now passed out of existence or merged into national organisations. Local record offices may have some material but the main source will often be the files on each society maintained by the Registry of Friendly Societies (which includes trade unions and other bodies), described in

Chapter 6, where the somewhat similar records of the Charity Commission are also mentioned (pp. 177-9).

The archives of local branches of the major political parties still appear mainly, where anything survives, to be in the custody of constituency parties or associations. The central records of the Conservative Party are in the Bodleian Library, Oxford, but these do not include local material. The Labour Party archives at its headquarters (150 Walworth Road, SE17) are accessible and the party has a policy of encouraging branches to preserve material. This has involved some measure of centralization and also deposits in local record offices.[8]

For the South Wales coalfield, a project based at University College, Swansea, in the 1970s sought to salvage documents, artefacts, printed books and oral recollections at a time when all were threatened by the run-down of local industry. This led to the establishment of the South Wales Miners' Library, whose archive holdings now form part of the collections of the college library and are much richer than comparable holdings in the local authority repositories in the region.[9]

An organisation with close links with both the trade union movement and the Labour Party is the Workers' Educational Association, the largest of the voluntary bodies in adult education, which works through a structure of regional offices and local branches, the latter staffed by voluntary officials. Surviving records at local level are probably still in the association's own hands, while information from this source can be supplemented for the inter-war period by Board of Education files now transferred to the PRO (p. 151).

One could extend this survey of the records of 'other' organisations (i.e. those which are not part of central or local government or the Church of England) almost indefinitely but in most cases the advice would be the same. If there is no material relating to a particular estate, family, business, church, trade union, club or whatever in the local record office then it may be worth contacting the organisation direct, possibly first discussing the matter with the archivist to see if anyone has made similar enquiries before and with what result. It is also important to remember that some parts of the country are served by more than one repository and that documents of a similar kind (even from the same source) may have ended up in any or all of them (cf. pp. 16-19). For certain classes of record the Historical Manuscripts Commission may be able to help and in a few cases the local archives of private organisations may have been transferred to a central repository. Another possibility, which is still all too common with much material of interest to local historians, is that the documents one is looking for are in the hands of a private individual who may be reluctant to admit even to their existence, much less allow use of them. This can be true not merely of the records of organisations mentioned in this section but also, admittedly less often, with Church and local government records. Under present legislation, there is usually little one can do in such situations except appeal to a collector's sense of public responsibility or, if that fails (as it usually does), keep a close eye on the death notices in the local paper.

A senior official of the Public Record Office has recently made a brave effort to set out the legislative provisions relating to archives in the United Kingdom so as to give the present situation the semblance of a policy, such as one finds in most European countries. An equally senior academic has also recently used the word 'anarchy' in discussing record keeping in this country, in an article dismissed by Mr Knightbridge as 'superficial'.[10] Few would suggest, however, that the unparalleled wealth of Britain's archives is matched by the quality of arrangements for their custody and study, at least at local level.

Public interest in the preservation of records dates, in roughly its present form, from the early nineteenth century, when a series of royal commissions was appointed to survey archives both in London and the provinces and to publish texts and calendars of some of the most important documents. The public records had, of course, been used by historians long before this and the official printing of records may be said to date from 1783, with the production of a remarkable edition of Domesday Book that has never been superseded.[11] The ad hoc work of the Record Commission was followed by the setting-up in 1838 of the Public Record Office, which gradually established itself as the repository to which all the records of the central courts and departments of state should be brought, including some (for example from the Welsh Great Sessions or the palatinate courts) which had traditionally been stored outside London. The PRO also took over the commission's work of editing and publication, establishing by the end of the nineteenth century the main series of lists, indexes and calendars which remain fundamental to the use of the medieval (and in some cases later) material at the office.[12]

After the second world war, the balance of the PRO's holdings shifted away from the records of the central courts and the State Paper Office towards documents transferred from the newer departments. This brought pressure on the office's resources from greatly increased numbers of readers who felt the PRO's traditional publishing policy offered them little and, particularly in the 1960s, found it difficult even to find a seat in the search-room.[13] More recent changes have much improved the situation. The transfer of departmental records to Kew now means that neither branch of the office is normally overcrowded; a programme of refurbishment at Chancery Lane has made the older building far more pleasant for both staff and readers; and the removal of the census enumerators' books to a special branch reading room (and, more fundamentally, their acquisition on microfilm by local libraries and record offices) has relieved a major source of discontent. The PRO has directed more editorial effort towards modern records, while readers themselves, assisted by PRO staff, have established the List & Index Society, which has made available cheap reproductions of search-room finding-aids, concentrating on classes outside the scope of the older *Lists and Indexes*.[14]

Another important aspect of the office's work in recent years has been the attention given to records created by government organisations other than the main departments of state. In some cases this has merely involved the recognition of other premises as approved repositories, allowing, for example, the Charity Commission to retain records at their own offices while ensuring the files are open to the public after 30 years. On the other hand, material has reached Kew from a number of bodies which considerably widens the scope of the PRO's modern holdings.

The department today operates under two main statutes, the Public Records Acts of 1958 and 1967, of which the former, based on the recommendations of the Grigg Committee of 1954, is the more important.[15] Essentially, documents deemed to be public records, including not only those created by central government and the superior courts of law but also, for example, those of such local courts as quarter sessions, petty sessions and those held by coroners, become available to the public 30 years from the date of their creation. This period may be extended in the case of records concerned with national security or other sensitive matters; it may also be shortened and there is now a considerable quantity of material at Kew less than 30 years old readily available to readers. Criticism of the Public Records Acts in recent years has centred mainly on the way in which record-creating departments, assisted and advised by the PRO, select documents for preservation in the first place. This concern led to the appointment of a committee chaired by Sir Duncan Wilson, which reported in 1981, whose recommendations, wherever they involved additional expenditure, the government has largely ignored.[16]

This controversy only marginally affects those who use the PRO for local studies. Neither at Chancery Lane or Kew (or even, for that matter, at the Census Reading Room at Portugal Street) should local historians find any reason to be dissatisfied with the service. The interest of nineteenth-century antiquaries in topography and genealogy led to the production of numerous lists of the older records which include the county to which a particular piece relates, while other classes are indexed by name. Much effort has gone into making available the records of the most important of the pre-1858 probate courts, with the registered wills now produced without delay on microfilm (p. 81). At Kew, most of the classes of likely interest to local historians have detailed lists, many of which have been published by the List & Index Society. Even the Record Users' Group, a body dominated by local, especially genealogical, interests, has found little to complain about recently, preferring to direct its fire at the more vulnerable target of the Registrar General (p. 119).

It is with record-keeping in the localities, which concerns local historians more directly, that there is currently much dissatisfaction, especially in some parts of the country. The two root causes of the problem are, one feels, the weak legislative framework within which repositories operate and the greatly increased pressure placed on record offices in the last ten years, which has coincided with a period of financial stringency and two attempts, neither wholly successful, to reorganise local government.

Although there were occasional suggestions in the nineteenth century that certain records, for example parish registers, should be collected into a central repository, the present pattern of local archive services has developed essentially from the establishment of county and county borough councils in 1888 (pp. 87, 130). The former inherited records from the court of quarter sessions while many of the larger towns engaged editors to publish texts of their charters and other records around the turn of the century. The earliest county record offices were established in Bedfordshire and Essex after the first world war, with the archivist located in the clerk's department, an idea gradually adopted by more counties and a few boroughs. Legislation in the 1920s enabled local repositories to be approved as places for the deposit of manorial documents (which in practice brought in other estate muniments as well) and to be appointed as diocesan record offices, where not merely diocesan but also parochial and other local church records might be deposited. After 1945 almost all English county councils established archive services until, on the eve of the 1972 reform, only the West Riding had not done so. On the other hand, although by this date county record offices formed a network covering virtually the whole country, there were numerous other repositories collecting local documents, including city record offices, the archive departments of county borough libraries, the reference or local studies sections of smaller libraries, museums, a few of the county antiquarian societies, and several universities.[17]

The 1972 Act divided local government outside London and the metropolitan counties between county and district councils, abolishing county boroughs and also the distinctions between different types of county district. The Act confirmed existing practice in conferring archive responsibilities on counties rather than districts, but there has been no judicial interpretation of ss. 224-229 of the Act to test the belief of some archivists that districts and parishes may not retain any documents beyond those needed for current administration, unless they have received dispensation under the Local Government (Records) Act, 1962, to run an archive service. A few districts have been so licensed since 1974 by the Secretary of State for the Environment but others either maintain a record office or at least possess large numbers of documents which they cannot possibly need for everyday use. District councils may in any case collect archives as part of a museum service. On the other hand, the Act removed library powers from districts (except for four special cases in South Wales) and this has enabled some archivists to extricate manuscript material from unsatisfactory surroundings in old borough libraries.[18]

The provisions of the 1972 Act concerning the six metropolitan counties are widely accepted to have worked badly; unfortunately, as far as archives are concerned, there is little reason to believe that the new arrangements, embodied in the Local Government Act, 1985, which came into effect on 1 April 1986, will be any improvement. In five of the counties the county council established a record office, alongside old established former borough libraries, all of which had traditionally collected documents as well as books. The West Midlands MCC, however, was never convinced of the need to provide an archive service and the districts were left to manage as best they could.[19] The other areas now face a similar future, unless the districts can be persuaded to combine to provide (or retain) a joint service. Since all have libraries with archive collections (but not all with archivists), this seems unlikely.

The situation in Wales requires special explanation, mainly because of the existence of the Department of Manuscripts and Records of the National Library of Wales, which collects material from all thirteen historic Welsh counties and whose holdings of family and estate records are especially strong. The department is in addition the only recognised repository for the provincial, diocesan, capitular and archdiaconal records of the Church in Wales, although the Llandaff chapter act books are in the Glamorgan Record Office. Until 1976 it was also the only approved repository for the ecclesiastical records of Welsh parishes, many of which have since been deposited in local authority offices (p. 94). The history of the department since its establishment in 1907 demonstrates all the strengths and weaknesses of central, as opposed to local, custody of local records.[20] A large amount of material is available under one roof alongside a fine reference collection, where it is cared for by high calibre professional staff spared the frustrations of working in local government; the collections are fully catalogued and reprographic facilities are comprehensive. Against this must be set the difficulty of access, since Aberystwyth is a hundred miles fom the main concentration of population in South Wales, with no reasonable public transport. Perhaps more serious is the effect of the department in draining away from local hands documents that in England would be in a county office. This, combined with the small size of most Welsh counties before 1974, discouraged several from even establishing an archive service. The National Library provided shelter for some material from these counties but could hardly provide a full service on an agency basis.

The reorganisation of local government in Wales essentially involved the amalgamation of the rural counties into larger units and the division of Glamorgan into three; Monmouthshire merely suffered minor boundary changes and acquired a new name. Dyfed, Gwynedd and Clwyd all operate archive services from more than one centre, with offices in each of the historic county towns, while Powys has continued the policy of its predecessors (Brecknock, Radnor and Montgomery) of not providing an archive service. Although the county has now appointed an archivist, who has taken some documents into custody, he has as yet few resources and no staff. In Glamorgan the three successor county councils agreed to maintain a joint service based on the existing Glamorgan Record Office in Cardiff. Hopes for a unified service, however, have been frustrated by the establishment of a record office by Swansea City Council (without authority under the 1962 Act from the Secretary of State and despite the existence of a branch repository in the city of the county service) and by the continued retention of manuscript material in Cardiff Central Library, notwithstanding the unsatisfactory physical conditions, lack of archive trained staff and a decision by South Glamorgan County Council to transfer such material to the archive service.

There is nothing in the sketchy statutory framework within which record offices operate either to control the proliferation of repositories or to enforce a minimum standard of service. Local historians whose work takes them mainly to one office may find little to complain about; those who use a number of places will have their own private league table of the good, the mediocre and the best avoided. When users complain about the deteriorating quality of service archivists normally point to cuts in local government expenditure and the increased burden placed on them by the growth of interest in genealogy. These are valid points but the profession seems less inclined to explain why, for example, it is necessary for public funds to provide three separate repositories in the comparatively small city of Swansea or why it was necessary in 1974 to establish a new South Yorkshire Record Office less than a mile from a city library archive department of international standing. If local record keeping could be reorganised on the basis of provision by a single authority in each county or metropolitan district the savings in staff and premises would, I suspect, enable those offices which survived such inconceivable trauma to offer a much better service.

The fullest guide to the multiplicity of repositories which now exists is that compiled by Janet Foster and Julia Sheppard, which includes most, if not all, the places a local historian is likely to visit.[21] I have assumed readers will use their book alongside this one, since it is obviously impossible to include here detailed references to the whereabouts of each office, nor details of published guides to their contents. Indeed, one of the problems of writing any general manual for local historians is the sheer diversity of experience in different parts of the country. Not only does the structure of record keeping vary, especially in the larger towns and in Wales, but so does the survival and, in some cases, creation of local records. Some investigators will discover that circumstances in their county differ from the general pattern, that documents I have referred to do not exist for their community, or that there is some valuable local source which I have not mentioned. There is no absolute defence to criticism of this kind: one cannot include every peculiarity and few, if any, local historians can claim a detailed knowledge of every county. Some of what appears here is inevitably coloured by my own experience of conditions in the East Midlands and South Wales, together with knowledge gleaned from colleagues elsewhere and published work on other regions.

Where it is possible to provide advice of more general value is in discussing sources at the PRO. It may be objected that the book would have been better described as a guide to local material in central custody, since much of the text is devoted to this subject. That, however, would miss the point that central and local sources must be viewed together as two aspects of a single process. Just as one cannot fully understand local administration without knowing something of the general framework within which it operated, so it is impossible to view the history of local communities purely from the centre, without seeing how policy was executed locally.

I have taken the realistic view, based on personal experience, that the extent to which any set of records relating to the entire country is worth searching for local references is largely a function of their arrangement and the nature of the available finding-aids. I have therefore tried to make sensible suggestions as to which classes can be searched most usefully for particular persons or places. Where appropriate, these comments are coupled to details of published lists, whether these are to be found in the old PRO *Lists and Indexes,* the volumes of the List & Index Society or elsewhere. There are also cross-references to the major series of PRO 'green calendars' and Record Commission volumes.[22] It should be stressed, however, that this book has not been compiled merely from published finding-aids but has entailed scanning virtually all the typed and manuscript lists at both Chancery Lane and Kew. In some cases I have drawn attention to material available only in the search-rooms or, at Chancery Lane, to volumes in the IND (i.e. index) series, the large collection of contemporary finding-aids which for certain classes have yet to be superseded. Several of the PRO *Handbooks* are of value to local historians, as are most of the leaflets prepared by staff as short guides to particular topics.

The best overall guide to the office, which has been used extensively here without specific references in each case, remains, in my view, that issued by HMSO in 1963 and 1968.[23] The first volume, describing documents at Chancery Lane, is probably the clearest introduction one can find anywhere to the complexities of medieval administration and most of the information is still up-to-date. The second and third volumes, dealing mainly with departmental records, have been overtaken by later accessions, including material from many departments not mentioned at all in these books as well as further transfers from those already represented at the office in the 1960s, although the introductory paragraphs outlining the development of each ministry retain some value. A new *Current Guide* is being compiled on a word-processor, output from which is issued from time to time on microfiche. This, however, is less convenient to use than hard-copy and the sections produced so far mostly deal with modern records. It is thus unfortunate that Volume I of the old *Guide* has been allowed to go out of print.

Readers not familiar with the overall structure of the PRO's holdings and finding-aids or with the mechanics of using the place may find it helpful to read Chapter 6 of my earlier book, information in which is still broadly accurate. Changes in the last few years mainly affect Chancery Lane, where refurbishment is now almost complete and an automated document requisition system has been installed similar to that at Kew.

References to PRO finding-aids have, as far as possible, been worked into the text, an arrangement which will, I hope, give the book more practical value, and a separate index has been compiled (Appendix 1) which lists all the PRO classes referred to, together with details of published lists. The bibliographical notes, grouped together on pp. 196-219, are therefore confined mainly to works on the history of the various officials and institutions whose records are mentioned and to more specialised guides to particular documents. Most of these topics have an extensive literature and to cite all of it would clearly be impossible. I have tried to choose a limited number of sound, up-to-date references in each case, preferably works which themselves have good bibliographies. Preference has also been given to material specifically concerned with records, their location and exploitation. On the other hand, the notes would have been swollen enormously had I included every published example of certain documents, especially those, such as IPMs, feet of fines or tax assessments, which have long been favourites of local record series. Nor do such references seem necessary, given the availability of a full bibliography, recently updated, arranged largely by county and impeccably indexed.[24] Local record publications have been included only where they appear to be of exceptional interest, although editions covering the whole of the country (or, in some cases, the whole of Wales) have been included. With a handful of exceptions, I have only cited works which I have myself examined.[25]

The general arrangement of the text is chronological, with chapters subdivided on what seem the most sensible lines in each case. Classes of material which extend over more than one of the three main periods into which the text has been split are generally described in that in which they first appear, with suitable cross-references given later. For reasons given at the start of Chapter 2, less space has been accorded to the middle ages than later but, overall, the book attempts to provide an account of records likely to be of interest to local historians from the eleventh century onwards. I have taken as a terminal date the structural reforms of the Conservative government of 1970-74, in which the Courts Act, Local Government Act, National Health Service Act and Water Act all wrought extensive changes to local administration and record-keeping, even if some of them have proved less durable than was hoped at the time. This takes the story beyond the date to which public records and local authority records are normally available for study but makes it possible to draw to a close an account of changes which affect the whereabouts of material.

Perhaps, finally, I might suggest for whom this book may be of some use. To me, the phrase 'local historian' refers to those interested in investigating the history of a local community or some aspect thereof, whether this interest is a part-time pursuit or done in the course of their full-time employment. I fail to see the value of using the term as a pejorative antonym for 'professional historian', partly because many of the latter are interested in local history and partly because the subject remains a branch of the discipline to which amateurs can make a genuinely useful contribution. Nor do I see any need to re-christen local history 'regional history' when it is pursued by those employed in higher education, as though this gives the activity a necessary degree of scholarly standing which it would otherwise lack.[26] On the other hand, few colleagues who share my specialist interest are likely to find much that is new in these pages and the book will probably be of most interest to their students, whether these be undergraduates asked to write a dissertation on some local topic, postgraduates beginning research, or those attending extramural classes. Given the limited funds which most undergraduates have to spend on books and the declining number of full-time postgraduates (not to mention falling library budgets in most institutions), the publisher's best hope for this book probably lies in the third category, who are more numerous than the second and generally better off than the first. My previous book was intended as a simple introduction to local history for extramural students and others with a similar interest in the subject: as extramural work moves increasingly into the field of courses leading to the award of certificates, diplomas and, in a few departments, higher degrees based on part-time study, a more systematic guide to one important area of source material may be welcome.

Chapter Two
THE MIDDLE AGES

The sources for medieval local history outlined here are rather different in character from those described later in the book. Firstly, the vast majority are in central rather than local custody: although there was an elementary system of local administration in England from before the Norman Conquest, there are no corresponding archives of local records to illustrate its workings, as there are for later centuries. Most of what is known about the activities of local representatives of the crown derives from records either created at the centre or transmitted from the localities and preserved centrally. Only since the sixteenth century has there been sufficient continuity in local administration for documents to accumulate in each county and remain in local custody. Medieval local archives are chiefly those created by institutions that were in part private, even if they were also partly public in character and function. Into this category fall the boroughs of England and Wales, some of which survived to be incorporated into the modern system of local government; the dioceses, chapters and archdeaconries of the Church; and, more tenuously, the manors held by individuals and corporations.

Other local archives might have survived had the sixteenth-century changes in government and society not been so sweeping. Thus, although the records of the three palatinate jurisdictions – Durham, Chester and Lancaster – retained their separate identity long after the institutions themselves had lost their quasi-independence, those of the marcher lordships of medieval Wales abolished by Henry VIII did not and are now largely lost, with surviving documents widely dispersed. Similarly, the destruction of the religious houses and the subsequent sale by the crown of their lands and other possessions led to the break-up of their muniments. Thus, since only a few private landowners have flourished without interruption since the middle ages, the continuity of ownership desirable, if not essential, to the creation and preservation of long series of documents recording the acquisition and management of landed estates has been largely restricted to a limited number of institutional owners, chiefly the Crown and the Church, together with Oxford and Cambridge colleges and a few other corporate bodies.

The second consideration is more practical. The study of medieval records requires technical skills that will never be universal among professional historians, much less those for whom history is an amateur pursuit. It is a commonplace that one cannot make effective use of records without knowing something of the history and working of the institutions which created them and, whilst the mechanics of a nineteenth-century department of state may seem complex, its records normally present few problems of language or legibility. They may be formidable in their bulk (although so may some medieval material) but are rarely difficult to read. Even sixteenth- and seventeenth-century documents are, for the most part, written in English in a hand that can be mastered with a little practice. This is not true of earlier records, many of which, whether of central or local provenance, are written in Latin (or less commonly French) in a hand that requires considerable practice. Even then, most people can still only read such documents comparatively slowly, looking at each word or phrase for items of interest, rather than quickly scanning each membrane of a roll in the way in which one can turn the leaves of a modern file. There may still be those who, like J.H. Round, can sit down with a medieval account roll and browse through it as though it were this morning's newspaper but they must now be few, added to which modern medievalists rarely have the leisure to devote to searches at the PRO which Round appears to have enjoyed.

This problem is especially relevant to local history for two reasons. One is the point already made that much of the source material is in central custody and thus relates to the entire kingdom. In some cases, the documents may be arranged by county or in some other way that makes it fairly simple to locate references to a particular place. If not, the class may not be worth searching, since its bulk will make such a task impractical except for someone with unlimited opportunities to visit the PRO or a bottomless purse from which to buy microfilm to read at home. Almost by definition, the local historian is unlikely to qualify under either heading. If a searcher is interested in a particular person or family then proportionately less material will generally be worth examining. For example, there is a reasonable chance that an assize roll will mention most places of any size in the county in which the justices were sitting, but only if the object of a genealogical or biographical enquiry is already known to have had criminal tendencies and to have been living in that county at about the right date will it be worth struggling through the roll. Closely related to this is the problem of comprehension, since so many local searches amongst the records of central government, at whatever date, involve trawling large numbers of documents in the hope of finding material of interest. Ten boxes of departmental files arranged by subject may not seem, from their description in the class-list, to be of much value for a particular topic but they can be searched in a day or two; a similar quantity of fifteenth-century King's Bench plea rolls, which may be of just as much potential interest, will take far longer to check. Neither document is arranged to facilitate local searches but the greater difficulty of reading a plea roll means that such documents will always be less fully exploited than more recent classes.

Conversely, medieval history, whether local or general, has been far better served than later studies by the publication of documents in full, calendars and other finding-aids. It was natural that the early nineteenth-century Record Commissioners should direct most of their energies towards the printing of some of the oldest public records, a policy continued by the PRO until well into this century. In some respects, the scope of official publishing remained narrow, concentrating especially on the administrative, rather than judicial or financial, activities of the medieval crown, but one can also discern some response to the needs of those with topographical or genealogical interests, as in the publication of inquisitions *post mortem*. Similarly, while non-official editorial work at national level also tended to deal with records of crucial importance to an understanding of the machinery of government, as illustrated most obviously by the work of the Pipe Roll Society, local societies did much to make available, not always in impeccable editions, documents of value to their members interested in people and places. As a result of a century of enterprise of this kind, a greater proportion of medieval public records are accessible in print than those of later centuries, generally in a form that makes local searches straightforward (i.e. they are competently indexed) and makes recourse to the original unnecessary (i.e. they are either transcripts or calendars). On the other hand, one should not underestimate the sheer volume of medieval material, much of it of considerable local interest, that remains largely inaccessible for reasons already suggested, including, for instance, many of the detailed accounts submitted to the Exchequer or the records of the courts which heard pleas either at Westminster or in the localities.[1]

Alongside the work of editing and publication, there also developed in the late nineteenth century the modern scholarly study of medieval administrative and legal history, the products of which may be offputting to the reader with a lay interest in local history but which nonetheless have provided a fairly full picture of the mechanics of government. Few branches of the administration have not been studied in detail, either at the centre or in the localities. The same cannot be said of more recent times: some of the departments mentioned in Chapters 5 and 6 have yet to be the subject of full-scale histories and there are few general studies of modern local authorities. A century of scholarship has also made it possible to produce reliable textbooks on medieval central government that provide local historians with sufficient background to understand references to topics in which they are interested amongst central government records.[2]

This chapter has thus been included with the modest aim of providing a simple guide to those classes of the medieval public records which are likely to be of interest for local studies and are relatively easy of access. As in the rest of the book, the material is arranged by administrative provenance, with the historical background to the documents explained as briefly as possible, together with an indication of where one can discover more. Finally, I have said something of medieval material in local custody, or at least of local origin.[3]

The Chancery

Although the Exchequer was the first branch of the *curia regis* to become a sedentary department, rather than constantly attendant on the king, it was the Chancery that stood at the centre of the fully developed medieval administration.[4] The Chancellor, the keeper of the Great Seal used to authenticate written expressions of royal will, and his staff of clerks were gradually distinguished from the king's immediate household and in the fourteenth century became domiciled in Chancery Lane. The Great Seal was thus no longer immediately available to the court and was superseded in everyday use first by the privy seal and later by the signet seal, whose keeper evolved in the sixteenth century from king's secretary into secretary of state (p. 52). The use of the Great Seal became increasingly formal and the Chancery accordingly ceased to be the central organ of royal administration. Decline in this respect was compensated for by the increasing jurisdiction exercised by the Chancellor in matters for which the common law could not provide a remedy. Although originating in the fourteenth century, the Chancery's equitable jurisdiction did not fully blossom until the sixteenth, from which date it became the court's most important function, overshadowing both its administrative duties and its common law jurisdiction. Since most surviving equity records date from the reign of Elizabeth and later, they are described in the next chapter (p. 73).[5]

From the reign of King John, the Chancery adopted the practice of enrolling copies of documents issued under the Great Seal and the parallel series of records thus created are amongst the best known and most accessible sources for medieval local history. As in later centuries, much that happened in the localities was the consequence of action taken at the centre, whether it was the appointment or dismissal of royal officials, the issue of instructions to such men, the granting of privileges or lands to corporations or individuals, the granting of pardons to wrongdoers or a wide range of other expressions of royal will.

The most solemn Chancery instrument was that entered on the Charter Rolls (C 53), which extend from the beginning of John's reign to the early sixteenth century. They include grants of land and privileges and, as well as original grants to boroughs, confirmations or inspeximuses of previous grants. Although a comparatively short series (there are only 200 rolls, compared with more than 5,000 patent rolls and over 20,000 close rolls), the charter rolls should be searched in any thorough local study since they are all in print: those for John's reign were published by the Record Commission in 1837 and the remainder in six volumes of PRO calendars between 1903 and 1927.

Renewals of privileges not found on the charter rolls may be entered on either the Cartae Antiquae Rolls (C 52) or the Confirmation Rolls (C 56). The former consist of transcripts of documents from the reign of Richard I to that of Edward II on a series of 46 rolls, the first ten of which were printed by the Pipe Roll Society (New Series, 17); for the remainder there is a descriptive list on the Round Room shelves. The Confirmation Rolls (1483-1625) contain a considerable number of entries of local interest but the only published calendar is that for 1509-14 included in the *Calendar of Letters and Papers, Henry VIII*. Otherwise, one has to search a manuscript list, reasonably well indexed, in the Round Room.

Before the establishment of the Confirmation Rolls renewals may be found on either the Charter Rolls or the Patent Rolls (C 66), one of the two major series of Chancery enrolments, whose name derives from the letters whose texts are recorded being issued 'open', addressed to all. During the middle ages the Patent Rolls contain a wide range of entries concerned both with public business and grants to individuals and corporations. After 1516 grants formerly enrolled on the Charter Rolls were transferred entirely to the Patent Rolls, although the documents were still known as 'charters'. Until the Civil War commissions of the peace, of sewers, of oyer and terminer and those for charitable uses, as well as various special commissions, were also enrolled, adding to the wealth of local detail. From the seventeenth century the rolls ceased to contain the breadth of material of earlier periods, although the series continues almost to the present day. For John's reign and the start of Henry III's (to 1232), a complete transcript was published by the Record Commission and then the PRO; thereafter a series of PRO calendars is complete to 1558, apart from the reign of Henry VIII, when the Patent Rolls were included in *Letters and Papers*. The series will continue on traditional lines to the end of Elizabeth's reign but no further, in view of the diminishing importance of the rolls for mainstream government. For the period 1580-94 an index of grantees named on the rolls has been issued by the List & Index Society (141, 167), which has also printed a calendar for the first 15 years of James I, with an index (97, 98, 109, 121, 122, 133, 134, 157, 164, 187, 193). Apart from these, the main finding-aid for the later rolls is a series of volumes in the Long Room, together with numerous pieces from the IND group (see LIS 166). Some 93 additional rolls form the separate class of Patent Rolls (Supplementary) (C 67), some, but not all of which, are included in the published calendars.

Gaol delivery, assize and similar commissions entered on the back of the patent rolls are generally excluded from the published calendars but are of some value to local historians. Otherwise, these volumes, and the parallel series for the other Chancery enrolments, can usually be relied upon as a summary of the original documents, although in the past (but not today) the accuracy with which personal names were transcribed and, more important, place-names identified, sometimes left a good deal to be desired.

The Close Rolls (C 54) were, as their name implies, originally intended for royal acts of a more private nature. From early in the fourteenth century business of this kind was diverted to the Privy Seal and under the Tudors the Close Rolls ceased entirely to be used for the enrolment of administrative instruments. Their use as a registry for private deeds, however, grew during the same period and continued until 1903 (p. 57). For the earlier period, when, like the Patent Rolls, the series contains a wide range of documents, many of them of local interest, there are published transcripts for 1204-72 and then a calendar which ends at 1509, the latter including (to 1435) the small class of Close Rolls (Supplementary) (C 55).

The other series of enrolments in the medieval Chancery worth checking for local references are the Fine Rolls (C 60), recording payments to the crown in return for the renewal of charters or grants, or the enjoyment of lands, office or some other privilege. The rolls begin in John's reign and end in 1641; there is a published transcript for John's reign, continued as excerpts for Henry III, then a series of calendars to 1471, while for the years 1547-53 the Fine Rolls are included in the published calendar of Patent Rolls. For other periods there are calendars, with indexes, in IND 17350-52, for which see LIS 166.

Apart from the enrolments, the best known Chancery classes are probably the inquisitions taken locally by the escheators following the death or lunacy of those who held lands in chief, i.e. directly of the king, or who were believed to do so, with the purpose of establishing the terms on which the land was held, the name and age of the heir and, most important, what benefits might accrue to the crown. In particular, if the heir was a minor, the lands remained in wardship until he came of age. The documents, which survive from the reign of Henry III down to the abolition of feudal tenures in 1660, are principally inquisitions *post mortem,* which have been used by genealogists since at least the seventeenth century, with collections of abstracts for particular counties or families often appearing in antiquarian collections under the older name of 'escheats'. Several other kinds of inquisition were originally intermixed with the IPMs, notably inquisitions *ad quod damnum,* taken to establish whether the crown would suffer any loss if a proposed grant of a market or fair, alienation of land or other privilege, were allowed. In addition, other material once among the IPMs has been placed in a class of Miscellaneous Inquisitions.

Because of their genealogical interest, the inquisitions are accessible in print. Those now grouped as IPMs, Series I (C 132 to C

141), from Henry III to Richard III, are calendared either in Record Commission publications or PRO volumes; the remainder, Series II (C 142), are listed in alphabetical order of tenant in *Lists and Indexes* 23, 26, 31 and 33. These bring together references not only to inquisitions filed in the Chancery but also the copies transmitted during certain periods to the Exchequer (E 150) and the Court of Wards (WARD 7; cf. p. 68), both of which are often easier to read, having been subject to less handling and (in the *Guide's* memorable phrase) 'the injudicious use of restorative fluids'. The lists also include inquisitions taken by the escheators in the palatine counties and the Duchy of Lancaster (p. 38). A more detailed calendar of the Series II IPMs was later published by the PRO for Henry VII's reign. Both these volumes and the earlier ones have been criticised for omitting two features of the original documents of local interest: the extents of land held by the deceased sometimes returned by the jury and the names of the jurors themselves.[6] The PRO have now relented in the first case but resisted in the second, arguing that the indexes to the volumes would be hopelessly overloaded if thousands of additional names were abstracted. It is worth remembering, therefore, that a photocopy of an original IPM may yield more local detail than even a modern calendar entry. It is also important to bear in mind that valuations placed on estates in IPMs are artificially low and not a reliable guide to landed wealth.

For the inquisitions *ad quod damnum* (C 143) from Henry III to Richard III (later ones being generally intermixed with the IPMs) there is a calendar in *Lists and Indexes* 17 and 22; for the Miscellaneous Inquisitions (C 145) for the same period a series of calendars is in progress; and for the small class of Criminal Inquisitions (C 144), which goes down to Henry VI's reign, a list in the Round Room identifies the counties represented in each bundle and piece.

Although the common law jurisdiction of the Chancery was never extensive the earlier proceedings are worth checking for cases of local interest. Both C 44 (Edward I to Richard III) and C 43 (Henry VII to James I) have published lists (List & Index Society 67), which give the names of the parties, a brief indication of the matter at issue and the county involved. The later proceedings (C 206), which continue to the nineteenth century, are not listed topographically.[7]

Another type of document of potential interest, arising either from the court's common law jurisdiction or proceedings under the law merchant, are the extents, returned usually by the sheriffs, of lands and goods belonging to debtors, which date from the early fourteenth century to the Civil War and are now grouped into two classes, C 131 and C 239, of which the second has been re-assembled from debris in C 47, Chancery Miscellanea, and included with several other such classes in List & Index Society 130. For C 131 there is only a searchroom list but for neither is there an index of names. Chancery Miscellanea itself, which has been reduced in bulk as some of the documents have been identified and re-classified, is briefly described in the *Guide* (vol. I, pp. 36-8) and more fully in LIS 7, 15, 26, 38, 49, 81, 105 and 145, the last containing a key to new references for documents transferred. Among material of topographical interest still in C 47 are the certificates returned in 1388-9 by gilds and chantries, listing their ordinances and, in some cases, their lands. Where a detailed return survives, it is likely to add greatly to what is known from locally preserved documents of the history of a small town or parish fraternity (p. 42).[8]

Finally, the group contains a large collection of deeds, arranged in four classes (C 146 to C 149), of which the last are modern (from 1603), for which there is no list. The first 8,060 deeds in C 146 are included in the *Catalogue of Ancient Deeds* (vols. I-III, VI), with the remainder described in two typescript volumes in the Round Room that might usefully be issued by the List & Index Society. There is a card index to persons and places mentioned in this list (which includes C 148 as well as C 146 but not C 147) in the Long Room, where there is also an index to C 147.

The Exchequer

The Exchequer was in origin the *curia regis* sitting for the transaction of revenue business, a gathering from which officers of state with no special function there gradually withdrew, leaving the Treasurer to preside, with the Chancellor represented by a clerk who ultimately became Chancellor of the Exchequer. The department was the first branch of the court to acquire its own institutional identity and its own premises, where the proceedings were divided into two parts, an Upper Exchequer, in which crown debtors were called to account, and a Lower Exchequer, or Exchequer of Receipt, where money due from accountants was actually paid in. Like the Chancery, the Exchequer had jurisdiction over those who had dealings with it and was thus a court of law as well as an administrative department.

Originally, the only accountants who came to the Exchequer were the sheriffs of counties and bailiffs of liberties and franchises; by the early fourteenth century, as other source of crown revenue developed, the court became responsible for these also. During the later middle ages and the early Tudor period, the crown also relied on a more personal system of financial organisation, the Chamber, which grew up alongside the Exchequer, whereby money was received, spent and accounted for without passing through the older procedure. The developments, culminating in the creation of the Court of Augmentations (p. 64), were brought to an end when that court was abolished in 1554 and its activities absorbed into the Exchequer. Some elements of Augmentations practice survived, however, adding another layer to an already elaborate structure.

The sixteenth century also saw the growth of equity jurisdiction in the Exchequer, possibly as an inheritance from Augmentations, while from the seventeenth century the department was increasingly superseded as the mainspring of central government finance by the Treasury (p. 58), a process formally completed in 1833. Exchequer equity jurisdiction was merged with that of the Chancery (which had always been more important) in 1841, while the common law side survived to be absorbed into the reformed High Court in 1873 (pp. 76, 180).

Because of the great antiquity of the Exchequer and the successive reorganisations of its structure over a long period, the department's records are not only voluminous but immensely complex, added to which comparatively few have been published. This section attempts to do no more than suggest some classes of medieval material in which documents of local interest can be located without excessive searching.

The group includes, of course, the oldest items amongst the public records, the five volumes of Domesday Book (E 31), compiled in 1086-7, the text of which is readily accessible in modern facsimiles and translations, together with an enormous interpretative literature.[9] Two centuries later, in the 1270s, somewhat similar enquiries were instigated by Edward I after his accession to establish what privileges private lords held throughout the kingdom, which resulted in the compilation of the Hundred Rolls (so-called since the information was supplied initially by juries for the hundreds or wapentakes of each county) and the resultant Quo Warranto proceedings, intended to determine 'by what warrant' privileges were enjoyed. Both sets of returns were published in full by the Record Commission, the fullest being the Hundred Rolls of 1279 for several counties in central England, where the amount of detail is comparable to that in Domesday.[10]

The earliest continuous series of documents is also to be found amongst the Exchequer records, the pipe rolls (E 372), of which the first dates from 31 Henry I (1130-31), with an almost continuous sequence from 2 Henry II (1155-6) to the abolition of the Pipe Office in 1832. The rolls are a record of accounts audited in the Upper Exchequer, at which each sheriff or other accountant had to appear. They are not, as has often been stressed, a complete record of either crown income or, much less, expenditure, but rather of money received from one class of accountant and expenditure authorised against that income. They are, however, the only public records to span a large part of the twelfth century, until the Chancery enrolments begin in John's reign, and, moreover, have now been published down to the early years of Henry III.[11] They may thus be checked easily enough for references to local communities, especially those which were on the royal demesne; for many parishes they supply the earliest post-Domesday place-name form.

Of more value for most local studies than the primary accounting records, of which the pipe rolls are the oldest class, are the subsidiary documents returned by sheriffs and others in support of their accounts, which are often themselves buttressed by further vouchers. The bulk of these are arranged in one of the best known Exchequer classes, E 101, aptly named Accounts, Various, which is described in fair detail in *Lists and Indexes* 35, *L&I Supplementary* 9, Part 1, and various typescript lists in the Round Room. The class is subdivided into a number of sections, of which those relating to works and buildings, the army and ordnance, and the royal forests are probably the most promising for local historians. Classified separately but similar in purpose are the accounts rendered by sheriffs of the income from manors and other property in their hands (E 199), to which may be attached writs and returns, extents, inquisitions and other documents. The class is listed by county in List & Index Society 127. Until the reign of Henry III the sheriffs were also responsible for income from lands temporarily in crown hands as a result of forfeit or escheat; from the 1230s separate officials, known as escheators, were appointed for individual counties or pairs of counties.[12] Their accounts form E 136, with subsidiary documents in E 153 and E 137, all of which are listed by county or escheatry in the class-list. The inquisitions *post mortem* sent in with the accounts are now filed separately (E 149), to form Series I of the Exchequer IPMs. Series II are duplicates transmitted from the Chancery from the reign of Henry VII onwards (E 150); both are included in the published calendars and lists (pp. 27-8). Other inquisitions returned to the Exchequer, which now form E 151 and E 152, are described in *Lists and Indexes* 22.

Receipts from customs duties levied on imports and exports from the reign of Edward I were accounted for by local collectors and other officials, whose records (E 122) are the main source for the medieval history of individual ports. After 1565 the class contains only subsidiary documents as the accounts themselves were superseded by the port books (pp. 58-60) as the primary record of the movement of goods and shipping.[13] Of wider local interest are the accounts returned to the Exchequer in connection with various medieval taxes, including the hidage and carucage levied on lands not held by military service; tallage paid by estates forming part of the ancient demesne of the crown and by boroughs; scutage paid for non-performance by those who held land by military service; subsidies of a tenth, fifteenth or some other fraction of moveable wealth granted at different dates by parliament; and poll taxes, also levied with parliamentary authority.[14] All the documents surviving from these various impositions are grouped together as E 179, which is arranged by county and then date and listed in LIS 44, 54, 63, 75 and 87, in which pieces supplying the names of individuals as well as the total assessment on each vill are identified. The class continues into the Tudor period and beyond, ending with the hearth tax and other experiments of the later Stuarts (pp. 60-62).

Documents returned by the sheriffs, escheators and other local officials range from simple summary accounts, through detailed nominal lists to those which are, in effect, estate records relating to property permanently or temporarily in crown hands. Several classes of this kind are to be found in the Exchequer group, others were removed early this century to the 'Special Collections' of material arranged by type rather than administrative provenance. The latter includes court rolls (SC 2), rentals and surveys (SC 11 and SC 12) and ministers' accounts (SC 6), some of which in each case belonged originally to the Exchequer, some to other departments. The court rolls are listed in *Lists and Indexes* 6, the rentals and surveys in *L&I* 25 and *L&I Supplementary* 14, and the ministers' accounts in *L&I* 5, 8 and 34. Other material of the same sort can be found in the palatinate and Duchy of Lancaster groups (pp. 36-9); the Augmentations and Land Revenue sub-departments of the post-medieval Exchequer (pp. 64-7); and the records of several modern departments concerned with crown lands (pp. 167-9). Medieval material still kept amongst the King's Remembrancer's records include two classes of extents and inquisitions (E 142 and E 143), of which the former is included in *L&I* 25, whereas for the latter there is only a summary in LIS 108, while a small collection of extents of the possessions of foreign religious houses in England in the thirteenth and fourteenth centuries is now E 106 (see LIS 91). Two other classes (E 119, E 120) contain some Duchy of Cornwall records of similar date.

The Exchequer group also includes the most important of several classes relating to the administration of the medieval royal forests. The documents in E 32 include records of forest eyres, inspections and inquisitions and are listed by county in LIS 32. For an overall view of what is available relating to the forests between the thirteenth and eighteenth centuries a more valuable means of reference is an unprinted compilation in the Round Room which brings together documents from E 32, E 36, C 47, C 99, C 154, C 205, CHES 33 and DL 39 in a single list also arranged by county.[15]

The largest class of deeds in the group is E 210, comprising over 11,000 pieces, about a tenth of which are described in the *Catalogue of Ancient Deeds,* vol. III, the remainder in typed lists in the Round Room, which are also the means of reference to E 212, E 213 and E 214, the last a small collection of post-1603 conveyances. A calendar of E 211 has been printed as LIS 200; it would be helpful if those for neighbouring classes could be treated likewise. Amongst the Treasury of Receipt records are five other series (E 40 to E 44), of which most of E 40 is included in the *Catalogue* and the rest in LIS 151, 152, 158 and typescript lists. There are also a handful of deeds in the Pipe Office sub-group, of which E 354 has a typed list, while E 355 is uncatalogued.

The Exchequer was the smallest of the medieval common law courts, although the plea rolls begin in the 1230s and its separate jurisdiction survived until 1875 (p. 180). Files of bills and writs exist from the early fourteenth century and from the sixteenth there are a number of subsidiary classes. Finding-aids can be found on open shelves in the Long Room but not in print. In the post-medieval period the Exchequer of Pleas was used particularly for suits concerning tithe (cf. p. 165) and a list of cases of this kind, which may be of particular interest to local historians, was printed in the second *Deputy Keeper's Report:* a copy of this is in the Round Room.[16]

Like the other older departments, the Exchequer group includes a collection of bound volumes now classed as 'Miscellaneous Books' (E 164, the contents of which is summarised in the *Guide* vol. 1, pp. 62-3). Among the most useful for local studies are two containing details of a tax levied on churches in England and Wales in 1291 by Pope Nicholas, which was printed in full by the Record Commission as *Taxatio Ecclesiastica* (1802) and in many cases provides the earliest reference to the existence of a particular parish church.

Administration of Justice

The general framework within which justice was dispensed by the crown in the middle ages is well known.[17] From the mid-twelfth century the work of the *curia regis* was divided into pleas heard by justices sitting at Westminster, those heard by itinerant justices and those heard, notionally, before the king himself, of which the last evolved into the court of King's Bench, the highest court of the realm other than parliament. In its developed form, King's Bench heard both criminal cases, especially those concerning breaches of the king's peace, and personal actions between individuals, although the records of the 'Crown' and 'Plea' sides of the court are themselves only separated from the reign of Queen Anne. From the late twelfth century, when the records begin, to the end of Henry III's reign, plea rolls from what later became the separate court of Common Pleas and some of those of the justices itinerant, as well as those of the court *coram rege,* are grouped together as Curia Regis Rolls (KB 26). The class is summarised in *Lists & Indexes* 4 and *L&I Supplementary* 1 and a number of rolls (or selections therefrom) have been printed by the Record Commission, Pipe Roll Society and Selden Society. Publication has been continued by the PRO in a series of transcripts which has now reached the 1240s.[18]

From the reign of Edward I King's Bench plea rolls form a separate class (KB 27), which continues without a break until the death of William III, with a roll for each term the court sat in which cases are divided into civil and criminal (i.e. the 'Crown Side' or 'Rex Roll'). From 1702 the two types of business are kept on separate Crown Rolls (KB 28) and Plea or Judgment Books (KB 122), of which the former continue to 1911 and the latter to 1875 (p. 180). For the post-medieval period there are a number of subsidiary classes on both the Crown and Plea sides of the court, whereas before the sixteenth century the rolls are flanked by only four other types of document: indictments (KB 8 to KB 12), controlment rolls (KB 29), writs (KB 136, KB 138) and essoins (KB 121). The first include indictments, presentments and convictions removed into King's Bench from quarter sessions or other inferior courts, while the controlment rolls are in the nature of memoranda kept by the king's attorney to note the progress and outcome of crown cases.

It would be unrealistic to suggest that King's Bench records are easily accessible for local studies except for the period, chiefly in the twelfth and thirteenth centuries, when much of the material has been published. The court heard cases from all parts of the kingdom and thus the number relating to any particular county in a given term or year will inevitably be small. There are, however, various manuscript indexes to the cases in the IND series, described in List & Index Society 180, which make it possible to search for cases involving particular individuals or families. List & Index Society 106 contains a class-list for the group as a whole.

A separate royal court of justice sitting at Westminster may be traced from Henry II's reign. Although originally its jurisdiction was unlimited, from the reign of Edward I the work of the court was increasingly restricted to common law actions between private subjects and and thus became known as the court of Common Pleas. The earliest plea rolls are included with the Curia Regis Rolls (KB 26) but from the accession of Edward I to the reform of 1873, when Common Pleas became a division of the High Court (p. 180), there is an unbroken series of Placita de Banco or de Banco Rolls (CP 40). Except for a couple of years at the start of Edward III's reign (1327-8), for which the rolls are indexed topographically in Lists & Indexes 32, there are no published finding-aids for CP 40. The manuscript indexes are described in List & Index Society 180. From the sixteenth century the plea rolls, and their accompanying essoin rolls (CP 21) are joined by an increasing number of subsidiary classes.[19]

Although the plea rolls are of limited usefulness for local studies, the records of the court include another series of documents which, together with the inquisitions *post mortem* (p. 27), are amongst the public records most heavily used by antiquaries for centuries. The fine, or final concord, was an agreement drawn up to mark the conclusion of a fictitious suit between private parties, the true purpose of which was to effect the conveyance of real property. The parties were given leave to terminate the suit by a fine, a document prepared in triplicate recording the sale and purchase of an estate. Two copies of the agreement were handed to the parties while the third, the 'foot', was retained by the court, thus preserving a record of the transaction in case a dispute over title should arise. Conveyancing by fine offered greater security than the use of private deeds, which might be lost, and was therefore judged in many cases to be worth the additional expense. The resulting archive of feet of fines (CP 25), with subsidiary material in CP 24 and CP 26 to CP 30, extends from the late twelfth century to 1834, when fines, and a somewhat similar post-medieval device, the 'recovery' (p. 69), were abolished. Although thousands of indentures of fines can be found in family and estate collections in local record offices, it is the series preserved centrally that is of greatest value and has been most heavily exploited. Fines contain rather less topographical detail than some other types of conveyance but provide a considerable amount of genealogical information, especially for the lesser medieval gentry, whose own estate papers only occasionally survive. A few of the documents have been published either by the Pipe Roll Society or the Record Commission; far more have been put into print by local societies, at least for the middle ages. There are, in addition, unpublished finding-aids in the IND series (see LIS 180), making it possible to use the material even for counties where local enterprise has been lacking.[20]

Fines and recoveries were also executed in the courts of the palatinate counties, the Duchy of Lancaster and the Welsh Great Sessions (pp. 36-40, 73), creating additional series which either supplement or replace those in Common Pleas for certain parts of the country.

The third major category of medieval common law records in the PRO are those making up the JUST group, which contains rolls from various types of itinerant court. The earliest of these was the general eyre, a court held locally at intervals of several years by royal justices, dealing mainly with serious crimes or other matters which had arisen since the last such hearing; the rolls thus have criminal and civil sides in the same way as those of King's Bench (p. 33). The earliest eyre from which records survive is that of 1194 and for all counties except Cheshire at least one roll exists for some date between then and 1294, when the system came to an end, apart from an attempted revival in 1329-31, and a few isolated eyres in particular counties, notably Kent. The eyre rolls, like other material in JUST 1, were included in *Lists & Indexes* 4, where the documents are listed topographically, and will generally be the earliest record that survives of the sitting of a royal court in a particular county. The records of the general eyre have recently been the subject of a PRO Handbook and an increasing number have been published, often through the combined efforts of the late C.A.F. Meekings, his successors at the PRO and local societies.[21]

JUST 1 also contains rolls from assize hearings between the early thirteenth century and later fifteenth, the predecessors of the material preserved by the clerks of assize from Elizabeth's reign (pp. 69-71), and from oyer and terminer hearings, a type of jurisdiction later merged with assize commissions. Both are examples of professional justices visiting the provinces to review the work of local peace officers and to hear criminal and civil pleas which could not be dealt with locally. Alongside the plea rolls are gaol delivery rolls (JUST 3), a class which also includes indictments, lists of jurors and other subsidiary documents, and the main class of coroners' rolls in the PRO (JUST 2).

The Counties Palatine, Duchy of Lancaster and Wales

Three areas of northern England stood partly, but not wholly, outside mainstream royal administration in the middle ages. The oldest of the exempt jurisdictions was the palatinate of Durham, held by the bishops of that see from the time of Anthony Bek (1283-1311), which extended over a considerably greater area than the modern county. The judicial supremacy of the bishops was ended in 1536 (27 Hen. VIII, c.24), but the courts remained in their hands until the 1830s (6 & 7 Will. IV, c.19). Even then, the Court of Pleas and the Palatine Court of Chancery continued as separate institutions, the former being merged into the High Court in 1873-5 (p. 180) and the latter surviving until the Courts Act, 1971.[22]

The records of the palatinate were initially transferred to the PRO in 1868. A few years later, material relating to the administration of the episcopal estate, as distinct from the courts, was passed to the Ecclesiastical Commissioners, who had succeeded the bishops in the immense possessions long held by the see. Most of these muniments have since been returned to Durham and are now at the Prior's Kitchen, a repository maintained by the university. Other palatinate records were scheduled for destruction in 1912, some of which were instead transferred to Gateshead Public Library, where they remain.

The documents now making up the Palatinate of Durham group at the PRO are judicial, rather than administrative, and mirror in miniature some, but not all, the elements of central government. Thus the Chancery classes include inquisitions *post mortem* and enrolments on patent and close rolls as well as records arising from the separate equity jurisdiction of the Durham Chancery. The judgment rolls contain both pleas heard by the Court of Pleas and also recoveries (p. 69) and enrolled private deeds. The group also includes material relating to the sitting of assize judges at Durham from the sixteenth century down to the reorganisation of circuits in 1876 (p. 70).

The earldom of Chester, which included both the modern county and Flint, was annexed to the crown in 1327 but remained a separate palatine jurisdiction throughout the middle ages.[23] The Act of 1543 establishing the courts of Great Sessions in Wales (34 & 35 Hen. VIII, c.26; cf. p. 72), placed Flint, Denbigh and Montgomery, together with Chester itself, in a Chester circuit of that court, presided over by the Justice of Chester, an office which survived until the abolition of Great Sessions in 1830. Although in a few cases Welsh material is to be found in the Palatine of Chester group at Chancery Lane or palatinate documents among Great Sessions records now at the National Library of Wales (p. 72), in general the two archives were kept separate from the mid-sixteenth century.

The records of the palatinate were removed from Chester to the PRO in 1854; those that are now in the CHES group are listed in *Lists & Indexes* 40, while others have been placed in four of the Special Collections classes: ministers' accounts (SC 6), court rolls (SC 2), rentals (SC 11) and surveys (SC 12), or in E 101, Accounts, Various. The palatinate group itself chiefly contain judicial material, either from the Exchequer Court which, like its counterpart in London, had both a common law jurisdiction over debtors (cf. p. 33) and equity jurisdiction (p. 76), or from common law hearings before the Justice of Chester. The equity material mostly dates from the sixteenth century and includes a range of documents similar to those found on the equity side of the Exchequer in London; the common law pleadings extend from the mid-thirteenth century to 1830. Besides the main series of rolls, there are separate eyre rolls, recording pleas heard by the justices at itinerant courts, as well as subsidiary classes, such as gaol files, indictments and fines. Administrative classes include enrolments of charters, letters patent and other documents from the early fourteenth century to 1830 and inquisitions *post mortem* for both Chester and Flint from the late thirteenth.

The third of the palatine counties was Lancaster, raised to this status in 1351 when Henry, Earl of Lancaster, was created duke, with power to have his own chancery and appoint justices to hear common law pleas. The palatinate was extinguished by Henry's death in 1361 but revived by a grant to John of Gaunt in 1377. Since the accession of Henry IV in 1399 the dukedom has remained in royal hands but has retained a separate administrative structure to the present day. The distinct judicial system also survived, the common law and criminal jurisdiction until 1873 and the chancery court until 1971. Records of the palatinate and of the Duchy of Lancaster are grouped separately at the PRO, on the grounds that the former are essentially 'public' but relate only to the palatine county, while the remainder are 'private', consisting either of estate muniments or the proceedings of a duchy court which had equity jurisdiction in all matters affecting lands belonging to the duchy, not merely those in the county. This division has been criticised by the modern historian of the duchy, who argues that the records of the Duchy Chamber are no less public than those of the palatine courts. Sir Robert Somerville also questions the traditional view that the records of the duchy, which had estates in almost every county in England and Wales and a correspondingly complex administration, replicate in miniature those of the kingdom, since there was no separate exchequer.[24]

Whatever view one takes of the present classification, it is clear that while palatinate records (listed in *Lists & Indexes* 40) are mainly of interest to local historians in Lancashire, those in the duchy group (*L&I* 14) include a wealth of material on all parts of the country. The palatinate group is similar to those for Durham and Chester, in that some classes, such as close and patent rolls or inquisitions *post mortem*, are administrative, and some judicial. As well as pleadings in both the chancery and common law courts, there are various subsidiary classes, including feet of fines from 1362 to 1834. From 1422 until the nineteenth century there is also a separate series of assize rolls for the county. Some of the classes in the Duchy of Lancaster group also relate mainly, if not wholly, to the palatinate, such as the plea rolls from the Duchy Bench for 1351-60 (DL 35), chancery enrolments of the fourteenth and fifteenth centuries (DL 37), or papers relating to the appointment of sheriffs (DL 21) or justices (DL 20) in Lancashire.

The duchy records of most local value are those relating to the administration of its estates and litigation arising therefrom in the Court of Duchy Chamber, which evolved from an administrative Duchy Council. The latter are similar to those on the equity side of the Exchequer (p. 76) and begin in the reign of Henry VII; the former include court rolls (DL 30) (listed with those in SC 2 in *L&I* 6), deeds (DL 25 to DL 27), ministers' accounts (DL 29, for which see *L&I* 5, 8 and 34), rentals and surveys (DL 43: *L&I* 25), leases (DL 14, DL 15), and maps and plans (DL 31). Apart from the last two categories, all these series run from the middle ages down to the nineteenth century and should contain some material, possibly a great deal, relating to any estate held by the duchy. Even today, when other crown lands are in the hands of either the Forestry Commission or the Crown Estate Commissioners (pp. 167-9), those of the duchy are separately managed. Other duchy records are similar to those found on the King's Remembrancer side of the Exchequer or the Chancery, such as extents for debt (DL 23; cf. p. 28), chantry certificates (DL 38; cf. p. 65), parliamentary surveys (DL 32; cf. p. 66), forest proceedings (DL 39; cf. p. 32), inquisitions *post mortem* (DL 27; cf. p. 27), special commissions (DL 44; cf. p. 77) or enclosure awards (DL 45; cf. pp. 89, 166). Most of these are post-medieval, but may conveniently be mentioned here; several reflect the greater intensity with which Henry VII and Henry VIII sought to exploit the land revenues of the crown, of which the duchy was an important part. Further archival legacies of this policy are considered in the next chapter (p. 64).

The other royal dukedom which has survived as a separate unit with extensive landed possessions is Cornwall. In this case, however, most of the records remain in the hands of the Duchy Office, although they are accessible. They relate chiefly, but not exclusively, to Cornwall and the West Country. There are a few medieval estate records at the PRO in E 119 and E 120 and later material in E 306, while the present duke has presented some muniments relating to

Welsh estates to the National Library.[25]

Record sources for the history of medieval Wales are widely scattered, complex in character and have suffered an unhappy archival history.[26] While in some respects the principality has benefited from its close proximity to England, in other respects the reverse is true. At the beginning of this century, after most material previously stored in unsatisfactory conditons in different places in Wales had been gathered together at the PRO, Welsh records were grouped with English documents of similar type (for example, medieval plea rolls), without respect to their separate provenance, while other items were transferred to the Special Collections. More recently, the division of the Principality of Wales group into two, with the bulk of the records transferred to the National Library at Aberystwyth, far from cognate English material and inaccessible to most potential readers, has created fresh problems. In the case of private muniments, whether of families or corporations, the situation is complicated by the overlapping activities of the disproportionately large number of repositories with which the country is now burdened (p. 17).

Sources prior to the Edwardian conquest are few: only after the Statute of Rhuddlan of 1284 is there any quantity of material or any systematic survival of distinct classes. The statute divided the principality into three areas: in the south and east control was left in the hands of the marcher lords, whose administrative, financial and judicial powers excluded almost wholly those of the crown. In consequence, English central government records are of little help for the study of this region before the abolition of their separate jurisdictions in 1536. Although the lordships survived into modern times as great estates, they were shorn of their chanceries, exchequers and courts, the records of which are for the most part lost, with surviving material widely dispersed as the estates have changed hands and been broken up. Some documents have reached the PRO, as have thousands of other private muniments by various routes, others are in the British Library Department of Manuscripts, but a large proportion are in either local repositories (in both England and Wales) or at the National Library, with little in the way of published finding-aids.

North and west Wales were brought more closely under royal control. The county of Flint was annexed to the palatine liberty of Chester (p. 36), while the rest of the region became the principality of Wales, a crown possession normally enjoyed by the heir to the throne. The principality was divided into five counties, of which Cardigan and Carmarthen formed West Wales and Anglesey, Caernarfon and Merioneth formed North Wales. The administrative hub of these shires was not London, however, but Caernarfon in the north and either Cardigan or Carmarthen in the west. Despite this, a considerable quantity of financial records survive for the later medieval principality, although the chancery enrolments are almost wholly lost and the plea rolls, recording hearings before Welsh justices prior to the establishment of the Great Sessions in 1543 (p. 71) are comparatively few in number. Most of this material is in the PRO, chiefly divided between the Exchequer, Duchy of Lancaster and Special Collections groups, with the plea rolls included in *Lists & Indexes* 4. For the principality, if not the March, many of the classes of English central government records mentioned earlier in the chapter contain some material on Wales, although generally it is no easier to locate references to Welsh communities, except where they have been separately calendared.

Local Administration

The rudimentary system of local government through royal officials which existed in most of England before the Norman Conquest was extended and improved in the twelfth and thirteenth centuries.[27] Outside the counties palatine, Wales, London and the larger provincial towns, the basic unit remained the shire, in which the principal official was the sheriff, responsible for the implementation of policy and collection of revenue. He was also a law officer, presiding over the county court. From 1194 the sheriff was joined by a new official, the coroner, appointed primarily to enquire into causes of sudden or unexplained death, who gradually became more widely involved in local administration. During the thirteenth century another official emerged, the escheator, who undertook duties connected with the forfeit of lands of the crown as a result of treason, felony or lack of an heir and with wardship, the administration of an estate on behalf of the crown during the minority of an heir. A further development of the same period was the appointment of collectors of customs at each port around the coast and, in each county, of assessors or commissioners who assisted the sheriff in the collection of taxes.[28]

The main feaures of this structure are familiar. None of the officials, however, can normally be studied from material surviving locally, and their activities have to be reconstructed from the records of central government. Thus the Chancery enrolments (p. 25) contain numerous letters addressed to the sheriffs, either seeking information or giving instructions, while the Exchequer records include the accounts submitted by sheriffs, customs officers, tax collectors, escheators and other accountants (p. 31). Local officials also returned information to the Chancery or Exchequer in response to writs issued either in the course of routine business or on special occasions. The inquisitions *post mortem* held by the escheator on the death of a tenant holding in chief are an example of the first kind of enquiry; the Quo Warranto proceedings (p. 30) are an instance of a major investigation into conditions in many counties throughout the kingdom.

The local administration of justice must also be studied mainly from records preserved centrally. Besides the itinerant justices travelling the country to conduct either eyre or assize hearings (p. 35), the crown also, from the fourteenth century, appointed local lay justices to hear pleas and deliver gaols between sitting of the assize justices. These 'keepers of the peace', the predecessors of the justices who dominate local government between the sixteenth century and late nineteenth, would have kept some record of their proceedings. Such rolls, however, are not preserved with those of later periods after the court of quarter sessions was fully established (p. 86); the handful that survive have usually done so because the justices' decisions were reviewed by a higher court. Much the same is true of the work of the medieval coroner, details of whose inquests are most commonly to be found on rolls handed to the eyre or assize justices or, while it remained itinerant, those of King's Bench. Even much more recent coroners' records tend to be poorly preserved, since only in 1958 were they given the protection of the Public Records Act (p. 161).[29]

The two institutions, other than those of the Church (p. 48), whose medieval records may survive in local custody are the borough and manor. Both, especially the second, were only partly public in character, unlike those concerned with royal administration or peace-keeping.

A number of towns throughout England appear in Domesday Book as boroughs, wholly or partly distinct from the tenurial pattern in the rest of the county in which they were situated. During the following two centuries many more communities made the transition from rural vill to borough, while others tried and failed.[30] Some successful medieval towns later decayed and lost some or all of their special status, emerging into modern times merely as parishes (p. 91). Most, however, survived to be treated separately in the nineteenth-century statutes which created the modern local government system (pp. 99-102). The municipal corporations reformed in 1835 and 1882 could thus claim continuity from medieval institutions and, by the end of the century, most were showing some sign of interest in their history and records. Some, whether or not they formally provide an archive service, are still in possession of medieval documents; others have handed them over to county record offices, which may also have acquired items from boroughs which have no successors among modern local authorities.

All towns, including those already in existence in the eleventh century, received grants establishing or confirming their privileges during the middle ages, as they did in the sixteenth and seventeenth centuries and after 1835. Whereas later grants of this kind were invariably made by the crown, many small boroughs, including most in Wales, were established by private lords, from whom the burgesses received an initial grant of liberties. Such seigneurial boroughs usually then sought royal confirmation of their privileges. All grants of this kind tend to be called 'borough charters', although, in the case of those emanating from the royal chancery, only the earlier ones were enrolled on the charter rolls (p. 25). Later grants, which often merely confirmed rather than extended privileges, were usually entered on the patent roll. Where a borough has retained a measure of institutional identity since the middle ages the burgesses have usually managed to preserve their copies of such documents; alternatively a grant may be traced through its enrolment in Chancery. There may be a few instances where the grant was not enrolled and so the copy now in the hands of the grantees' successors forms a unique record. This is the case also with charters issued by private lords since, even if the grantor possessed a properly organised writing-office, the chances of its records surviving to the present day are slight. Thus many of the grants made by the marcher lords of South Wales (p. 39) are known only from copies preserved by the burgesses, whereas post-1536 renewals can normally be traced from Chancery enrolments.[31]

In some towns, the only medieval muniments inherited by the modern burgesses are a series of charters. Others, however, have a wider range of records similar to those found more commonly from the sixteenth century (p. 100). The proceedings of the common council or sittings of the borough court, including attendance lists and orders made by the council, may survive for the later middle ages, or there may be lists of admissions to the freedom of the borough. If the townsmen owned any land there may be leases, rentals or other estate records. The borough may also have enrolled for safekeeping private deeds executed by burgesses. Material of this kind is reasonably plentiful for the larger towns and cities but for smaller places (including the Welsh boroughs) little or nothing survives, if indeed the documents ever existed in the first place.[32]

Alongside the borough records themselves there may be material from the gilds, chantries and other fraternities which flourished in most medieval towns. The term 'gild' was used loosely in medieval communities to mean almost any kind of religious, craft, trade or social organisation; in small towns there may be little or no difference between the 'gild' (or gild merchant) and the 'borough'. Alternatively, a post-medieval corporation may have evolved from an earlier gild, on which the townsmen had previously relied for a measure of institutional identity. Most fraternities were in part religious organisations and suffered accordingly during the reign of Henry VIII or, more commonly, that of Edward VI, a period in which something of their activities can be discovered from the *Valor Ecclesiasticus* of 1535 and the records of the Court of Augmentations (p. 64). Before then, the crown conducted only one major enquiry into the local gilds, in 1388, the returns for which have already been mentioned (p. 29). Where gild muniments themselves survive they will most commonly be in the nature of estate records, including rentals and surveys of their possessions, deeds recording the gift of land in the first place and leases showing something of its subsequent management. It is also posible to find agreements between the gild brethren and priests who served them and statements of gild ordinances. For the craft gilds in the greater cities there may also be records of admissions, which are less commonly found for the typical parish gild in a market town. Conversely, where a small fraternity was dominated by a single family, some of its muniments may have survived in that family's own archives, especially if it inherited part or all of the gild estate after 1548.[33]

Manorial and Estate Records

Outside the larger towns the ubiquitous territorial unit throughout the middle ages was the manor, a term which referred both to a large house and to an administrative institution.[34] In its second sense, the word could apply to a great variety of estate, ranging in size from a few acres to over a hundred square miles. Although those responsible for the compilation of Domesday Book viewed the whole country as being divided into territories to which the name 'manor' could be applied, in reality there was already great diversity in size, value and structure. Nor was a manor necessarily rural: in many small towns the institution survived the establishment of a borough in the twelfth or thirteenth century and the two existed alongside until modern times. The complexities increased in later centuries as the manor ceased, in many parts of the country, to be an administrative entity while remaining a legal institution. Gradually the word acquired its modern meaning of a piece of landed property, with tenants, over whom the landlord exercised jurisdiction through a manor court. Such courts had been held long before but they now served to define the institution itself: if there was no court, there was no manor. Because of this shift in meaning, which the most recent account of the subject places in the mid-sixteenth century, the records can be viewed differently before and after this divide. In the middle ages, the manor was a unit of estate management and all documents produced as part of that process may be seen as 'manorial records'; from about 1540 only the proceedings of the manor court are so regarded and other material is placed in that omnibus category which dominates deposits in local record offices: 'estate papers'. This distinction is not without objections but serves to stress a shift in the character of the manor corresponding with the economic and social changes of the sixteenth century.

It is important to appreciate that, simply because the nature of estate management altered, the manor did not cease to exist. Even if courts were no longer held, the institution still existed in law and was unaffected, for example, by the abolition of military tenures in 1660. Nor were manors affected by the reform of land law in 1922, when copyhold tenure came to an end, although since that date there has been little reason for most manor courts to sit. The consequent threat to records, which might still be needed as evidence of title to former copyhold land, was appreciated at the time and by an amending Act of 1924 the documents were placed 'under the charge and superintendence' of the Master of the Rolls. Successive holders of that office have issued statutory rules for their control and custody: they must either remain in the hands of the lord of the manor or his steward (usually a solicitor) or be deposited in an approved repository; they may not leave England and Wales without the Master of the Rolls' consent, which in practice has never been given; they must be accessible to searchers and, if deposited, listed in prescribed form and a copy of the list passed to the Historical Manuscripts Commision. From these the HMC maintains, on behalf of the Master of the Rolls, a register covering the whole of England and Wales, indexed by parish, which also names the last known lord or his steward. These entries are often the best clue to the whereabouts of other estate records, especially in the case of material in local offices.

A large number of manors have in the past been held by the crown for either short or long periods; a rather smaller number still are. For these records may be found in the PRO, both in the Special Collections classes (p. 32), several of which consist specifically of court rolls, rentals and surveys, ministers' accounts and the like, or amongst the records of the Duchy of Lancaster (p. 37), or elsewhere (pp. 64-7, 167-9). Other manorial and estate records are in the British Library Department of Manuscripts, chiefly as a result of the break-up of estates in the sixteenth and seventeenth centuries and the dispersal of documents. In both cases, the material is included in the HMC's register and can easily be located. In this respect, manorial records are more fortunate than most other kinds of private muniment, since there is some degree of public control over them. In particular, it has been possible to prevent the removal of documents from the country by overseas purchasers of manors.

Professor Harvey's authoritative new account avoids the older, legalistic approach by turning first to estate records rather than court rolls. For many manors, both in the middle ages and later, there are documents known generically as 'surveys', the oldest (apart from a handful which predate the Conquest) in some instances being developed from information collected for Domesday. In the thirteenth century surveys of demesne lands (i.e. those parts of the manor farmed by the lord himself, rather than his tenants) were joined by 'extents', the essence of which was the inclusion of valuations of each part of the estate, including tenants' as well as demesne land. Extents were drawn up not merely in the course of day-to-day management but also, for example, as a preliminary to the leasing of a manor, especially by the crown or a corporate landowner, or in connection with an inquisition taken by the escheator after the death of a tenant in chief (p. 27). A more detailed later medieval survey was the 'terrier', a description following a topographical arrangement, giving as much attention to land held by tenants as to the demesne. Finally, a rental lists both parcels of land and income due therefrom, thus bridging the distinction between surveys and accounts.

The latter survive from the thirteenth century and are basically a record of transactions between the lord and his officials, who were responsible for income received and disbursements. The scale of record keeping obviously varied, depending on the size of the manor, whether it was held by a local resident or an absentee, and whether it formed part of a large estate, possibly with land in several counties. Manors which were part of larger units, especially those held by the crown or other institutional owners, are more likely to have detailed and well preserved records than those held by a country squire, whose steward may have had little need (or even the skill) to draw up elaborate accounts. At the opposite extreme, a great estate might have three levels of accountant: the bailiff of the individual manor, a local receiver to whom he was responsible, and a receiver-general who finally channelled the net income to his employer.

Better known and often better preserved than other muniments are the proceedings of seigneurial courts. Most relate to a single manor, less commonly to a court held for an honour, an estate made up of a number of separate manors, or to the court of a private hundred or wapentake. The popular term 'court rolls' is sometimes misleading: from the seventeenth century many stewards preferred to use bound volumes rather than membranes sewn into a roll. For some manors, both in the middle ages and more recently, there are long runs of well kept court records, especially where the estate was in institutional hands; for others there may be little or nothing. The keeping of manor courts declined during the sixteenth century, as agrarian and tenurial practices changed and local administration was taken over by the parish or township (p. 91), but in some areas, where, for example, customary tenures survived until 1922 or manorial commons were closely controlled, courts continued to sit into this century. A handful still do.

The privilege of holding a court to which tenants, free and unfree, could be summoned, was a basic right enjoyed by all lords of manors. The court administered the customs of the manor, which affected the villein tenants more than freemen, who could, if they wished, turn to the common law dispensed by the royal courts. In particular, tenements held 'according to the custom of the manor' (i.e. customaryhold or copyhold tenure) changed hands in the manor court: if a tenant died his heir would be admitted to the property there, or if he wished to acquire further land by purchase or exchange, or engage in any other kind of transaction, he could do so only with the consent of the lord given at the court. Thus manor court records of any date down to this century may provide considerable information about the history of individual properties.

Free tenants, on the other hand, were able to convey land without consent from their lord and dealings of this kind, whether in the middle ages or later, were recorded not in court rolls but in individual deeds which, for the most part, were not registered in any court, royal or seigneurial, local or central (cf. p. 47).

The other work of a manor court, which explains the survival of the institution in a few places today, concerned the organisation of farming and community life generally. Where the manor had extensive common lands, whether arable, meadow or pasture, there had to be some machinery for regulating the farming year, keeping animals off some areas at certain times and limiting the numbers allowed to graze at others, preventing the encroachment of private holdings on the commons, and appointing officials to administer the court's orders and by-laws, including a constable, who was to survive (as a parish officer) into modern times (p. 92), as well as those, such as haywards, whose functions disappeared with the decline of common-field farming.

Besides the right to hold a court customary, manor courts also enjoyed a wider jurisdiction which belonged to the crown but was granted to private lords. This privilege generally took the form of the right to hold a court leet, the term used in recent centuries, although in the middle ages the most common phrase in court rolls was 'view of frankpledge'. This referred merely to one part of the bundle of rights making up the frankpledge system, a network of mutual sureties between tenants which was already in decline by the thirteenth century, except as legal jargon. Some of the associated rights lived on far longer, such as that to try minor breaches of the peace, to maintain gallows and hang thieves caught red-handed, and to enforce the law relating to the sale of bread and ale. In theory, the court leet, with or without view of frankpledge, and the court baron were two separate institutions; in practice, on many manors a single court was held at which the two kinds of jurisdiction were exercised together.

Although the enclosure of common fields and wastes, the substitution of rack-renting and leasing for copyhold, and the rise of the parish as an agency of local government took away much of the work of the court baron, both it and leet not merely survived but in some areas flourished in the early modern period. Customaryhold continued to be administered by the court baron, while in many small towns the leet was, right up to 1835 or occasionally beyond, the only effective institution of local government, with elementary powers to control public health and trading standards which the post-medieval borough often lacked (p. 100). Manuals for stewards and guides to copyhold were published and, from 1733, the proceedings, like those of other courts, were recorded in English. On the other hand, even fewer manorial records of this period have been published than for the middle ages, since the material is so bulky and often relates to only a small area.

In many collections in local offices, as well as classes of the public records concerned with the modern crown estate (p. 167), manor court records are to be found alongside surveys, maps, rentals and other papers relating to the acquisition, management and (sometimes) disposal of a landed estate. It is thus slightly artificial to treat such material as 'manorial' only if it pre-dates 1540, since, for example, a nineteenth-century rent roll had exactly the same function as a similar thirteenth-century document, while many eighteenth-century estate maps are explicitly said to be plans of a particular manor, not a parish or some other area. The form the records take may change but their purpose does not, nor, generally, does their location.

An important constituent of such collections are title deeds, which also fill numerous classes at the PRO. It is impossible here to deal fully with deeds and their importance – indeed, a specialised work is badly overdue – but it is worth stressing that communities for which manorial records are poor may, conversely, be relatively rich in early deeds. In upland areas, where copyhold tenure and common-field farming were neither widespread nor long-lived, much of the land may have been held by free tenants whose manorial obligations were nominal and who from an early date conveyed land by deed of gift or some other instrument. Where they chose to proceed by fine in the court of Common Pleas, some record of the transaction should be preserved centrally (p. 34), but otherwise the only clue to thousands upon thousands of similar land deals is to be found in deeds now in local record offices, deposited there by landowners and solicitors; in old public library collections, where the arrangement is often very unsatisfactory; in the PRO, in the various classes of 'Ancient Deeds'; or in the British Library, where the documents are catalogued as 'Charters', mostly Additional Charters; or another national collection. Numerous calendars have been produced, either officially for the PRO or BL collections or privately, but the great bulk remains unpublished. The documents abound in topographical and genealogical detail but have received less attention from record society editors than manor court rolls. In any local study it is always worth checking available indexes for places, persons or families in which one is interested.[35]

There are a relatively small quantity of land charters surviving from before the Norman Conquest, mostly preserved in central custody. These have long been the subject of study and are well known for the inclusion in many of detailed descriptions of the bounds of the estate being conveyed. All known material of this kind has been listed and a full-scale corpus is in course of publication.[36]

From the sixteenth century to the late nineteenth deeds become bulkier and, it seems, more and more documents were needed to effect a transaction which in the middle ages required only a single item. Proportionately fewer deeds of this period have been published, or even listed: both in local offices and the PRO modern deeds lurk uncatalogued by the boxful, as they do in the deed registries of government departments and other public bodies, although their usefulness for topography and genealogy, as well as the history of individual properties or whole estates remains undiminished (cf. pp. 169-70). The necessity for such elaborate conveyancing would not have arisen had the state not tried, at various dates from the reign of Henry VIII, to devise a system of registration of title and had lawyers not successfully circumvented such efforts until the advent of modern registration in 1862. Some private deeds were enrolled in both local and central courts but only in a few counties was a universal system of registration adopted before this date (pp. 89-90).[37]

The Church

The records of the medieval church fall into two main groups. Firstly, there are those produced by the administrative and judicial hierachy of archdeaconries, dioceses and provinces, together with cathedral chapters, a structure which survived the Reformation and continues to the present day. Secondly, there are those belonging to the religious houses, great and small, which flourished in England and Wales in the middle ages but were swept away by Henry VIII, with their muniments lost or dispersed.

In general, the lowest tier of church organisation, the parish, did not create records before the mid-sixteenth century. Registers of baptism, marriage and burial were initated in 1538 and other material stems from Elizabethan legislation (pp. 94-99). For a few parishes churchwardens' accounts exist from as early as the fourteenth or fifteenth century, but these are exceptional; mostly they are found only from after 1550 or indeed much later (p. 95).[38]

Diocesan and capitular records, on the other hand, survive in England from the twelfth or thirteenth century, although in Wales only St Davids has any quantity of medieval material.[39] The administrative acts of the bishop in each see were recorded in a series of registers, volumes which sometimes replaced earlier rolls. They record, amongst other matters, the ordination of clergy, their institution to livings, the appropriation of benefices to religious houses and the receipt and return of writs from the royal chancery. A separate section of each volume may be concerned with the temporalities of the see and there may also be copies of orders made after episcopal visitations. By the late fifteenth century, the growing complexity of diocesan administration led to the subdivision of work between different officials whose records henceforth accrued separately; in addition, the practice arose of filing loose documents in support of acts noted in the registers, which marks the beginning of record keeping on more modern lines and was developed further in the century after the Reformation.

Medieval bishops' registers, like most other diocesan records, are now in archival custody (p. 107) and for many there are either published transcripts or typescript calendars in local record offices, so that recourse to the original in search of reference to a particular parish may not be necessary. The material as a whole has been fully described in a Royal Historical Society handbook.[40]

From a very early date archbishops, bishops and archdeacons exercised jurisdiction over their fellow clergy and, to some extent, the laity, which only finally ended in the mid-nineteenth century (p. 179). A series of courts extended from archdeaconry to province, with ultimate appeal until the Reformation to the Pope. Records of this jurisdiction in the middle ages survive for some dioceses, either in the bishops' registers or separate volumes. Like other judicial material of this period, the records of church courts are difficult to use for local studies unless they are published or calendared, although where finding-aids are available they are obviously worth checking. As in later centuries, it is the church's exclusive jurisdiction in testamentary matters that is perhaps most likely to yield documents of interest. In some dioceses wills proved in the bishop's court in the middle ages were entered in the registers before the main series of probate act books and filed wills begin, usually in the sixteenth century, and should be indexed, if not printed. The registered wills of the Prerogative Court of Canterbury, the highest probate court in the southern province, begin in 1383, although the documents do not become numerous until the sixteenth century (p. 81). There is, however, a published index for the early period, as there is for the smaller collection of medieval wills recorded in the archbishops' registers at Lambeth Palace. The earliest probate records of the Prerogative Court of York also date from the late fourteenth century.[41]

Documents relating to the temporalities of dioceses and chapters are broadly similar to other manorial and estate material (p. 43), but often better preserved. Besides the different types of estate material, there should be references to the administration of the capitular possessions in the chapter act books and, as well as loose deeds and leases, there may be a cartulary into which such items were copied for safekeeping.[42]

In the case of a religious house, of whatever size or order, the document most likely to have survived the vicissitudes of the Dissolution and later will likewise be a cartulary. The term is so often associated with monasteries, abbeys and similar foundations that it is perhaps as well to point out that other medieval landowners, lay and ecclesiastical, also compiled registers of the same kind, and that religious houses, again like their fellow landowners, would, at the time of their dissolution, have had a great mass of other estate records besides those considered sufficiently important to enter in a cartulary. Much of this material has disappeared since the Reformation, although for some houses there are surveys, rentals and other muniments, some of which owe their preservation to families who acquired former monastic estates to which the documents relate. The same is also true of some cartularies, although more commonly these passed into the hands of antiquaries after 1540 and have found their way into central, rather than local, custody, chiefly the British Library and Bodleian. There are complete lists of both religious houses and their cartularies, while short descriptions of the houses in each county are a standard feature of the *Victoria County History*, where this has been published. These accounts usually make use of the cartulary, if one survives, and many others are accessible through published editions.[43]

A cartulary, lay or monastic, was basically a register into which title deeds were copied, usually in somewhat abbreviated form, together with other important documents, such as surveys of the whole estate or records of legal proceedings concerning the property. The cartularies of religious houses generally record gifts, rather than purchases, whether of entire manors, individual pieces of land or spiritual possessions, such as benefices and tithes. Very often they begin with a major deed of gift from the founder, who provided the site and an initial endowment. They may also contain transcripts of royal or papal grants, bulls and similar items. For local historians interested in a particular parish, rather than the house itself, cartularies are a useful additional source of title deeds: sometimes, the original documents survive as well as the cartulary abstract and provide slightly more information; good modern editions where possible collate the register with loose deeds.

Cartularies are less commonly found for the gilds, hospitals and chantries established in most medieval boroughs. Here, however, there may be muniments incorporated into borough archives (p. 42) or a return to the crown enquiry into gilds of 1388 (p. 29).

Chapter Three
EARLY MODERN CENTRAL GOVERN-MENT AND THE LOCAL COMMUNITY

The 'Tudor Revolution in Government' first hypothesised thirty years ago by Sir Geoffrey Elton affected local communities just as it did the kingdom as a whole.[1] The sweeping changes in the machinery of government introduced by the early Tudors, consolidated by Elizabeth and retained in modified form until the Civil War greatly altered the way in which the crown dealt with the localities. At the same time, a system of local government evolved, its operation entrusted to individuals and institutions whose duties were mostly regulated by statute, augmenting, but not entirely superseding, the medieval pattern of administration through officials whose powers derived from grants by the crown or magnates rather than parliament. Such changes were especially marked in parts of the country which in the middle ages were counties palatine, partly exempt from royal jurisdiction, and in Wales, which was now assimilated into the pattern of government which most of the country had known since Norman times.

The Interregnum saw further changes affecting the localities, most of which were reversed with the restoration of Charles II. Between 1660 and the late eighteenth century innovations were few until pressure for reform began to assert itself from the 1780s. Apart from the establishment of separate departments for home and foreign affairs in 1782, reform before the 1830s was limited, certainly as it affected local communities. The three and half centuries between the accession of Henry VII and the Reform Act of 1832 thus have a measure of unity in administrative history, even if some Tudor innovations have antecedents which may be traced well back into the fifteenth century and some institutions established by Elizabeth survived almost until the death of Victoria.

As in other periods, central government in early modern times can be considered under three main heads: administrative, financial and judicial.[2] In all cases, links between crown and localities established in the middle ages were sustained by the Tudors and their successors, either through the same institutions or in new ways. Central control became considerably more rigorous under the Tudors, a rigour that was sustained by the governments of the Commonwealth and Protectorate. The links weakened after the Restoration and more especially after 1688 but did not wholly disappear, although that impression is sometimes given by the changing pattern of archival survival and, equally important, accessibility. Similarly, the great strengthening of central control which accompanied the creation of the modern system of local government after 1834 should not obscure the authority that could, if necessary, be exercised by eighteenth-century secretaries of state or the court of King's Bench over unco-operative justices of the peace, much less the extent to which central government continued to tax local communities or the frequency with which lawsuits of local interest were heard in the central courts.

Secretariat and Council

In the early middle ages the affairs of state, as directed by the king's council, were put in execution through the Chancery, with the Chancellor acting as the king's secretary. In time, the Chancellor ceased to be an officer of the royal household and became instead the head of an important administrative (and later judicial) department. The great seal, of which the Chancellor was keeper, was increasingly reserved for formal acts, and a privy seal was brought into use for instruments issued by the king or his council in the daily course of government. The keeper of the privy seal in turn went 'out of court', to be replaced by a new royal secretary, known from the early sixteenth century as 'secretary of state', who had custody of the signet seal. Between the reign of Henry VIII and that of Charles II this office likewise evolved from its origin as part of the royal household to become a central element in the administration. The work of the signet office became formal, although still remaining one of the responsibilities of the secretary, alongside a range of other functions.[3]

Since no statute limited or defined the duties of the office, it was in theory all-embracing and in practice its standing depended much on the prestige and abilities of the holder. In general terms, four main areas of activity can be identified. One was as a medium of communication between sovereign and subject, a relic of the office's origin as royal letter-writer. A second was to act as the king's representative on the Privy Council. The secretary of state was not the clerk of the council, which had its own secretariat and its own seal, but he became in this period its leading member, especially after the king ceased regularly to attend, and increasingly acted as its chief executive. His importance in parliament grew in a similar way. Two other functions were concerned with matters which remained largely the prerogative of the crown: the conduct of diplomacy and the maintenance of order.

From 1540 it was normal to appoint two secretaries of state, although this arrangement was not sanctioned by statute and the office remained one. In 1640 the secretaries' foreign business was divided between 'northern' and 'southern' departments, broadly separating dealings with protestant and catholic powers. Both continued to deal with domestic business until the office was re-arranged on modern lines in 1782, with one secretary taking responsibility for foreign affairs and the other for home policy (p. 162).

All aspects of the secretaries' work from Henry VIII's reign onwards, apart from diplomacy, brought them into contact with the local community. Letters and petitions intended for the king or council might come initially to the secretary; information sought by the council from localities might be returned to him and, although reported to the crown, the documents filed in the secretary's office. This was the case both with regular returns such as the muster certificates and the results of occasional enquiries, such as the census of inns and alehouses ordered in 1577; both are examples of the wealth of local information which can be found amongst the state papers, especially prior to 1660. Crown appointments of justices of the peace, lieutenants and sheriffs (p. 84), passed through the secretary's office; equally, the appointment of a clerk of the peace (p. 85) or a town clerk (p. 100) had to be approved, a requirment maintained even when close control of the localities withered after the Restoration. Requests from local officials for the use of troops were made to the secretary of state, since control of the army was a prerogative matter. More generally, secretaries of state, especially in times of tension or unrest, whether in Henry VIII's reign or George III's, sought to keep themselves informed as to what was happening in the localities, either through the lieutenants or a wider network.

Because the office was less formal in character than the Chancery, so record-keeping was less precise. There was no counterpart of the enrolment of documents (p. 25); indeed, to begin with, there was no state paper office and each secretary kept documents in his own hands. It is for this reason that many are no longer in official custody, although most that survive are now in the British Library, the Bodleian or a local repository. Those that did remain have long been divided into domestic and foreign series, even though the duties of the two secretaries were not separated until 1782; other papers, dealing with colonial matters, once formed a third series since merged with the records of the Colonial Office. The domestic series, which are obviously those of interest to local historians, begin in the reign of Henry VIII and continue in an unbroken sequence, in which papers are arranged roughly chronologically and bound into volumes, until 1782. Early Home Office papers (p. 162) are in fact similar to the domestic state papers of the earlier part of George III's reign.

The state paper office has been well served by editors, at least until the early eighteenth century. The calendars may vary in fullness and the reliability of personal and place-names, but they at least provide an index, if no more, to original documents. For the reign of Henry VIII, the *Calendar of Letters and Papers (Foreign and Domestic)* (1864-1932) includes not only all the papers in the PRO but also material from the British Library and elsewhere. It is an indication of the transitional state of government in this period that a calendar of the patent rolls (p. 26) is subsumed into this series, reflecting the way in which business might go through either the traditional channel or the newer office. After 1548 the functions of the Chancery and secretary of state are more distinct and calendars of the two archives have been published separately. All the state papers of Edward VI, Mary, Elizabeth, James I and Charles I are accessible through officially published calendars, while for the Interregnum the main *Calendar of State Papers (Domestic Series), Commonwealth* should be read in conjunction with the *Calendar of Proceedings of the Committee for the Advance of Money* (1888) and the *Calendar of Proceedings of the Committee for Compounding* (1889-92), of which the latter were once known as 'Royalist Composition Papers'. Both committees were concerned with the seizure and confiscation of the estates of 'delinquents' who had taken the royalist side in the Civil War or were papists or recusants. Where an estate was not confiscated it was subject to fining. Although much local detail is suppressed in the published volumes, they locate where fuller information on a particular family and its estates will be found. The Commonwealth Exchequer Papers (SP 28), dealing with the financial operations of the government between 1642 and 1660, are not in the calendars.

The calendars continue after the Restoration through the reigns of Charles II, James II and William III. Only two volumes have been published for Anne's reign, covering the years 1702-4. There is then a gap until a *Calendar of Home Office Papers of the Reign of George III, 1760 to 1775* (1878-99) begins, in which the term 'Home Office' is used to mean domestic, rather than foreign, papers in a still undivided State Paper Office. For the intervening period, the LIS has issued a Calendar of State Papers (Domestic) for George I's reign (1714-27) as volumes 139, 144, 155, 165 and 173, reproducing from typescript a work prepared on the same lines as the published calendars, including a full index. The original calendar was typed as long ago as 1928; it would be helpful if they dealt similarly with other volumes on the Round Room shelves, so that all the domestic series would be in print. The society has also issued a calendar of SP 46, State Papers, Supplementary, a miscellaneous collection of which only a few items actually originate from the State Paper Office (volumes 9, 19, 28, 33, 129, 143, 154, 178, 182). Only some of these are indexed but none would take very long to search for local references. Two other ancillary classes (SP 45, State Papers, Various, and SP 9, State Papers Miscellaneous) have no published calendar. LIS 179 prints a finding-aid for SP 5, a small class of papers relating to the suppression of religious houses in the mid-sixteenth century, consisting of only four volumes. Finally, SP 11 contains plans of fortifications, English and foreign, dating from the seventeenth century and later, which is worth checking for the topography of coastal towns.

During the sixteenth and seventeenth centuries the secretaries of state worked closely with the Privy Council, which evolved in the fourteenth century from a larger gathering of the king's advisers. Its secretariat was originally provided by the Privy Seal Office but from 1540 the council began to keep a register of its own and in 1556 acquired a seal. Like the secretaries of state, the council dealt with almost every aspect of government, from both an administrative and judicial standpoint. Under the Tudors and early Stuarts some of the judicial work was handled separately by the Court of Star Chamber (p. 78) or by the Court of Requests (p. 77), especially where the common law could not provide a suitable or quick remedy. Star Chamber was not revived after the Restoration but the Privy Council retained some judicial business as a court of appeal at a time when it was losing its administrative importance. Much of its work had always been done through committees, a system from which the modern cabinet emerged in the late seventeenth century as a small, more flexible body, which remained sufficiently informal for no record to be kept of its proceedings until 1916. Other council committees evolved into the Board of Trade (p. 171) and modern departments concerned with education (p. 142) and public health (p. 127).[4]

Between the accession of Henry VII and the Civil War the Privy Council was concerned with innumerable local matters. It received petitions from private individuals, officials and communities seeking redress, some of which were remitted to Star Chamber, others were dealt with by the Council. In turn, it issued orders to localities, either in execution of royal policy or seeking information. At times of disturbance or disorder the council was concerned to establish what was happening throughout the country. More generally, the renewal of local privileges, such as borough charters, was dealt with in the sovereign's name. At the height of its prestige, during Elizabeth's reign, there were few local concerns that might not, at some stage, come to the Council's notice. After 1603, and more especially after 1660, business became more formal, as actual policy was discussed elsewhere. Even in the eighteenth century, however, much of the routine involved the localities, with a flow of directions or requests for information in one direction and petitions for the renewal of privileges in the other. Sheriffs and other officials continued to be appointed by the Council. It was thus appropriate that, in the early nineteenth century, local efforts to meet the threat posed by cholera and yellow fever should be co-ordinated by the Privy Council, a function it had discharged in pulic health matters since the sixteenth century. Although eclipsed as a political institution by the cabinet, the council retained some administrative vitality.

Privy Council records are most accessible for the period in which its actvities were widest, making a search for references to an individual or place comparatively simple. Although its own register only begins in 1540, earlier records, from the period in which its secretariat was provided by the Privy Seal Ofice, can be found from 1386 onwards. These, together with the first register, were published by Sir N.H. Nicholas in *Privy Council of England, Proceedings and Ordinances, 10 Richard II – 33 Henry VIII* (Record Commission, 1834-7). From 1542 to 1631 the register is printed in *Acts of the Privy Council of England* (1890-1964), a series which has now apparently been given up. For 1637-45 the register was issued in facsimile (HMSO, 1967-8), with no attempt at indexing or editing; for 1631-7 it was reproduced on opaque 'microcards' (HMSO, 1962). Neither of these expedients is very satisfactory and nothing has been done to continue publication after 1645, except on the colonial side of the council's work.

Besides the registers, the main records of the Council before its nineteenth-century revival are the first 142 bundles of PC 1, a class of loose papers, mainly of the eighteenth century, earlier documents having been destroyed by fire in 1698. LIS 24 and 35 are lists of these papers, the first taken from a modern typescript, which is well indexed, while the second is an older manuscript schedule, endorsed 'Draft', which lacks an index. Both are worth searching for local material, since they deal with a period in which the council still received petitions, called for reports and handled the renewal of borough charters. It would presumably be possible to go from documents in PC 1 to the unpublished register (PC 2) to trace what action the council took in a particular matter.

During the sixteenth century, the council discharged some of its work through two regional bodies, the Council in the Marches of Wales and the Council in the North; there was an abortive attempt in 1539-40 to establish a Council in the West. The Council in the North ceased to meet after the outbreak of the Civil War and its proceedings are lost, although its history can be reconstructed from other sources. The Council in the Marches was revived after the Restoration and continued to meet until 1688. Two volumes of its records survive for the late sixteenth century, while its history can likewise be studied from other material.[5]

Although in most respects the Chancery was superseded in this period as the mainspring of government by the secretariat and council, the Chancellor retained some administrative functions which create records of local interest. Statutes of 1597 (39 Eliz., c.6) and 1601 (43 Eliz., c.4) gave him (or the Chancellor of the Duchy of Lancaster, cf. p. 37) power to enquire into charitable bequests through commissioners and to rectify abuses by issuing a decree which could be confirmed, modified or exonerated in the chancellors' courts. Arising from this procedure, which was superseded in the nineteenth century by powers conferred on the Charity Commission, set up in 1853 (p. 178), are series of inquisitions and decrees (C 93), confirmations and exonerations (C 90) and depositions taken at local inquiries (C 91). All three classes are listed by county in *Lists & Indexes* 10. The material is of obvious value for the history of local charities, since both oral testimony and documents (which may themselves now be lost) were produced at the inquiries.

Similarly, the Chancellor appointed commissioners to discover whether a particular person was to be certified a lunatic, since the crown had jurisdiction over the lands and possessions of such people. Early inquisitions of this sort are filed with the IPMs (p. 27) but from 1627 there is a separate series (C 211) which continues into this century. Although the law was modernised in 1842 and 1853, from which date there are other sources to check among the Ministry of Health records (p. 126), the Lord Chancellor's role in dealing with the judicial aspects of lunacy survived both these reforms and the major Lunacy Act of 1890, although after this date formal inquisitions were needed less often. The material in C 211 is arranged alphabetically to 1853, thereafter chronologically; a manuscript volume (IND 17612) is the main finding-aid for the earlier period.

Thirdly, from 1532 (23 Hen. VIII, c.5) commissions of sewers were issued more systematically than before to bodies of local officials in maritime counties charged with maintaining sea-walls, drains, ditches and rivers, whose own quasi-judicial proceedings are mentioned in the next chapter (p. 90). Related documents, including the original commissions, will be found in C 225, C 226, C 229 and C 191, which extend from the early seventeenth cetury to the later nineteenth.

Lastly, as the Close Rolls ceased in the early sixteenth century to be used as a means of enrolling administrative instruments, they assumed increased importance as a registry of private deeds, including both straightforward conveyances of lands and other transactions, such as enclosure awards, patents of invention, and deeds of gift conveying land for charitable purposes, such as the building of churches and schools in the nineteenth century. There are several series of manuscript finding-aids, arranged both by person and place, for this material in the Long Room.

Financial Administration

The early Tudor period saw major changes in the way in which revenue was raised and accounted for. Both Henry VII and Henry VIII greatly increased the resources of the crown, partly by making existing sources more productive but also by introducing new ones, chiefly, in the case of Henry VIII, the confiscation of church property. At the same time, both kings experimented with new and more efficient techniques of financial administration, by-passing the cumbersome procedures of the Exchequer. In the 1550s, these initiatives faltered and the new organs of 'chamber administration' devised by the early Tudors were absorbed into the older body. The techniques evolved by the new departments, however, were partly incorporated into the revived Exchequer, while many of their records were kept separately. In effect, a new layer of administration was added to those which had grown up in the middle ages, increasing the complexity of the records.[6]

Although most of the material described in this section originates from the Exchequer or one of the departments absorbed by it, a major theme of the second half of the period covered in this chapter is the rise of the Treasury as the main financial organ of central government. Early Treasury letters and papers (to 1718) are all accessible in printed calendars, which can easily be searched for local references. These volumes are indispensable in any study of public finance from 1660 onwards, although the editor's introductions should be treated more warily.[7]

When Henry Tudor became king the crown derived its income from four main sources. The sheriffs continued to bring to the Exchequer revenue from the crown demesne in their counties, together with fee-farms from incorporated boroughs and fines levied in the county courts, where these still sat (p. 40). Other traditional income came from bailiffs and escheators and was accounted for, as in earlier centuries, on the pipe roll of the Exchequer (p. 30). Secondly, the collectors at each port remitted customs dues, which grew as trade increased under the Tudors. Thirdly, the crown periodically sought parliamentary sanction to tax the wealth of its subjects through a levy of one-fifteenth or one-tenth of the value of the moveable property of each person assessed. Despite the efforts of both Henry VII and Henry VIII, revenue from this source did not grow in proportion to the increasing wealth of the country during the sixteenth century. Lastly, the crown, like any other great landowner, exploited its own estates. It was here that revenue increased most during the early Tudor period and where there was most innovation in procedure. Similarly, while other branches of the revenue all generate documents of local interest, it is the extension and more efficient management of the crown lands that, together with more rigorous exploitation of feudal privileges, produces the greatest quantity of material relating to local communities.

The Customs

The procedure by which the sheriffs accounted for their county farms and other traditional revenues hardly differed from that which evolved in the middle ages (p. 29), while it no longer represented an important part of the total revenue. Other Exchequer classes mentioned in the previous chapter (pp. 31-33) also extend into this period largely unchanged, including customs accounts (E 122), which give details of the trade of individual ports down to 1565; there is a list arranged by port in LIS 43 and 60. After this E 122 contains only subsidiary documents, as the port books (E 190) become the main source for the history of each port until the eighteenth century. A list of port books to 1700 was issued by the PRO as a one-off publication in the same style as that later adopted by the List and Index Society, which has completed the publication of the list to 1798 (volumes 58, 66, 80).[8]

For each port three series of books were compiled by local officials each year, covering the period Christmas to Christmas; in larger ports, especially after 1660, the books may only cover the half-year to or from Midsummer. One recorded the collection of import and export dues; another was kept by searchers concerned with cargo rather than revenue; and the third recorded coastal shipping, which was exempt from the payment of dues. In the latter case, the shippers had to enter into bonds undertaking not to unload at a foreign port; bundles of these 'coast bonds' survive in E 209 but only as unarranged debris. In the printed list the first two types of book, dealing with overseas trade, are listed together; often only one book, if that, will survive for any particular year. The class as a whole is not well preserved and many ports lack a complete series to 1798, when the system was ended. It is impossible in such cases to tell whether the later books have been lost after their return to the Exchequer or whether ports gave up keeping them well before 1798; the class includes a number of blank books which were returned but not filled in. From 1697 the Inspector General of Customs collected, from each custom house, details of the quantity and value of goods passing through each port, so as to produce a general statement of overseas trade. The surviving records from this exercise are arranged by country and commodity, the only other division being between the trade of the port of London and the 'outports', i.e the rest of England and Wales. The Inspector General's ledgers (p. 170) are therefore of no value for local studies, except for London, where the port books for 1697 and later were destroyed under schedule early this century precisely because the same information was supposedly available in the ledgers. The local officials at other ports must also have wondered why they were required to make two returns, to two different departments, of the same information and may have been disinclined to continue completing the port books. Since, however, the original returns from which the ledgers were compiled do not survive, the port books remain the only source of detailed information on the eighteenth-century trade of individual outports.[9]

Both the coastal and overseas books normally record the name of each vessel entering or clearing the port, its master, details of the cargo and the names of the merchants shipping the goods. The destination of outgoing vessels and port of departure of incoming ships are also recorded. Entries were made daily and while clearances normally apear once only, the arrival of vessels, especially from overseas, may be noted on several days, with entries for different ships intermixed, as they were unloaded and their cargo cleared customs. The day-book character of the documents tends to be obscured in printed editions which tabulate entries by ship but it is important to continue searching after a vessel's initial appearance. At first sight, well kept port books appear an immensely rich source for the trade of a port, theoretically listing every item of cargo shipped in or out, with a wealth of names of merchants, masters and ships, as well as coastal and overseas ports. In practice, it is very difficult to check their completeness, but where this can be done it soon becomes clear that the books are far from a complete record of seaborne trade.[10] Most, possibly all, ships were entered, but by no means every consignment was listed, nor every merchant. It seems highly unlikely that one can calculate the volume of trade, either in total or in a particular commodity, from the books, even for a single port over a short period. It is probably better to use them merely to give an impression of the general flow of goods in and out, including a rough idea of the relative importance of different commodities and a general picture of who were, at any one time, the leading merchants trading through the port. The books should be used in conjunction with any locally preserved documents and, for the eighteenth century, with correspondence between the local collector and London (p. 171). After 1798, and for some ports well before, one is entirely dependent on other material of this kind.

Taxation

The medieval practice of taxing one-fifteenth of the value of moveable property of men living outside the royal demesne and one-tenth of those living there or in cities and boroughs fossilised after 1334, with new impositions failing to yield increased revenue despite the growing wealth of the country. After 1500 an attempt was made to tax this wealth more effectively by introducing a new levy, in which either land or goods were taxed on a sliding scale imposed afresh on each occasion. The impost was known as a 'lay subsidy', since the clergy were assessed separately, and remained the standard form of direct taxation until the Interregnum. Its original flexibility, however, soon gave way to the same rigidity as had affected the fifteenth and tenth; after the accession of Elizabeth the sliding scale was abandoned in favour of a fixed assessment at the rate of 4s in the pound on land worth 20s or more per annum and 2s 8d in the pound on goods worth more than £3. The original plan of re-assessing a community on each occasion was also abandoned: the same group of 'subsidymen', as they became known, were assessed year after year by the petty constable in each township (p. 92), who remitted the money via the high constable of the hundred (p. 90) to commissioners for each county appointed in the authorising Act.

The detailed assessments of individual townships for the Tudor fifteenths and tenths and the subsidies will be found, like earlier tax returns (p. 31), in E 179, since the commissioners continued to account at the Exchequer. The documents are arranged by county and date, with individual pieces generally covering either an entire county or a single hundred or wapentake. There is a detailed list (List and Index Society 44, 54, 63, 75, 87), in which pieces that contain names, normally arranged under townships, are distinguished from summary accounts that do not. In general, the subsidy authorised in 1523 provides the fullest information for counties in southern and midland England and several editions of assessments from this have been published. For the north and for Wales, which was only brought into the English tax system after the Act of Union of 1536, the subsidy authorised in 1543 appears to be rather fuller. Later assessments have tended to be overlooked, although many years ago S.A. Peyton drew attention to their usefulness, and for a full local study one may as well look at all the material. Contemporary copies of assessments turn up fairly frequently in local record offices among the papers of families included in the commission or in some other context.[11]

For the ship money collected by Charles I in the 1630s there are no detailed assessments naming individuals comparable to those for the subsidies, although summary accounts survive to show how much each county paid. Similarly, during the Commonweath communities were taxed through 'monthly assessments', in which a quota was laid on each county and no lists of taxpayers were returned to the Exchequer. In both cases, however, there may be more detailed material for a particular place in a local collection. The Civil War also saw the introduction of the Excise but nothing of interest to local historians appears to survive before the nineteenth century (p. 171).[12]

During the reign of Charles II and later various expedients were tried in new attempts to tax the wealth of the country effectively and produce sufficient public revenue. The traditional form of subsidy was revived and then abandoned for good, while a poll tax was levied on seven occasions between 1660 and 1697. Assessments for the subsidies survive for some counties in E 179 and locally; for the poll tax material in the PRO (also in E 179) is limited but there may be more in local offices. In 1661 a 'free and voluntary present' to Charles II was authorised by parliament, to which most of the gentry (and in some counties others) subscribed; lists of contributors are again in E 179. Between 1695 (6 & 7 Will. & Mary, c.6) and 1706 a tax was levied on births, marriages, burials, bachelors over 25 and childless widows, from which no documents appear to survive in central custody but for a few places, including the City of London, detailed lists of inhabitants have come to light.[13]

The best known Restoration levy, however, was that on hearths first imposed by an Act of 1662 and continued at intervals until 1689. Apart from those exempt by reason of poverty, all householders were taxed at a rate of 2s per hearth on each occasion, assessment and collection at local level falling to the constables and sheriffs, who returned nominal lists which are now in E 179. This material generally exists for only two periods, 1662-65 and 1670-73, when the tax was collected through the traditional machinery. For the years 1666-69 and 1674-84 the tax was farmed and after 1684 was managed by a commission which also collected the Excise; for these periods only subsidiary documents were returnable to the Exchequer. Nevertheless, there should be at least one assessment (showing the amount each householder was supposed to pay) or return (listing what was actually paid) or both for each county and for some there may be several. The assessments may also list those discharged because of poverty or they may be listed separately. For some counties there are also returns of arrears of payments for 1662-65. Because of their obvious genealogical interest assessments and returns have been published for a number of counties, several with introductions by C.A.F. Meekings, whose own analysis of hearth tax collection between 1662 and 1669 has been issued by the LIS (153, 163). As with other taxes of this period, duplicate material can be found among the papers of families who served as sheriff or constable and at least one collectors' book survives as an unclaimed exhibit in an Exchequer revenue case.[14]

After the Revolution of 1688 a new type of direct tax evolved which combined elements of both the subsidy and assessment. In common with the subsidy of 1671 the tax authorised in 1692 (4 Will. & Mary, c.1) fell on personal estate, offices and land. It was similar to the three aids raised in 1688 for the collection of 1s, 2s and 1s in the pound, except that 4s, the rate adopted in 1692, was the highest level ever for an aid. It remained at this figure until 1696; the following year the government converted it to a 3s rate supplemented by a poll tax. In 1698 the tax was redesigned on lines similar to those used for the monthly assessments during the Interregnum and Charles II's reign, by which a fixed sum was charged on each county and the method of raising the money left to local custom. The two main forms of direct taxation employed since the sixteenth century were thus fused and in practice the new tax came to be regarded as falling solely on land. By 1702 the annual renewing Act (which remained the form of authorisation until 1798) was called the Land Tax Act. The tax was made perpetual in the latter year (38 Geo. III, c.60), with provision for redemption by a lump-sum payment, and the amount payable by each township permanently fixed. The 1949 Finance Act made redemption compulsory on the sale of property or the death of an owner and in 1963 all unredeemed tax was abolished.[15]

Duplicate assessments showing the amount of tax payable by each township were returnable to the King's Remembrancer on the same lines as before but these do not name individuals. Three classes (E 181, E 182, E 183) contain receivers' accounts for the land tax and other eighteenth-century assessed taxes, while E 184 has selected duplicates for 1798. More important are the documents transferred from the former Land Tax Redemption Office to Kew. IR 23 contains, with some gaps, a complete assessment for 1798, including names, and is especially useful for counties where the preservation of material locally is poor. The contracts by which taxpayers redeemed their annual liability in return for a single payment (a process known as 'exoneration') form IR 24, while information arranged by parish will be found in the Redemption Books in IR 22.

The bulk of surviving land tax material of local interest, however, is in county record offices, chiefly for the period 1780-1832, when duplicate assessments were deposited with the clerk of the peace as evidence of entitlement to vote in parliamentary elections in a period in which the county franchise was based on ownership of freehold land worth 40s per annum. In some counties duplicates were retained from an earlier date under an Act of 1745. They were not normally deposited for townships in parliamentary boroughs, where the franchise was different, although of course land tax was imposed on boroughs as well as counties. After 1832 the compilation of printed registers of electors and changes in the parliamentary franchise made deposit unnecessary. Later documents have in some areas been transferred to record offices by the local land tax commissioners or their clerk. Assessments for the period before 1780, except where deposit with the clerk of the peace was adopted earlier than in general, may have reached record offices with the papers of families who served as commissioners or sheriff or again from the commissioners' clerk. Odd assessments, for both land tax and other taxes of this period, also turn up in parish collections. A useful handlist has recently surveyed material in both central and local custody but less has been written on the administrative history of the tax at local level than on the hearth tax or lay subsidy. This is perhaps because land tax has received little attention from record societies: some editions of assessments for selected years might be useful not only for genealogists but also those interested in the administrative history of taxation. The major use, besides genealogy, to which land tax records have been put is in determining shifts in landownership during the period 1780-1830, especially as a result of enclosure, although their reliablity in this respect remains controversial.[16]

Several other assessed taxes were levied in the eighteenth century, of which only the window tax (strictly a tax on houses assessed by the number of windows), imposed by 7 & 8 Will. III, c.18 and later Acts, generates documents of local interest. There is no central archive of window tax assessments but examples can be found in family, parish or solicitors' collections. For the income tax levied on a temporary basis between 1799 and 1816 returns giving the names of individual taxpayers arranged by parishes survive in E 182, with summary returns in E 181, despite an undertaking after the tax was repealed that all such records would be destroyed. Another tax of this period, to which attention has recently been drawn, was that levied on shops in 1785.[17]

Land Revenues

It was here that Henry VII's attempts to increase the financial resources of the crown were most successful and where his new administrative methods proved most durable. Henry VIII further increased the land revenues, chiefly by the confiscation of monastic property, and the seizure of church estates was completed by Edward VI's dissolution of gilds and chantries. Later Tudor sovereigns reduced rather than increased the crown's estate, the remainder of which was largely disposed of during the Commonwealth. These sales were declared void at the Restoration but not all the property was recovered. William III made further sales, a process arrested by the Civil List Act (1 Anne, c.1), which prevented alienation for more than 31, or in some cases 50, years. Much reduced, the crown estate survives to the present day and is now administered by commissioners whose records, together with those of the Office of Land Revenue Records and Enrolments and the Office of Works (all at Kew), form the main sources for its modern history (p. 167). Earlier material is divided between a number of classes at Chancery Lane, reflecting the frequent reorganisation of the administrative structure in the sixteenth century and the tendency of earlier record keepers to group documents concerned with estate management by type rather than provenance.

From the start of his reign, Henry VII assigned certain revenues, including those from crown estates, to his own household rather than the Exchequer, introducing a swifter, more precise method of audit. His son continued the practice and by an Act of 1512 (3 Hen. VIII, c.23) appointed General Surveyors and Approvers of the King's Lands to manage the revenue therefrom. The General Surveyors were made perpetual in 1536 (27 Hen. VIII, c.62) and in 1542 were given the status of a court with power to punish defaulting accountants. Meanwhile, the revenues of the monasteries dissolved in 1536 (27 Hen. VIII, cc.27, 28) and 1539 (31 Hen. VIII, c.13) were entrusted to a newly erected Court of Augmentations of the Revenues of the Crown, which by further statutes of 1545 (37 Hen. VIII, c.4) and 1548 (1 Edw. VI, c.14) acquired the property of gilds, chantries, colleges and other religious foundations. In 1547 the two courts were amalgamated into a reformed Court of Augmentations, which was both an administrative and judicial department. In 1554 Queen Mary, by letters patent under the statute 1 Mary, c.10, abolished the court as a separate entity, annexing it to the Exchequer. Although its separate jurisdiction was ended, its administrative methods survived, while the auditors of the dissolved court formed a new sub-department of the Exchequer known as the Office of the Auditors of Land Revenue. Partly reformed in 1799 (39 Geo. III, c.83), the office, consisting now of only a single auditor, survived until 1832 (2 & 3 Will. IV, c.1). Records of the Court of General Surveyors, the Court of Augmentations and the

Auditors of Land Revenue are now to be found in both the Augmentations classes of the Exchequer (E 299 to E 330) and the Land Revenue classes (LR 1 to LR 16), while other material has either passed out of official custody (most commonly ending up in the British Library Department of Manuscripts) or has been placed elsewhere in the Exchequer group.[18]

The Augmentation Office classes contain a mass of material of local interest, which broadly falls into two categories. There are records concerned with the survey, acquisition and disposal of property formerly held by the church, plus documents, chiefly deeds, cartularies and other estate records, inherited by the office from former holders of lands which passed through Augmentations hands. In the first group come the certificates returned by commissioners listing details of the chantries, gilds and other minor foundations dissolved under the statutes of 1545 and 1547, which record the date of foundation and name of founder, the value of their lands and details of plate, jewels and other possessions (E 301). Somewhat similar inventories of the goods of parish churches and gilds made during the reigns of Edward VI and Mary can be found in E 117 and in some of the Augmentation Office Miscellaneous Books (E 315/495-515), both of which are listed by county in LIS 69; there is no published list for E 301.[19]

Most of the former church lands which passed to the Augmentation Office were initially leased, rather than granted in fee. 'Particulars for Leases', i.e. preliminary drafts, will be found in E 310; counterparts of leases made by the court during Henry VIII's reign are in E 299 and those for later reigns in E 311. Warrants for leases under the privy seal or some other authority form E 300, while enrolled leases are divided between E 315 and, for Elizabeth's reign only, E 309. A detailed list of the entire, extremely varied, contents of E 315 was issued as LIS 16 and for the other classes, like those concerned with grants of Augmentations estate, material relating to particular localities can be found fairly easily from a series of manuscript indexes, whose bulk unfortunately makes them unsuitable for reproduction. Deeds of purchase and exchange between the crown and religious houses make up two further classes (E 305, E 315), with leases surrendered by monasteries to the crown in a third (E 312).

Particulars for grants (as opposed to leases) of crown lands between the reigns of Henry VIII and Charles I now form E 318; those for Henry VIII only are listed by grantee's name in appendices to *Deputy Keeper's Reports* 9 and 10. E 319 is a small class of similar particulars concerning lands belonging to schools. For the major sales of the Commonwealth period a variety of classes need to be checked, details of which are given in PRO Leaflet 54. Among the more important are surveys taken by parliament under two Acts of 1649 to establish the extent of the estate of Charles I, his queen and the Prince of Wales, which are listed in *Lists and Indexes* 25 and calendared in appendices to *Deputy Keeper's Reports* 7 and 8. Duplicates of some of the surveys will be found amongst Duchy of Lancaster records (DL 32) and in the miscellaneous books of the Auditors of the Land Revenue (LR 2/276-304).[20] Particulars were then drawn up for the sale of the estate (E 320) and in some cases counterpart conveyances survive in E 304. Contracts for sale will be found in SP 26/1-4, some of which are entered in E 315/173-4, which are not indexed. Certificates as to sales are in E 121 (listed in LIS 91), while particulars for the sale during the Interregnum of fee-farm rents reserved on sales before the Civil War now form E 308, with counterpart deeds of sale in E 307.

Other Augmentations classes of local interest include counterparts or transcripts of leases made by monasteries before their dissolution in E 303 (which is arranged by county) and E 118; original deeds of surrender by heads of religious houses (E 322, listed in *Deputy Keeper's Report* 8); and several classes of deeds, most of which originally belonged to religious houses. The largest collection forms E 326, of which the first 4,000 are calendared in *Catalogue of Ancient Deeds,* I-III (1890-1900) and the remainder in LIS 95, 101, 113 and 124, of which the last is the index. Volume 137 in the same series contains a calendar of deeds in E 328, again with an index; there is no published list of E 327 or E 329, nor for a small collection of 'modern' deeds in E 330. There are also several classes of deeds on the King's Remembrancer side of the Exchequer, many of which were originally acquired by the Augmentation Office. Again, the largest of these (E 210) is calendared in the published *Catalogue,* while LIS 200 contains a calendar of E 211, a supplementary class of large documents. There are no printed lists for E 212 or E 213, while the modern (i.e. post 1603) deeds in this series (E 214) are listed in a volume available in the searchroom only. E 132 is a small class of transcripts of deeds, many recording grants to religious houses, described in LIS 108. Among the Augmentation Office miscellaneous books are further deeds bound into volumes (E 315/31-54) as well as royal charters and other documents, mostly relating to religious houses (E 315/29-30), while are included in LIS 16. The same class also contains other estate records inherited by the office, such as cartularies, rentals, surveys and ministers' accounts, of which the first are described in the printed list and the others included in *Lists and Indexes* 25 and 34.

The remaining classes are either of limited local interest or inadequately indexed to facilitate searches. Thus the proceedings of the court as a judicial tribunal, divided between loose papers in E 321 and yet more of the miscellaneous books (E 315), lack any topographical finding-aid, whereas E 306, which contains most of the limited quantity of Duchy of Cornwall records not at the Duchy Office, mainly relates to estates in Cornwall. (Some records of the medieval duchy are in E 119 and E 120; cf. p. 38.) The 42 boxes of 'Miscellanea' (E 314) lack any printed list; conversely, it may be worth checking the published index to E 313 (LIS 185), a small collection of original letters patent.

The Land Revenue classes are fewer in number and less complicated in arrangement; there is also a published class-list covering almost the whole group (LIS 53, 57), although in some cases it is necessary to consult IND volumes at Chancery Lane to identify material relating to specific places. This is true, for example, of LR 1, a series of books containing enrolled grants, leases and other documents relating to the crown estate, mainly from the mid-sixteenth century down to the abolition of the office in 1832. Particulars for grants and drafts of particulars in LR 10 are, however, arranged topographically and described in detail in the list. Other grants, leases and particulars are entered in some of the miscellaneous books (LR 2), which are also well listed. The second major class of record are the accounts of the receivers of land revenue, declared before the Auditors, and documents subsidiary thereto. Two of the three series of accounts (LR 6 and LR 7, extending from the mid-sixteenth century to 1832) are listed topographically in LIS 53; for LR 12 one has to use IND 7655 and 7656. The 'views of accounts' (LR 8) are listed by county and some local detail is also given in the list of vouchers to the accounts (LR 5). To identify the exact contents of documents in LR 9, auditors' memoranda, IND 7659 has to be sent for. There is a separate class of accounts kept by the Surveyors General of Woods and Forests from the Restoration to 1810 and the Commissioners of Woods, Forests and Land Revenues from then until 1832 (LR 4; cf. p. 168), in which material relating to individual forests can be located without difficulty.

As with the Augmentations records, the Land Revenue group contains muniments inherited from religious houses and elsewhere. There are court rolls in LR 3, listed by county, and estreats of rolls in LR 11, for which the list is divided between the two printed volumes. Rentals and surveys among the miscellaneous books (LR 2) are described in both the class-list and *Lists and Indexes* 25. Finally, there are some small classes of deeds, of which the largest (LR 14) has a printed calendar (LIS 181), the other two (LR 15 and LR 16) do not.

The records of another Exchequer sub-department, the First Fruits and Tenths Office, may also be mentioned here; although not strictly part of the land revenues of the crown, the income accounted for by the office arose from Henry VIII's attack on the church. The payment of 'annates' (the profits of a benefice during the first year after the death or resignation of an incumbent) to the see of Rome was ended in 1532 (23 Hen. VIII, c.20); three years later (26 Hen. VIII, c.3) another Act directed that these 'first fruits' should be paid to the king, together with a sum equal to one-tenth of the value of each benefice. Commissioners were appointed to value church possessions for these payments, the results of which form the *Valor Ecclesiasticus* of 1535 (E 344), normally consulted in the six-volume Record Commission edition (1810-34), which contains details of the income of all parish churches, many chapels and a wide range of gilds and chantries as well as the larger religious houses. In 1541 (32 Hen. VIII, c.45) a new Court of First Fruits and Tenths was established to administer the revenue, which was abolished under the Act of 1 Mary, st. 2, c.10, and made a branch of the Exchequer. In 1704 first fruits and tenths were vested in a corporation known as Queen Anne's Bounty (2 & 3 Anne, c.20), which established a fund to augment the income of poor livings from payments by those with a larger income. Records of Queen Anne's Bounty, which in 1948 was merged with the Ecclesiastical Commissioners to form the modern Church Commissioners, have been transferred to Chancery Lane as QAB 1, for which there is a search-room list, including an index of parishes. Records of the older department, some of which extend well beyond 1704, form the Exchequer classes E 331 to E 347, for which there is no published list.[21]

The main series of local interest are those which name individual incumbents and livings. Among the most useful is E 331, returns by bishops and the deans and chapters of London, Salisbury and York of the institution of incumbents between 1544 and 1912, which is arranged by diocese and then by date, for which there are name indexes in the IND group. Certificates returned by bishops seeking exemption from payment of first fruits and tenths, mainly after the Restoration, when a large number of benefices were vacant, form E 333, which is listed by county and parish, while a bundle of returns by sheriffs to the Commonwealth and Protectorate governments (1651-8), listing names of benefices and incumbents (E 339), is also arranged topographically.

Finally, material in two other groups reflects the crown's attempts to increase its revenues from land during the Tudor period. The Duchy of Lancaster was included in the previous chapter (p. 37), since its oldest records are medieval, but several classes begin in the sixteenth or seventeenth century as the crown sought to exploit more effectively its enormous landed wealth. Secondly, from Henry VII's reign onwards, the crown enforced its rights of wardship over the heirs of tenants holding in chief, a development culminating in the establishment of the Court of Wards and Liveries in 1541 (32 Hen. VIII, c.46). The court was abolished in 1660 as part of the Restoration settlement which swept away feudal tenures (12 Charles II, c.24). Its surviving records include a considerable quantity of unsorted miscellanea, for which there is a typed list in the Round Room, plus some court proceedings, such as depositions (WARD 3) and decrees and orders (WARD 1), as well as surveys of lands in wardship (WARD 4 and 5). There are also duplicate IPMs sent from Chancery in cases where the heir was a minor (WARD 7), which are included in the general list (p. 28), and a large number of deeds and other estate muniments put into court as exhibits and not reclaimed (WARD 2). Two well known studies provide a sound introduction to the group and the class list is in print as LIS 18.[22]

Administration of Justice

Common Law

The three courts sitting at Westminster in the middle ages – King's Bench, Common Pleas and the Exchequer – continued into modern times with their procedure, and thus their records, largely unchanged, although the amount of business heard by each court varied over the centuries. The classes in which cases of local interest may be traced extend in several instances from the thirteenth or fourteenth centuries down to the nineteenth with few breaks (p. 33), although for the more recent period there is a wider range of subsidiary classes alongside the main series of plea rolls. The material does not, frankly, become any easier to use for local studies, since the finding-aids remain limited in scope and unpublished. One development in the Elizabethan Court of Common Pleas worth mentioning was the establishment of a separate series of Recovery Rolls (CP 43), on which some documents formerly included on the plea rolls (CP 40) were henceforth enrolled, in particular, 'common recoveries', judgments arising from a collusive suit entered into between parties seeking, typically, to circumvent an entail on a freehold estate. Recoveries are somewhat similar in purpose to the fines found among the Common Pleas records from the twelfth century (p. 34) and the two were often used together. Both were abolished in 1834. By contrast with the fines, however, little has been done towards the publication of local series of common recoveries, examples of which often turn up in estate collections in county record offices.[23]

There were more marked changes in the administration of common law in the localities. The general eyres (p. 35) ceased in the fourteenth century and the court of King's Bench was rarely itinerant after 1400. Some civil pleas were held by local lay justices, who also delivered gaols on occasion, but during the fifteenth century the practice became established of judges from all three common law courts riding circuits twice a year to hear pleas of assize and deliver gaols. Indeed, by 1330 assize circuits that remained virtually unaltered until 1876 were already well defined. The assize judges heard civil pleas under the *nisi prius* procedure which would otherwise have gone to Westminster and increasingly took murder and other serious felonies (as well as minor criminal cases) out of the hands of the justices of the peace (cf. p. 86). They were also used as part of the mechanism of supervision of local government. The justices transmitted specific instructions and general political sentiment from the centre, as represented by the Council, to the localities, as personified by the JPs in quarter sessions.

Before 1876 there were six assize circuits in England outside London and Middlesex. The Midland Circuit included Lincoln, Nottingham, Derby, Warwick and (until their transfer to the Norfolk Circuit in 1863) Northampton, Leicester and Rutland. The

Norfolk Circuit included (besides those added in 1863) Buckingham, Bedford, Huntingdon, Cambridge, Norfolk and Suffolk. Essex, Hertford, Kent, Surrey and Sussex made up the Home Circuit, while Berkshire, Oxford, Hereford, Shropshire, Gloucester, Stafford and Worcester formed the Oxford Circuit, to which Monmouthshire was added by 34 & 35 Hen. VIII, c.26, which established a separate Court of Great Sessions for the other Welsh counties (p. 71). The more remote counties of the north (Yorkshire, Durham, Northumberland, Cumberland, Westmorland and Lancashire) formed a Northern Circuit, those of the west (Hampshire, Wiltshire, Dorset, Somerset, Devon and Cornwall) a Western Circuit. In 1876, in the only change in assize procedure in a period in which the superior courts in London were far more radically reformed (p. 180), the Norfolk and Home circuits were abolished and a South Eastern Circuit set up, containing counties from the other two, less Northampton, Leicester, Rutland, Buckingham and Bedford, which went into an enlarged Midland Circuit. The north was divided into Northern and North Eastern Circuits, the latter including Northumberland, Durham and Yorkshire. Wales, which under the Act of 1830 abolishing Great Sessions (11 Geo. IV & 1 Will. IV, c.70) formed a single assize circuit, was divided into North and South Wales. Finally, in 1893, Surrey, omitted from the changes of 1876, was added to the South Eastern Circuit.

Thus modified, the assizes survived until the Courts Act, 1971, merged their jurisdiction with that of quarter sessions, whose judicial and licensing work was left unscathed by the setting up of elected county councils in 1888 to take over their administrative functions (p. 87). Whereas quarter sessions records have always been in local custody, those of the higher courts accumulated in the hands of the clerk of assize for each circuit, from whom the older material was transferred to the PRO early this century and is now arranged according to post-1876 circuits. Some earlier documents relating to circuit justice will be found amongst King's Bench records and others relating to civil pleas heard by the assize justices were returned either to King's Bench or Common Pleas.

Despite the importance of the assize courts, which for more than five centuries formed the apex of the local judicial pyramid, their records are not especiallly well preserved, nor easy to use for local searches. Nothing survives from the Midland Circuit before 1818, while only for the Home Circuit is there any sixteenth-century material. Even after 1600 many classes have large gaps. Finding-aids are limited, except for the Home Circuit, where Prof. J.S. Cockburn, as well as providing the standard account of assizes in the early modern period, has edited several volumes of calendars.[24] Certainly in the nineteenth century and sometimes the eighteenth, a local newspaper will provide a fuller account of a particular case than can be reconstructed from the records, including speeches by counsel and the judge, the demeanour of the prisoner in criminal cases and public reaction to the verdict or sentence. Major political cases heard by circuit judges can also be followed in *State Trials* and for others, civil or criminal, local interest sometimes warranted the publication of lurid pamphlets.

Assize business divided into two parts. On the Crown Court side a single judge heard criminal cases by virtue of a writ of gaol delivery, i.e. those committed to gaol since the last assize for offences too serious to dealt with at quarter sessions were brought before him, tried and, if found guilty, sentenced. Until the nineteenth century this normally meant execution, although often the sentence was commuted. Before the establishment of the modern appeal procedure, convictions on the Crown side of assize could be reversed by King's Bench, to whom a case was remitted for review by a writ of *certiorari*. Where records of the criminal work of assize courts survive, they include indictments, setting out the alleged offence, with the verdict entered on them; gaol books or calendars, listing prisoners to be tried; witnesses' depositions; and minute books, recording sentences. Coroners' inquisitions can also be found among the indictments or filed separately.

Civil, or *nisi prius,* business was concerned with actions between private parties on a variety of matters concerning real or personal property, such as trespass, breach of contract, assault or libel. The technical term derives from the fiction that these were cases set down to be heard at Westminster, where the sheriff had to produce jurors on a certain date, 'unless before' then the case was heard on circuit, which in practice it was. Proceedings were more dignified than in the Crown Court, parties were heard by counsel and there was concern for points of law rather than merely fact. Most, if not not all, the published reports of assize hearings before modern times are for civil cases. Conversely, fewer records survived in the hands of the clerks of assize. Documents received from King's Bench or Common Pleas were returned after the hearing with a note of the judgment endorsed (the *postea*), where they now form KB 20, CP 41 and CP 42, or were handed to the parties, leaving only an entry in the minute book of the circuit court as a brief record of the proceedings.

The evolution of the superior common law courts in Wales followed a different course.[25] Under the Statute of Wales (12 Edward I) six counties were established (Anglesey, Carmarthen, Caernarfon, Merioneth, Flint and Cardigan) and provision made for the appointment of assize justices. Surviving medieval Welsh assize rolls can be found among the records of the Justices Itinerant (pp. 35, 40). The rest of the country was shired by Acts of 1536 and 1543 (27 Hen. VIII, c.26, and 34 & 35 Hen. VIII, c.26), the second of which grouped the counties into four circuits, each with a Court of Great Sessions exercising criminal and civil jurisdiction, whose justices were to sit twice annually in each county. Chester, Flint,

Denbigh and Montgomery formed the Chester Circuit; Anglesey, Caernarfon and Merioneth a North Wales Circuit; Brecon, Radnor and Glamorgan a Brecon Circuit; and Carmarthen, Pembroke and Cardigan, plus the county corporate of the town of Haverfordwest, made up a Carmarthen Circuit. The chief official of each, in whose hands records of both criminal and civil hearings accumulated, was the prothonotary, an office which for the Chester Circuit was combined with that for the Palatinate of Chester, which included Flint, and whose justice became a judge of the Chester Circuit. As a consequence, both palatinate and sessions records were kept at Chester and some of the latter form part of the Palatinate of Chester rather than Principality of Wales group in the modern PRO classification (pp. 36-7).

From the end of the seventeenth century Great Sessions also exercised equity jurisdiction, which evolved without statutory warrant, possibly following the abolition of the Council in the Marches of Wales in 1688 (p. 56), whose court had enjoyed both equity jurisdiction and appellate jurisdiction in some common law causes from Great Sessions, of which the latter after 1688 passed to King's Bench. In 1830 (11 Geo. IV & 1 Will. IV, c.70) Great Sessions was abolished, with pending common law suits transferred to the Exchequer and equity cases to Chancery or the equity side of the Exchequer. Both Great Sessions and Palatinate of Chester records were moved to the PRO in 1854, apart from some documents from the North Wales Circuit, which in 1930 passed to the University College of North Wales at Bangor among a solicitor's papers, where they form the Porth yr Aur collection. Subsidiary documents dating from after 1660 were scheduled for destruction by the PRO early this century but, after protests from Welsh scholars, were presented to the nascent National Library of Wales in 1909-10, to become the first major manuscript accession, while retaining the PRO number WALE 13. In 1963, after renewed agitation from the Board of Celtic Studies of the University of Wales and others, further Great Sessions records in the WALE group (but not the group as whole, nor any Great Sessions material in the Chester classes) were transferred to the NLW under the Public Records Act, 1958. The classes involved are briefly described in the present PRO *Guide* (vol. I, pp. 168-71), which was then going through the press, and this entry remains the most extensive published finding-aid for the Great Sessions records. Despite an undertaking by the Board of Celtic Studies to produce a series of plea roll calendars, neither they nor the National Library have done anything with these documents that could not have been done in London, where they would have been easier of access and remained alongside cognate material. The difficulties of achieving consistency when attempting to transfer records of regional (rather than national or local) interest to a provincial repository is highlighted by the fact that Welsh Office records are at Kew (p. 138), while those of the Palatinate of Chester remain at Chancery Lane: the Chester Record Office, housed in the building in which the palatinate records were kept for hundreds of years, has not been selected as a suitable repository today.

Great Sessions records are similar in character to those of the assize courts but better preserved. For each county there are good runs of plea rolls from around 1543 to 1830, or from an earlier date for shires established by the Statute of Wales, all of which are listed in *Lists and Indexes* 4. Those for Chester and Flint form CHES 29 and 30, the others are WALE 16 to 26. In both cases there are supporting gaol files (CHES 24 and WALE 4) and other subsidiary documents, including 'Crown Books', containing minutes of both civil and criminal cases on the common-law side of the court (WALE 14, WALE 28, CHES 35 etc). A series of 'Calendar Rolls' (WALE 7) contains enrolled indictments and pleas of the crown, giving the names of those indicted and the offences with which they were charged; they also contain abstracts of coroners' inquests. From the start, Great Sessions allowed suitors to levy fines and recoveries on lines analogous to the procedure in Common Pleas from the twelfth century (p. 34), so that for each county there are original documents (WALE 3) and enrolled fines (WALE 2), while for the Carmarthen Circuit from 1657 there is a series of remembrance rolls of recoveries (WALE 5). The miscellaneous documents which escaped destruction in 1909 (WALE 13) are office papers of various prothonotaries.

On the equity side there are entry books of decrees and orders for each circuit from the early eighteenth century (WALE 10), original pleadings from 1689 (WALE 11 and 12), and a handful of unclaimed exhibits (WALE 27). The Exchequer Court at Chester exercised similar jurisdiction in the palatinate and later the Chester Circuit; its equity records, similar again to those of the equity side of the Exchequer at Westminster (p. 76), form CHES 6 to 16. The Wales group also includes three series of deeds (WALE 29 to 31), about half of which originate from the palatinate. Finally, the transfer of 1963 took 249 bundles and volumes of 'Miscellanea' (WALE 28) to Aberystwyth, which have yet to be described in print.

Equity

During the later middle ages the Chancellor alone came to deal with certain petitions seeking redress in matters where the common law could not provide a remedy. His equitable jurisdiction thus became distinct from that of the Council, whose judicial activities were in part hived off to Star Chamber (p. 78). The separation of the Chancellor's jurisdiction from that of the Council was probably made complete by the statute of 3 Hen. VII, c.1, and from the beginning of the sixteenth century the work of the Chancery as an equity court expanded greatly. Indeed, as its administrative functions fossilised and its common law jurisdiction remained limited (p. 28), equity business became by far the court's most important activity.[26] In 1873 it was remodelled as the Chancery

Division of the Supreme Court of Judicature (p. 180) but the records continue with little discontinuity into the twentieth century.

The equity side of Chancery heard a vast number of suits of considerable local interest, since many concerned inheritance, landed property, debts, marriage settlements, probate and other family business. Unfortunately, once one passes the mid-sixteenth century, the published finding-aids become fewer and better at identifying names of parties than places, while after about 1660 one becomes entirely dependent on a formidable array of unpublished indexes at Chancery Lane, some on open access in the Long Room, others in the IND series, of which the latter can be located from the Catalogue of Lists and Indexes, Chancery and Exchequer (LIS 166). PRO Leaflet 32 provides a characteristically clear, concise guide to the main classes and finding-aids; it does not perhaps emphasise quite how long one can spend, especially for nineteenth-century cases, simply searching indexes before locating a single relevant document.

The records themselves may be divided into three categories. There are preliminary written statements by both plaintiff and defendant, sometimes with further rejoinders or replications from both sides, setting out the complaint and the answer thereto. Evidence might then be collected from witnesses, either in the form of depositions (answers to questions submitted by both sides), affidavits (sworn statements), or documents assembled by the Chancery Masters in the course of preparing reports to the court on the facts of the case. Plaintiffs might also submit exhibits, some of which were not subsequently removed. Finally, the court issued a decree or order, embodying its decision, or a report on a matter arising from a suit on which they could not pronounce a judgment.

For the relatively small amount of pre-1558 material (which now forms C 1) *Lists and Indexes* 12, 16, 20, 29, 38, 43, 50, 51, 54 and 55 provide a list from which cases relating to particular persons or places can be identified; some suits are printed at greater length in three Record Commission volumes and another issued by the Selden Society.[27] From the reign of Elizabeth the series divides into C 2 and C 3, which continue in parallel down to Charles I and the Commonwealth respectively. For this period there are indexes, rather than lists, in *Lists and Indexes* 7, 24, 30 and 47, plus List and Index Society 202 and some privately produced volumes.[28] From the early seventeenth century, the proceedings split into six, as each clerk in Chancery began to file cases separately in his own division (C 5 to C 10); after 1714 the arrangement changes to three consecutive series (C 11, C 12, C 13). For C 5 there is an index in *Lists and Indexes* 39, 42, 44 and 45 and for C 9 one issued by the British Records Society. Beyond that there are only manuscript indexes at the PRO, none of which is much help in tracing localities rather than individuals. From 1842 the 'Modern Series' proceedings form three consecutive classes (C 14, C 15, C 16), indexed in volumes in the Long Room, which continue until the abolition of the court. Similar records from the Chancery Division are in J 54, starting in 1876, for which there are indexes in the Long Room for the first three years; thereafter the documents are filed in alphabetical order within each quarter.

From the mid-sixteenth century it is generally easier to locate a case from the decrees and orders and then search for other papers than start with the proceedings. Entry books of decrees and orders from 1544 to 1875 form C 33, continued from 1876 by J 15, both indexed in volumes in the Long Room. These are supplemented by reports or certificates issued by the court (C 38, C 39, J 57), which also begin in 1544 and are indexed (from 1606) similarly. Decrees and orders which were enrolled, so as to make the judgment more authoritative, are in C 78, the main series from Henry VIII to 1903, and C 79, a supplementary series covering the same period. LIS 160 and 198 make available a list and index of the main class as far as the reign of Elizabeth. Appeal from enrolled decrees was to the House of Lords but for unenrolled decrees appeal lay to the court itself by petition. Documents of this kind survive from 1774 in C 36 and J 53, and include petitions for winding up associations or seeking the appointment of new trustees to administer an estate as well as those arising from litigation.

Depositions taken from witnesses in Chancery suits consist of lists of questions prepared by both sides and answers thereto, prefaced by the deponent's name, parish, age and occupation, which gives them a usefulness beyond the information they provide concerning the case at issue. Those taken in London are called 'Town Depositions' (C 24) and extend from the mid-sixteenth century to 1853, after which they are filed with the pleadings. 'Country Depositions' taken elsewhere are now C 21 and C 22, again starting in the sixteenth century but continuing only to 1714, when they too are filed with the pleadings. The country depositions are indexed in volumes in the Long Room; for the town depositions, and the equivalent modern material in J 17, IND volumes have to be sent for. Affidavits sworn by witnesses are in C 31 (1611-1875), with registers for the period 1615-1747 in C 41; J 4 continues the series to 1925. The only finding-aids are IND volumes, described by the PRO as 'rough and ready'. Documents used by Chancery masters for their reports, which survive only for the nineteenth century, form C 117 to C 126, again indexed in closed-access volumes, while masters' exhibits, some of them dating from the middle ages, fill another 15 classes (C 103 to C 115, C 171, J 90), some of which are listed in LIS 13, 14 and 197; the latter, covering J 90, is particularly full and worth checking for business history as other well as other local studies.

For the historian interested in a particular place it is difficult to make use of Chancery equity proceedings after the published lists which include topographical details cease. Since there is no general index even of plaintiffs' names (much less defendants') it is also impossible to make a quick search for a specific individual after about 1600. On the other hand, odd papers from a Chancery suit often turn up in local record offices, among solicitors' collections, in family and estate material or in business records. A single decree, master's report or some other subsidiary document will not in itself supply much information but can be used as a way into the court records, since it will normally supply a date and a plaintiff's name, the two details without which a search is unlikely to be fruitful. Perseverance among the complex network of unpublished finding-aids may then yield rich pickings. Chancery proceedings are perhaps most commonly associated with the history of landed estates but can also be a valuable source for the history of trade and industry in the eighteenth and nineteenth centuries when most companies were partnerships in which disputes often ended in equity litigation.

During the sixteenth century the Exchequer, which had sat as a common law court since the early middle ages (p. 33), acquired a parallel equity jurisdiction, possibly in part as an inheritance from the Court of Augmentations after its absorption into the Exchequer in 1554 (p. 64).[29] The equity side of the Exchequer never attracted as much business as the Chancery and in 1841 (5 Vict., c.5) its jurisdiction was transferred to the busier court. Proceedings on the equity side of the Exchequer were similar in form to those in the Chancery, with written submissions in English, called bills and answers; depositions by witnesses; and decrees and orders by the court. The court's registrar was the King's Remembrancer and the records filed in his office. They are far less voluminous than the equivalent Chancery classes and thus easier to search; although after about 1700 most cases seem to be concerned with tithes, church livings and a few other issues, before then the court handled a wider range of business, including many cases of local interest.

The earliest bills, answers and depositions, spanning the reigns of Henry VII, Henry VIII, Edward VI and Mary, form a small class (E 111), listed in detail in the published King's Remembrancer class-list (LIS 91, 108). Later bills and answers are in E 112, which for the reign of Elizabeth only is listed by county in the same volume. Other calendars, also by county, are on the Round Room shelves, but these are described as incomplete in the Catalogue of Lists and Indexes (LIS 166), which identifies more reliable IND volumes. The other approach is through the decrees and orders, which survive both as entry books (E 123 to E 127) and original documents (E 128 to E 131). The latter are listed but not indexed; for the entry books there are calendars in the Round Room which give the name of parties to each case and the counties to which the issue relates, but in addition there are better, if less accessible, finding-aids in the IND series. Minute books recording decisions in both equity and revenue cases from 1616 form E 163.

Several classes contain evidence presented in equity proceedings. The earliest affidavits are combined with other material in the 220 bundles of 'Bille' (E 207), for which LIS 91 merely provides the covering dates of each piece; after 1774 they are filed separately (E 103) but still only listed by date. More useful are the depositions taken by the court, either by the barons themselves (E 133) or by commissioners (E 134), of which the latter are more numerous and were calendared chronologically in *Deputy Keeper's Reports* 38-42. A volume on the Round Room shelves (which the LIS might with advantage publish) contains slips from these calendars rearranged by county, together with those from a similar list of E 178 (originally published in *DKR* 37), which are returns to special commissions of inquiry initiated by the Exchequer, with the commissions attached. Although not connected with equity proceedings, these are quasi-judicial in character and abound with local topographical and personal information. Also on the searchroom shelves are older manuscript lists of both E 133 and E 134, arranged by date but giving brief details of the parties and premises involved; they remain the best means of reference to the barons' depositions.

Subsidiary classes worth checking in a detailed search include a short series of early nineteenth-century petitions (E 185) and a rather larger quantity of reports and certificates (1648-1841) in E 194, for which again see LIS 108.

The other equity court in this period was Requests, which evolved from an informal committee of the Council 'for the expedition of poor men's causes', providing a service in civil matters comparable to the criminal work of Star Chamber (p. 78). Although its activities gradually widened, it remained principally a court offering equitable jurisidiction for suitors too poor make use of the Chancery whose cases were too petty to be heard in Star Chamber.[30] The court continued to sit until 1642 but was not revived at the Restoration; its records are not extensive but the main class (REQ 2), consisting of some 800 bundles of bills, answers, depositions and other documents, is worth searching for cases concerning people or places in which one is interested. *Lists and Indexes* 21 is a printed calendar of the first 136 bundles, which is continued by typed and manuscript volumes in the Round Room, all of which give the names of parties, a brief indication of the issue involved and the county to which each case relates. Searches would be made even simpler if the LIS published the finding-aids for the later bundles; the material would also be well suited for a local record series, since the documents contain a good deal of human interest and large numbers of names of comparatively modest individuals, while remaining manageable in bulk.

Prerogative, Conciliar and Regional Courts

Of the other royal courts of early modern England, the records of two are likely to be of value to local historians generally, while for some parts of the country those of the palatinate courts which retained their separate identity after the counties themselves were brought fully under crown control will obviously be worth searching.

The Court of Star Chamber developed, like Requests, from a committee of councillors sitting as a judicial tribunal to deal expeditiously with matters brought before the Privy Council, especially where the enforcement of law and order was involved. The name derived from its meeting place in the Camera Stellata at Westminster. Initially popular as source of quick redress in private disputes for which common law procedures were too slow or inflexible, Star Chamber fell into disrepute in the early seventeenth century as an instrument of royal prerogative and was abolished in 1641 (16 Charles I, c.10). There was no attempt at revival after the Restoration. Procedure was by bill and answer, as in the equity courts, with evidence taken on deposition. No decrees and orders have survived and the documents are arranged in chronological order, with a separate class number assigned to each reign from Henry VII (STAC 1) to Charles I (STAC 9); the bulk of the material dates from the time of Elizabeth and James I. *Lists and Indexes* 13 provide a chronological list of cases to 1558, for which an index of persons and places is supplied by *Lists and Indexes, Supplementary,* 4 Part 1. The remaining parts of the latter series form an index of persons (only) to STAC 5, which now contains nearly all the Elizabethan records of the court, STAC 6 (Elizabeth I, Supplementary) having been merged with it. A chronological calendar, giving brief details of the matter at issue and the county as well as the names of parties, is available in manuscript in the Round Room for both STAC 5 and later classes. For proceedings during the reign of James I and (despite its title) Charles I, an index of persons was compiled in 1975 using a computer, from which the output is arranged in a rather complicated form. There are a couple of volumes of published reports but, as with Requests, Star Chamber records have yet to attract the attention of record society editors, despite the number of local disputes with which the court dealt. As G.E. Aylmer observes, it would seem odd today for the Cabinet or Appeal Court to discuss matters that now come before a magistrates' court or district council, but it was often at this level, especially during the reign of Elizabeth, that Star Chamber (or the Council as a whole) intervened. An index of places for the post-1558 material would help considerably in making the documents more accessible.[31]

The two regional offshoots of the Privy Council, the Council in the Marches of Wales and the Council in the North, have already been mentioned as administrative bodies (p. 56). Both also exercised criminal and civil jurisdiction but in neither case do any systematic records survive. In the three palatinate jurisdictions of Durham, Chester and Lancaster the separate courts which had existed in the middle ages continued to sit until the nineteenth century, in the case of the two latter for the counties concerned, while the palatinate of Durham extended over a larger area than the county (pp. 36-8). In all three cases the records include common law and equity proceedings comprising a similar range of documents to those from the Westminster courts (pp. 69-77): pleadings, affidavits, depositions, decrees and orders and various subsidiary classes. There was a separate equity court for the Duchy of Lancaster, an institution distinct from but closely related to the palatine county, which sat at Westminster and was known as the Court of Duchy Chamber of Lancaster. Its jurisdiction extended to all matters arising in lands held by the duchy, not merely those in the palatinate, and its records are located accordingly (DL 1 to DL 9; DL 48 and DL 49).

A summary list of all palatinate records, together with those of the principality of Wales and honour of Peveril, was published in *Lists and Indexes* 40; for some classes there are calendars appended to various *Deputy Keeper's Reports* (cf. *Guide,* vol. I, pp. 172-82), while pleadings and depositions in the Duchy Chamber were calendared in a three-volume Record Commission publication.[32] Some subsidiary Durham records scheduled for destruction were transferred to Gateshead Public Library in 1912, otherwise efforts to return the documents to repositories in the counties to which they relate have been unsuccessful, by contrast with the removal of Great Sessions records to Aberystwyth (pp.72-3).

The other group in *Lists and Indexes* 40, the records of the court of the honour of Peveril, has attracted little attention from local historians, even those in Derbyshire and Nottinghamshire parishes within its former jurisdiction. The only historical account of the honour after it reverted to the crown in the fourteenth century appears to be that appended to *Deputy Keeper's Report* 16, written shortly after the court was abolished in 1850 (12 & 13 Vict., c.101), and its records form a single class (PEV 1) of 62 pieces.[33] They at least are in the PRO, whereas the records of the Stannaries Court, which had jurisdiction over those engaged in tin-mining in Devon and Cornwall and was abolished by the Judicature Act of 1873 (36 & 37 Vict., c.66), remain in the custody of the Duchy of Cornwall (together with most of the duchy's administrative and financial records), since the Lord Warden of the Stannaries was appointed by the duke.[34] A somewhat similar court still exists in the lead-mining district of the Low Peak, whose Barmaster is appointed by the crown in right of the Duchy of Lancaster. The Barmote Court records are mostly at Chatsworth House, the home of the family which has leased the duchy's rights in this respect since the seventeenth century.[35]

Lastly, two central courts dispensing civil law should be mentioned briefly. The High Court of Chivalry, presided over by the Earl Marshal, enjoyed some vitality in the century before the Civil War which it has not experienced since, except on one celebrated occasion in 1954. Its records are at the College of Arms, together with those of the heralds' visitations of the sixteenth and seventeenth centuries and other papers concerned with the administration of heraldry in England and Wales.[36] More important, the High Court of Admiralty had jurisdiction in cases involving piracy, privateering and other offences on the high seas. Records of its criminal proceedings (HCA 1) are listed in LIS 45, to which there is an index (LIS 46) worth checking for material on ports or maritime counties. There are also published lists of prize papers for the period 1739-1817, with indexes, in LIS 93, 112, 183-4 and 194, but these name ships rather than places. Otherwise searchers are dependent on finding-aids available only at the PRO, which are listed in LIS 180.[37]

Ecclesiastical Courts

Alongside the lay courts existed a parallel structure of ecclesiastical jurisdiction at both national and local level. The diocesan and archidiaconal courts are included in the next chapter (p. 105); here it is worth mentioning three superior church courts whose records may occasionally be of interest to local historians and one which should be included in any systematic search for material on a particular place.

The highest ecclesiastical court in the land, after the break with Rome, was the High Court of Delegates, established to supersede papal jurisdiction in appeals from the lower courts; it also had appellate jurisdiction from the High Court of Admiralty, High Court of Chivalry and the courts of the two university chancellors. The records, the earliest dating from the 1530s, include minutes of proceedings, depositions and answers and various miscellaneous papers. There is a thorough modern history of the court but no published finding-aid for the documents. In 1832 (2 & 3 Will. IV, c.92) the powers of the court, including appellate jurisdiction from the Admiralty, were transferred to the Privy Council and a small group of records (PCA 1-5) survive from the work of the Judicial Committee of the Privy Council under this Act, which in 1873 was transferred to the newly established Court of Appeal.[38]

Beneath the Delegates in the southern province sat the Court of Arches, whose records are at Lambeth Palace Library, and also, between the 1580s and 1641, a High Commission for Causes Ecclesiastical, whose records are largely lost. There was a separate commission for the northern province, whose records are better preserved and are now at the Borthwick Institute, York. Commissions also sat in each diocese but only for Chester, Exeter, Kent, Norwich, Salisbury and Winchester in the southern province and Durham in the north do act books survive.[39]

Of vastly greater interest to local historians are the records of the Prerogative Court of Canterbury, the senior probate court in the southern province from the middle ages down to January 1858, when ecclesiastical probate jurisdiction was abolished (p. 179).

Before this date the bulk of wills were proved in local church courts (p. 106) but where the estate included goods in more than one diocese or in both provinces executors were supposed to seek probate from the PCC; a similar court sat for the northern province (p. 83). The PCC also had jurisdiction over the estates of Englishmen dying overseas, including seamen who died on board ship, and was often preferred to a local court in difficult or contentious cases because of the greater solemnity of its judgments. Especially in the first half of the nineteenth century it grew in popularity at the expense of the local courts, many of which were moribund well before 1858. During the Interregnum all the church courts were suspended but a court continued to sit in London in place of the PCC to deal with probate, whose records were merged with those of the ecclesiastical court after the Restoration, so that, in effect, PCC records for the years 1653-60 include all wills proved in England and Wales. After 1858 the documents passed to the newly established Court of Probate, whose successor transferred them to the PRO in 1962, since when a major programme of sorting, listing and repair has greatly extended the range of material available.[40]

Like the local probate courts, the main business of PCC was the granting of probate and administration in 'common form', i.e. in simple, uncontested cases. Alternatively, grants might be made in solemn form, by affidavit, where executors or administrators expected litigation to ensue. The court also called executors and administrators to account and handled some testamentary litigation, although many disputes, especially where real property was involved, were heard in Chancery (p. 74).

Surviving PCC wills date from 1383; earlier wills proved in the Archbishop of Canterbury's court are at Lambeth Palace (p. 49). The main series of PCC wills are those preserved as registered copies, entered chronologically into bound volumes (PROB 11), now produced to searchers on microfilm; original wills, where they survive, are in PROB 10 and can only be seen at the PRO at seven days' notice. The working indexes to PROB 11 are manuscript Register Books (PROB 12), photocopies of which are on open access at Chancery Lane. A series of published volumes of varying reliability, available in main reference libraries, makes searches down to 1700 easier, but from 1701 to 1749 and from 1801 to 1852 one is dependent entirely on the registers. For 1750-1800 the Society of Genealogists is in the process of publishing an index, while for 1853-8 an index was printed by the Court of Probate on similar lines to those produced annually since 1858 (p. 179). Records of grants of administration by PCC survive from 1559 and from then until 1630 and for 1649-60 there are published indexes; otherwise PROB 12 remains the only finding-aid. The original letters of administration were returned to the administrator and only the act book recording the grant (PROB 6) is produced to searchers; surviving administration bonds are not yet available. Probate act books (from 1526) form a separate series (PROB 8, indexed in PROB 12 and the published volumes), entries in which may sometimes supply more information than is given either in the will or the probate sentence normally entered in the register after the will.

From 1796 duty was payable on legacies and residues of personal estate, regulated initially by 36 Geo. III, c.52, but extended by later Acts. A much wider succession duty was introduced in 1853 (16 & 17 Vict., c.51), payable on the gratuitous acquisition of property on death, whether personal, real or leasehold. Registers listing bequests chargeable with these duties between 1796 and 1894 now form IR 26, kept with the PCC records at Chancery Lane, rather than Kew, where most other Inland Revenue classes are to be found, and are indexed in a series of manuscript volumes (IR 27) on open access in the Probate Room. Only after 1853 do the registers list most, although still not all, grants, but from 1796 may provide a convenient short cut in locating a will proved either in PCC or a local court. The registers themselves list the name of the deceased, the date of the will and probate, names and addresses of executors, and details of duty paid. In the case of administrations they normally provide more information than the court's own record of the issue of letters of administration. The books are closed for 75 years from the date of compilation and their use requires a little practice, since the information is presented in tabular form, with a formidable range of abbreviations, but are an important additional finding-aid for the last half-century of church probate. List and Index Society 177 covers both IR 26 and IR 27, with an explanatory note on their contents.

Inventories exhibited in the PCC were not filed with the original wills, as was usually the case in local courts. Many pre-1666 inventories were apparently destroyed in the Great Fire of London and others suffered from the neglect meted out to PCC records after 1858. What survives has been sorted into four main classes (PROB 2 to PROB 5); other inventories are preserved in some of the records of litigation in the court. Early inventories up to 1660 form a class of about 700 documents (PROB 2), for which there are lists and indexes at the PRO; a series covering the years 1718-82 (but not including all material for that period) is now PROB 3, listed in LIS 85 and 86. The two largest classes are parchment inventories post-1660 (PROB 4), which are office copies of paper inventories files in PROB 5. For the former there are lists and indexes at the PRO; for the original inventories one can use LIS 149.

Records of litigation survive from the sixteenth century. The best starting-point is generally a reference to a sentence or decree in either the will register (PROB 11) or the calendar (PROB 12), which will supply the title of the cause. Early papers (1642-1722) are in PROB 28, listed in LIS 161; those for 1783-1858 are PROB 37, for which LIS 174 provides a list. An alternative approach is to check indexes to exhibits between 1722 and 1858 (PROB 33), available on the searchroom shelves, which relate to documents preserved in PROB 31 and PROB 37. For early exhibits (PROB 36) an index is available at the PRO; for exhibits filed with inventories between 1662 and 1720 (PROB 32) there is a list in LIS 204. None of these finding-aids is comprehensive and the only complete record of proceedings is, as in other courts, to be found in the act books (PROB 29) or the loose acts themselves (PROB 30), to which there is no overall index.

PCC wills have long been used by genealogists in tracing relatively wealthy families; local historians, conversely, have tended to use the records of local courts to reconstruct life in sixteenth- and seventeenth-century communities. Although, for any town or village, there will always be far more material in the diocesan or archdeaconry court than PCC, wills and (where any survive) inventories preserved centrally may be of considerably greater individual interest, since the testators will be wealthier and inventories may list the contents of identifiable large houses. For any thorough study at least the more accessible PRO classes should be searched. In particular it is worth remembering that PCC wills do not somehow stop in 1700; on the contrary, they remain a considerably under-appreciated source for eighteenth-century local history, as do the inventories. The lack of published indexes for this period is thus an irritating obstacle to their use.

A prerogative court of probate sat at York for the northern province, whose records are at the Borthwick Institute there. They include wills and administrations from the 1380s to 1857, for which there are published indexes down to the 1680s. Either of the standard guides to probate records will explain the complex relationship between the different ecclesiastical jurisdictions in the province: two other courts, for example, made probate grants during visitations or vacancies or on appeal from the lower courts.[41]

Chapter Four

EARLY MODERN LOCAL GOVERNMENT

During the sixteenth century a structure of local government was created which was to survive, modified, augmented but in essentials unaltered, until the early nineteenth. The institutions established by the Tudors and the records they created are among the most familiar topics discussed in this book; much of what follows here will already be well known to many readers and some of it is covered more fully in works on the county, parish, borough and so on. In particular, the period from 1688 to the beginning of statutory reform in 1834-5 was the subject of the Webbs' monumental history, which is unlikely ever to be superseded.[1] Whereas Chapter 5 deals with each main function of modern local government in turn, as most were originally the responsibility of a single authority set up for the purpose, the material here is arranged by institution, since, with the exception of turnpike trusts and a few similar bodies (p. 103), each dealt with a range of functions and their records are best treated together.

The Counties

By the sixteenth century most of England except the far north had long been shired. The counties palatine of Chester, Durham and Lancaster were finally brought under crown control by Henry VII and legislation of 1536 (27 Hen. VIII, c.26) and 1543 (34 & 35 Hen. VIII, c.26) completed the process begun by Edward I of dividing Wales into counties on English lines. The chief administrative official in the medieval county was the sheriff; as the early Tudors consolidated their control of Wales and the palatinates the sheriffs there were henceforth appointed by the crown and not by private lords. Until the middle of the sixteenth century, some counties were paired under a single sheriff; conversely, London and a few of the larger boroughs had secured not merely the privilege of paying a fee-farm rent separate from the county farm but of having a sheriff of their own, whose authority excluded that of the sheriff of the county within the borough.

Ancient though the office was, its administrative importance was by the sixteenth century greatly reduced. The county court over which the sheriff presided was virtually obsolete, while the farm for which he accounted at the Exchequer formed an insignificant element of crown revenue (p. 29). Some parliamentary taxation continued to be remitted until the late seventeenth century through a structure which included the sheriff (p. 62) but otherwise his duties were largely ceremonial, part of the ritual which attended sittings of the assize (or great sessions) justices in each county (pp. 69-73). The small amount of administrative work associated with the office came to be undertaken by an under-sheriff, normally a local attorney. For this reason, shrieval archives are rarely found in county record offices, although some solicitors' collections may include records created by their work as under-sheriffs.[2]

The other ceremonial office of modern times, the lord lieutenancy, is, by contrast, a Tudor creation. Lieutenants were initially appointed either for counties or groups of counties on a temporary basis; only in the seventeenth century did the pattern emerge of appointment for life for a single county. They were originally responsible for military arrangements in each area and remained in charge of the militia until the nineteenth century; as the office evolved, however, it formed part of the general pattern of local government. In particular, the Elizabethan and early Stuart Privy Council relied heavily on the lieutenants for local news, especially where religion, the maintenance of law and order, the economy or public health were concerned, and at the same time used them as a means of disseminating information, especially to the justices of the peace (pp. 55, 86). In addition, the lieutenants were also drawn into local government as commissioners for the collection of taxes. After the Restoration, and more especially after 1688, the office became less onerous and more one of honour, traditionally held by the greatest landowner in the county. He remained responsible for the militia but his main function was as the medium of communication between the JPs and central government, now usually represented by the secretary of state rather than the Privy Council (p. 53).

By the end of the seventeenth century it was normal to combine the lieutenancy with the technically separate office of *custos rotulorum*, the 'keeper of the rolls', i.e. the records of the court of quarter sessions in each county, which were in practice in the custody of the clerk of the peace, the court's principal officer. Ironically, although lords lieutenant retain this additional title to the present day (and a few still chair the archives committee of their county council), lieutenancy records themselves do not survive in great quantity. Before the Civil War the main source for their activities are generally the papers of the Privy Council and secretaries of state with whom they corresponded (pp. 52-56). For the later period, there may be material on the county militia, especially during the Napoleonic War when the lieutenants' duties in this respect became more important, including nominal lists, minute books and possibly correspondence, both with central government and the deputy lieutenants within the county. After 1782 their dealings with Home Office can be followed through that department's records (p. 162). In recent times, the clerk of the peace (since 1972 the clerk of the county council, a post normally held jointly with the older office after 1888), has acted as clerk to the lieutenancy and there will be material in official custody, some of which may be available for search. Older papers, however, may have come to the office as private deposits by families whose members have served as lieutenant or deputy lieutenant, or from solicitors who have acted for such families.[3]

A far more important development than the appointment of lieutenants was, of course, the increased responsibility given to the justices of the peace over whom they presided. The medieval 'keepers of the peace' evolved under the Tudors into modern JPs, charged with a wide range of administrative tasks as well as extensive criminal jurisidiction. By the outbreak of the Civil War they were well on the way to becoming the 'rulers of the counties', a role which they wholly assumed after 1660. Although the justices displayed remarkable flexibility in adapting to changing times, enabling them to retain their powers until almost the end of the nineteenth century, some aspects of their work remained medieval in character, especially the combination of judicial and administrative work in one office and the use of judicial forms to discharge administrative duties.[4]   Under a statute of 1361 (34 Edw. III, c.1), and in some counties from an earlier date, the justices sat four times a year in a court of quarter sessions to hear and determine criminal cases or to remit capital offences and some other felonies to the next assize court (p. 69). Increasingly, this work was overshadowed by an administrative burden, much of it supervisory but some involving direct action. To meet the costs of this work they were empowered to levy a county rate.

Justices of the peace were appointed not only for counties but also for many boroughs, whose charters normally provided for the mayor to be a JP *ex officio* during his mayoralty and for a year afterwards, so that there were always two in the borough, usually exercising petty sessional jurisidiction either concurrently with the county justices or exclusively. Larger towns had a commission which gave their justices jurisdiction over felonies as well as misdemeanours, enabling them to sit in quarter sessions as well as petty sessions and to exclude the county magistrates entirely. In boroughs without an exclusive commission the town clerk was normally clerk to the magistrates; in larger towns a clerk of the peace was appointed with powers and duties similar to those of counties. Quarter sessions boroughs normally also levied their own rate in place of the county rate. Although, when investigations were made in the early nineteenth century, only 17 boroughs were found to be 'counties unto themselves', i.e. wholly independent of the county officials with their own clerk of the peace, sheriff and, in a few cases, lieutenant, some 40 towns had exclusive commissions of the peace and a still larger number were not assessed to the county rate. There is thus no precise definition of a 'county' in this period, since different towns enjoyed a varying degree of independence. Throughout this section, the functions (and records) ascribed to counties should be understood to include not merely the geographical counties but also the larger towns and the separate ridings and parts into which Yorkshire and Lincolnshire were divided.[5]

Once the basic structure was established of a body of unpaid lay justices, men of social standing and landed wealth, some of them legally trained, there was little fundamental change until the late nineteenth century. Between the 1830s and 1880s, when other local institutions were reformed, the justices in quarter sessions survived, acquiring new duties but shedding none of their traditional prestige. Only in 1888 were their administrative functions transferred to elected councils in each county and large town, the origin of the modern administrative counties and county boroughs which existed until 1974 (p. 130). Their judicial and licensing powers were untouched, while responsibility for the police was divided between the JPs and the councils through standing joint committees (p. 157). Even then, the separation in most counties outside the major conurbations was more apparent than real. The clerks of the peace normally became clerks of the county councils and standing joint committees; many justices were elected to the new councils; and the inclusion of nominated county aldermen on the new authorities enabled others to become members. This continuity also meant that the county councils inherited the older records of quarter sessions, although more recent judicial material henceforth accumulated separately. In other respects, however, the Act marks the turning-point between traditional county government and the modern system of elected authorities.[6]

Quarter sessions continued to sit as a criminal court until the Courts Act, 1971, amalgamated their jurisdiction with that of the assize courts to form the present network of Crown Courts, presided over by circuit judges. The office of clerk of the peace was also abolished in 1971 and remaining quarter sessions records transferred to county record offices or other approved repositories. In general, they are amongst the best arranged of any in a local office, since they are the nucleus around which other material has been gathered. For many counties there are published guides and for some detailed calendars. Conventionally, the records are divided into three catgories: judicial, administrative and enrolled (or deposited). The third group is distinct enough but the other two overlap because so much of the administrative work was conducted judicially.[7]

The main record of the court in session is normally a file or roll for each sitting; in some counties these have been broken up and their contents rearranged by subject and in all courts an increasing proportion of material was filed separately as the roll became bulkier. Besides lists of jurors, constables and the like and writs to the sheriff to summon attendance, the rolls contain the presentments or indictments on which subsequent action was based. An individual might be presented for keeping a disorderly alehouse or failing to attend church, while a parish would be presented for failure to repair a bridge or highway. Criminal actions were initiated by indictments, which give details of the alleged offence, sometimes supported by depositions or 'informations' supplying evidence. Those who had been kept in gaol until their case was heard were listed in a 'gaol calendar', which usually reiterates details of the charge. The file may also contain certificates recording summary convictions by one or two justices out of sessions and removal orders made on the same basis which had been appealed to the sessions (pp. 98-99). From 1673 those holding civil or military office had to supply a certificate confirming their allegiance to the Church of England under the Test Act (25 Ch. II, c.2) and from 1688 (1 Wm & Mary, c. 18) dissenters' meeting houses were certified by quarter sessions (or by bishops, p. 105). Both these, as well as memorials and petitions from individuals or communities, may be on the files or kept separately.

The judgment of the court in criminal cases was recorded by the clerk in a minute book, a rough record kept while the court was in session; a more formal note of administrative decisions was kept in the order book, whose contents tend to be dominated by poor law business but which also deal with the repair of highways, bridges and county gaols; levying of rates and payment of accounts and salaries; setting wage and land carriage rates; regulating fairs and markets; appointing constables; and (in the nineteenth century) supervising asylums (p. 124). These volumes form the main record of the court as an administrative body, to which the minutes and sealed orders of the county council after 1888 are the natural successors.[8]

The statute of bridges of 1531 (22 Hen. VIII, c.5) established that those not customarily maintained by individuals, parishes, hundreds, boroughs or other bodies were the responsibility of the justices. Highways, on the other hand, were maintained by the parish under a statute of 1555 (2 & 3 Ph. & Mary, c.8), with the justices supervising their work (p. 97). After 1835 a succession of Acts tried, with limited success, to transfer responsibility to district boards set up by quarter sessions. Only in 1888 did the county, through its elected council, take responsibility for main roads as well as bridges (p. 140). In addition to presentments as to highways out of repair and orders for their maintenance, there may be papers, such as plans, specifications and reports from the county surveyor, on county bridges, together with orders for their repair and the levying of rates therefor.[9]

The only other buildings for which quarter sessions were usually responsible before the nineteenth century (when the establishment of lunatic asylums and, more particularly, police forces greatly extended the county estate: cf. pp. 124, 157) were a gaol and, in some cases, a county hall. There may be prison records at least for the nineteenth century, up to 1877, when all establishments were transferred to the Home Office (p. 158), including details of individual prisoners as well as accounts, returns and reports by the governor and by committees of visiting justices.[10]

The main licensing function of the justices was concerned with the keepers of inns and alehouse who, under an Act of 1552 (5 & 6 Edw. VI, c.25), had to provide two sureties for good behaviour. Early 'victuallers' recognisances' may be found on sessions rolls but are more likely to survive in separate registers for the eighteenth and early nineteenth centuries; they supply the name of the parish in which the house stood, its licensee and his sureties and, possibly, the inn-sign, making them a useful source for the period immediately prior to the general availability of local directories. In recent times, licensing has been transferred to petty sessions. Less well known are the registers supposed to be kept by the clerk of the peace between 1563 (5 Eliz., c.12) and 1772 (12 Geo. III, c.71) of 'badgers', 'higglers' and and other itinerant traders licensed by quarter sessions. Had they survived more widely (most seem to be for the eighteenth century) the study of inland trade before the Industrial Revolution would probably be slightly easier.[11]

Documents enrolled, registered or deposited with the clerk include some of the most heavily used quarter sessions classes, including, for example, the duplicate land tax assessments of 1780-1832 (p. 63). Registration locally sometimes preceded central registration, as in the case of charities, registered under Acts of 1786 (26 Geo. III, c.58), 1812 (52 Geo. III, c.102) and 1853 (16 & 17 Vict., c.137), and friendly societies and similar organisations from 1793 (33 Geo. III, c.54), for which later records are at the PRO (p. 177). From 1710 (9 Anne, c.27) the Game Acts required lords of the manor to notify the appointments of gamekeepers; the resulting registers of deputations are generally used to trace owners of manors rather than their keepers. Besides the sacrament certificates already mentioned (p. 88), dissenters and Roman Catholics may also be traced in various seventeenth- and eighteenth-century lists, as can their estates and places of worship. There are also two important classes of maps and plans: those attached to enclosure awards made under local Acts from the mid-eighteenth century or the General Inclosure Act of 1845 (8 & 9 Vict., c.118) and those deposited prior to an application to Parliament for powers to build a turnpike road, canal, dock, railway or other public undertaking. After 1792 a second copy of plans of canals etc was deposited with the Clerk of Parliament, which should now be in the House of Lords Record Office. Copies of awards under the General Inclosure Act will also be found in the Ministry of Agriculture group at Kew (p. 166).[12]

Finally, a statute of 1535 (27 Hen. VIII, c.16) requiring the enrolment of deeds of bargain and sale either with the clerk of the peace or at one of the courts at Westminster might have led to the creation of a national land registry providing a simple, sure means of transferring titles in real property as early as the mid-sixteenth century. In practice, the ingenuity of conveyancers ensured that this did not happen and in most counties comparatively few deeds were enrolled. Nor was a central registry set up, although some private deeds continued to be entered on the back of the close rolls (p. 57). Registration was established in the three ridings of Yorkshire and in Middlesex early in the eighteenth century, which ended only as the modern system, which originated in 1862 (25 & 26 Vict., c.53), gradually became more comprehensive. The records of the Yorkshire registries have since passed into the custody of the archive services of Humberside and North Yorkshire county councils and that maintained until 1986 by the former West Yorkshire Metropolitan County Council; the Middlesex material was until the same date in the hands of the record office provided by the former Greater London Council.[13]

From at least the sixteenth century the justices also exercised summary jurisdiction in cases of petty crime outside quarter sessions. In some matters a single justice could act alone, in others a minimum of two were required, one of whom had to be legally trained. Some poor law business, chiefly the granting of removal orders (p. 98), was also dealt with in this way, with the decisions reported to the next sessions. From this practice evolved the court of petty sessions in the eighteenth century, from which in turn the modern magistrates' court has developed (p. 160).

In some counties the petty sessional divisions corresponded with the older hundreds or wapentakes into which the counties had been divided since early medieval times. Otherwise, the hundred had ceased to be a living administrative unit well before the Tudor period; its only official to survive into modern times, the high constable, was in practice appointed by quarter sessions, not the hundred court. Apart from accounting to the sheriff for the collection of rate and taxes, the constable's other duties were connected with the judicial work of quarter sessions. The office survived until the late nineteenth century but had long been superseded by the establishment of modern police forces under Acts of 1839 and 1856 (p. 156).[14] On the other hand, most county records continued to be filed by hundred well into the nineteenth century.

In maritime counties, commissions of sewers were appointed under a statute of 1531 (23 Hen. VIII, c.5), charged with draining low lying land liable to flooding. Commissioners were drawn from much the same class as the justices and, like quarter sessions, courts of sewers conducted administrative business in a judicial manner, assisted by a jury. They were abolished by the Land Drainage Act, 1930 (20 & 21 Geo. V, c.44), and their work transferred to internal drainage boards or river authorities, themselves now part of the regional water authorities (p. 194). The older records, consisting mainly of order books, possibly supplemented by engineers' reports and other papers from the eighteenth century and later, should have passed to the successor authorities and may now be in local record offices, together with the older records of the drainage boards, whose activities may also be studied from Ministry of Agriculture files at Kew (p. 166). Alternatively, solicitors whose predecessors acted as clerks to the commission may have deposited material in local offices. Some original commissions and other documents can be found in three Chancery classes (p. 57).[15]

Before leaving the county, it is important to add that during the Civil War local government through the justices was disrupted. In particular, in areas controlled by Parliament, county committees were established whose proceedings, where they survive, are a major source for local administration in these years. The Royalists attempted, with less success, to set up similar committees in counties in their hands. Papers from these bodies may have reached local record offices from families whose ancestors served on them and for several counties there have been detailed studies of local government during the Civil War and Interregnum.[16]

Manor, Parish and Township

During the sixteenth century the manor, as a ubiquitous unit of local territorial and social organisation, fell into decay in most areas, while remaining in existence as a legal institution (p. 43). This decline was not universal and in some places manor courts continued to sit into the present century. Some courts leet retained genuine vitality in both rural and urban areas until the nineteenth century, not least as the only agency with responsibility for public health. In general, however, the Tudor period saw the replacement of the manor by the parish as the institution responsible for day-to-day local administration. Thus emerged a two-tier pattern of local government, the basis on which the nineteenth-century reforms were erected.

By the sixteenth century the whole of England and Wales had long been divided into some 11,000 parishes, which formed the lowest link in a chain of ecclesiastical organisation stretching through the deanery, archdeaconry and diocese to the province and, until the 1530s, to the Pope in Rome. A structure of lay administration was grafted on to an institution originally intended for other purposes by the establishment alongside the older office of churchwarden, whose responsibilities were confined to the upkeep of the church and its services, of those of overseer of the poor and surveyor of highways. The ecclesiastical and civil sides of the parish were not wholly separate, since the wardens were, *ex officio*, also overseers, and all the officers were either appointed or nominated by the parish in vestry assembled, a general meeting of householders.

On the other hand, while the churchwardens were also responsible for their actions to the archdeacon and through him the bishop, the overseers and surveyor were accountable to the justices.[17]

The parishes established in the early middle ages, whose boundaries remained largely unchanged until the nineteenth century, varied greatly in area and population. In upland districts, where the population was thinly scattered, many were too large to form a single administrative unit. The practice thus arose, confirmed by statute in 1662 (14 Ch. II, c.12), of dividing parishes into smaller areas for poor relief and, in rather fewer cases, the maintenance of highways. In England these subdivisions were usually called 'townships', in Wales 'hamlets'. Both appear to be ancient units into which a parish naturally divided: some corresponded with manorial boundaries and some contained chapels built in the middle ages to supplement the parish church. Townships might also form part of the ecclesiastical organisation of the parish through an arrangement by which each provided one churchwarden, appointed at a meeting analogous to the vestry. Both overseers and surveyor were empowered to levy a rate to meet the charges of their office and, where a parish was divided, a rate was assessed separately in each township. This occurred most commonly in the case of the poor rate and by the nineteenth century a 'parish' was, for civil purposes, an area which was, or might be, separately assessed for the poor rate, a concept quite different from that of a parish in ecclesiastical law. Matters were further complicated by the existence of 'highway parishes', where a separate highway rate was levied for an area whose boundaries differed from those used for the poor rate, and by the re-arrangement of ecclesiastical boundaries in response to the changing distribution of population.

The only manorial official to be absorbed into the new pattern of local government was the constable, appointed in the middle ages by the leet. Where these courts ceased to sit, the appointment was made instead by the justices, an arrangement recognised by statute in 1662 and made universal in 1842 (5 & 6 Vict., c.109), under which the overseers of the poor were to draw up lists of eligible candidates. Before this date it is misleading to describe the office as that of 'parish constable', since in some parts of the country constablery boundaries conformed neither with those of parishes nor townships but reflected an older tenurial geography; the traditional term 'petty constable' is preferable. By 1842 the office was already in decline: appointments could not be made under this Act if the County Police Act, 1839 (2 & 3 Vict., c.93) had been adopted locally, while the establishment in all counties of forces under the Act of 1856 (19 & 20 Vict., c.69) made them wholly redundant (p. 156). The office was finally abolished in 1872 (35 & 36 Vict., c.92).[18]

During the nineteenth century the parish gradually lost the other functions laid on it three hundred years earlier, while remaining the basis of the rating system and church organisation. Concern at this loss of local autonomy, fuelled partly by a misunderstanding of the nature of communal institutions in the middle ages, eventually resulted in the establishment of 'civil parishes' by the Local Government Act of 1894 (56 & 57 Vict., c.73), which finally separated the lay and ecclesiastical elements of local administration. The whole of England and Wales was divided into some 14,000 such units, whose boundaries generally followed those of existing poor law parishes, while the opportunity was taken to remove the remaining anomalies of divided parishes and extra-parochial places which had survived earlier reforms. Civil parishes which were not coterminous with county or municipal boroughs or urban districts (where the existence of a civil parish remained purely titular) were designated 'rural parishes', in which most local government was undertaken by rural district councils (p. 115). Some minor powers, however, were entrusted to 'parish councils', which were elected in places with a population of 300 or more and might, with the support of the ratepayers and consent of the county council, be elected in those where the population was between 100 and 300. Parishes which did not have a council were to hold an annual 'parish meeting', which was also to be called in other parishes to elect the council. Henceforth, the vestry was concerned solely with church matters, until it was largely eclipsed in this respect too by the establishment of parochial church councils, elected bodies intended to give lay members of the Church a greater role in the running of parishes.[19]

The Local Government Act, 1972, retained parish councils and meetings, although the word 'community' was substituted in Wales. More confusingly, parish councils in places which had previously been administered by urban district councils or municipal corporations were allowed to adopt the title 'town council' and describe their chairman as 'town mayor', affectations which encouraged some to retain former UDC and borough records.

The 1894 Act gave county councils a general supervisory role over civil parishes, including their records. The Act also provided, in some cases, for the transfer from the incumbent or parish clerk to the clerk of the parish council (or the chairman of the parish meeting, where there was no council) of all documents in his custody other than ecclesiastical records. In practice, documents were rarely handed over, because of either inertia or ill-feeling, and most remained in church custody, alongside more modern material created by the PCC and other organisations, while the records of civil parish councils and meetings consisted merely of minutes, accounts and correspondence. To a small extent before the war and a greater extent since, parish councils were persuaded to deposit material in county record offices; one interpretation of the 1972 Act is that it requires minor authorities to transfer all non-current records to county councils, since they alone are empowered to provide archive services (p. 131). More has arrived from parish councils since 1974 but much remains in the hands of council clerks, who normally hold part-time appointments and often lack proper storage facilities.

The custody of ecclesiastical parish records in England is now governed by the Parochial Registers and Records Measure of 1978, under which parishes may only retain material if they can provide suitable accommodation. Since the equipment required is far too expensive for most parishes to contemplate the great majority of registers are now in archival custody. The legislation replaced an earlier Measure of 1929 (19 & 20 Geo. V, No 1), which allowed (but can hardly be said to have encouraged) parishes to deposit records in repositories nominated by diocesan bishops (p. 107). Deposits of this kind have brought into local offices both registers and other ecclesiastical records and also large quantities of civil material not separated from the other documents after 1894.

The Church in Wales was disestablished and partially disendowed by the Welsh Church Act 1914 (4 & 5 Geo. V, c.91) and thus not affected by the Measures of 1929 and 1978. In 1950 agreement was reached between the Church in Wales and the National Library by which parish records might be deposited at the Library. This was supplemented in 1976 by another, under which the documents might alternatively be deposited in county record offices. Since then, most registers have been transferred to local offices, except in Powys, where the National Library remains the only approved place of deposit.[20]

All registers, of whatever date, whether in clerical or archival custody, are open to public search in both England and Wales, although incumbents are entitled to charge fees for the production of those in their custody. Under the agreements of 1950 and 1976 Welsh repositories are required to provide parishes with a bound facsimile of each book, which may often be easier of access for the local historian.

Since English and Welsh parish records are similar in type (although those in England are generally better preserved) and since ecclesiastical and civil records normally accumulated together until 1894, all may be dealt with here, although the former are not strictly concerned with local government.

The longest series of ecclesiastical records are normally the registers of baptism, marriage and burial ordered to be kept in all parishes in 1538, although only a few survive from this date. In Wales, especially, there may be nothing before 1660 or 1700. Until 1812 baptisms and burials were entered in blank books and the amount of information recorded varied, depending on the inclination of the incumbent or parish clerk. Printed forms were introduced in 1813 (52 Geo. III, c.146), alongside those which had been used for marriages since 1754. In 1837 the Church of England was brought into the new system of marriage registration and incumbents have since kept duplicate registers, one of which is sent to the superintendent registrar of the district when full (p. 120). Baptism and burial registration were not affected by the legislation of 1836 and have continued on similar lines to the present day. As new parishes were established in the nineteenth century, registration was established on the same basis as in medieval parishes. Some older chapels (which typically became new parishes) may have registers of their own, at least of baptism and burial. Registration in the Church in Wales since its disestablishment has followed Church of England practice, apart from the use of bilingual forms in recent years.

From the late sixteenth century parishes had to return a transcript of their register to the archdeacon at his (theoretically) annual visitation, a practice that died out during the nineteenth century at a date which appears to vary between dioceses. These copies are known as 'bishops' transcripts', since they were filed in the diocesan registry, and in some cases fill gaps left by the loss of original registers. They are now in diocesan record offices in England and at the National Library in Wales (p. 108).

Parish registers have been quarried by genealogists interested in tracing particular families probably since the sixteenth century; from the early nineteenth attempts have also been made to extract statistical data relating to birth, marriage and death and the size of the population. Both techniques have reached new levels of sophistication in recent years; the original source material, now increasingly saved from further damage by the use of facsimiles or microfilm in record offices, retains the same strengths and weaknesses as it has always had.[21]

The other main class of material connected with the church itself are the accounts kept by the churchwardens. Until 1868 (31 & 32 Vict., c.109) the wardens were allowed to levy a rate, payable by all who lived in the parish, irrespective of whether they were churchgoers; since then the main source of income for most parishes has been weekly offerings by worshippers. Churchwardens' expenditure, both today and in the past, is mostly on the supply of consumable items needed for services, cleaning, decoration and maintenance. From time to time, major repairs or even the total rebuilding of the church may have taken place, the accounts for which, certainly until book-keeping became more sophisticated this century, will probably be found amongst the routine entries. A few parishes have churchwardens' accounts from the mid-sixteenth century; in most cases they are far less well preserved. As new parishes have been set up since 1800, wardens have been been appointed for their churches also and accounts kept, including those built after the abolition of rates.[22]

If an incumbent and churchwardens wish to make structural alterations to their church, including the addition or removal of window-glazing, monuments, furnishings or the like, they must seek the permission of the bishop, who grants a 'faculty', signifying consent to the proposed change. Documents of this kind survive in most dioceses from the eighteenth century, if not earlier, and there may be copies in parish collections. Especially for the nineteenth century, which saw so much church building and restoration, faculty papers can be a useful source for the architectural and decorative history of the fabric, since they often include plans and specifications, which identify the architect and artist to be employed.

Most parishes have received charitable benefactions since the sixteenth century, most commonly consisting of a capital sum entrusted to the incumbent and churchwardens, who distribute the income therefrom annually. Some parish records include papers relating to these charities, most commonly accounts, unless income and expenditure were merged with the churchwardens' other transactions. In the early nineteenth century parliament appointed commissioners to enquire into local charities, whose reports are a major source for this subject, especially where no material survives locally; since 1853 a permanent commission has kept a central register of trusts, which is the other main source (p. 178).

Papers concerned with the incumbent himself rather than the church include periodical statements of the property belonging to the living, which today are taken whenever a vacancy occurs and are mainly inventories of the church, the parsonage house and their contents. These are the modern successors of earlier glebe terriers, when the property included land and buildings besides the parsonage. Terriers may contain useful details of the parsonage house itself and the documents as a whole are a good guide to the wealth of the living. Copies were deposited with the diocesan registrar as well as in the parish chest and the central collection (p. 104) may supplement what survives in a particular parish.[23]. Occasionally, mainly in the nineteenth century, insurance polices provide a similar description of the parsonage and its contents. The parish collection may also include induction and institution papers for past incumbents and stipendiary curates' licences, both of which again are registered amongst the diocesan records, as well as correspondence or other personal items.

Older accounts of ecclesiastical parish records tend to be concerned mainly with the registers, churchwardens' accounts and other formal documents which are supposed to survive (but frequently do not) in parishes which have existed since the middle ages. Much of the present network of Anglican parishes, however, dates from nineteenth-century changes in boundaries as the Church awoke to its responsibilities in new towns and industrial districts. Such places may be severely deficient in material of the kind traditionally thought of as 'parish records', but may conversely be rich in printed ephemera, parish magazines, the minute books of clubs and societies and other papers which bring to life the work of the incumbent and his congregation. In many communities, the building of a new church was accompanied, frequently in close physical proximity, by the establishment of a National school, which may since have closed or passed entirely into the hands of the local education authority, or it may still be a voluntary aided or controlled Church school. Where links between parish and school have remained close, an important element in the nineteenth-century records of the parish may be papers relating to the building and management of the school, which will supplement what is available elsewhere (p. 148).

Vestry minutes, which occasionally survive from the seventeenth century but more commonly (if at all) from the nineteenth, form a bridge between the ecclesiastical and civil life of the parish, since until 1894 the meeting dealt with business of all kinds. After the establishment of parish councils and parish meetings the vestry minute books may have been handed to the new authority or, more likely, used for the minutes of the annual 'Easter vestry' held by the church, to which the traditional gathering now withered. Since the setting-up of parochial church councils, the vestry has tended to be seen as a kind of AGM for the church and its minutes are often kept in the same book as that used for quarterly or monthly PCC minutes.

In parishes in which each township kept its own poor and possibly dealt with other civil matters meetings analogous to the vestry may be recorded in a 'township book'. Alternatively, especially in urban parishes in the nineteenth century, a 'select vestry' may have been established, formed by members elected from the parishioners at large in places where the traditional meeting was impractical.

Each of the parish officers appointed or nominated by the vestry may have left records which now form part of a parish collection. Alternatively, as is the case more often than some textbooks acknowledge, there may be nothing remaining from three centuries of local administration. Where a parish was divided into townships there may be separate archives for each, possibly preserved by a successor parish council.

The petty constable, whose area of jurisdiction may or may not have coincided with that of the parish or township, was responsible for maintaining law and order, a duty which included some share in the enforcement of the poor law (p. 98) and organising the militia, and for the collection and remittance of taxes. The office was unpaid but the constable could recover his expenses from the poor rate, and accounts showing receipts and disbursements occasionally survive.

The office of surveyor of highways was established by a statute of 1555 (2 & 3 Ph. & Mary, c.8), which remained the basis of highway law until 1835. Each parish appointed a surveyor annually, who was to supervise the maintenance of roads in the community through the voluntary labour of the inhabitants. In practice, statute labour was soon commuted into cash payments, which provided an income from which labourers were hired. Under an Act of 1691 (3 Wm &

Mary, c.12), which transferred the appointment of the surveyor from the vestry to the justices, parishes were permitted to levy a rate as an alternative to statute labour or a cash commutation. The reform of 1835 began the process by which the actual upkeep of the roads was taken away from parishes and placed in the hands of salaried surveyors employed by larger authorities (p. 138), but did not end the parochial basis of highway rating, nor the appointment of parish surveyors. A parish collection may include surveyors' accounts or there may simply be some post-1835 ratebooks. Many parishes, however, remained responsible for their roads well after this date and here accounts may be more informative. The system was modified from the early eighteenth century by the creation of turnpike trusts, charged with the maintenance of specified stretches of main roads (p. 103), although this did not relieve the inhabitants of each parish of liability to see that the road was maintained.

Parochial responsibility for poor relief was consolidated by a statute of 1601 (43 Eliz., c.2), which formed the basis of the law until 1834, subject to only one major modification, the Act of 1662 (14 Ch. II, c.12) allowing parishes to be divided (p. 92), which also established the law of settlement on lines that were to last well into the nineteenth century.[24] The Act of 1601 required each parish to appoint two or more overseers of the poor to act together with the churchwardens, who were overseers *ex officio*. The poor were to be relieved through the payment of doles or, wherever possible, set to work. The overseers' expenses were to be met by a rate, which soon became the most important tax levied on the community and one whose astronomical growth in some parts of the country in the early nineteenth century provided the main impetus behind the reform of 1834 (p. 112). Surviving records may include accounts showing the receipt of poor rate and its disbursement on outdoor relief and other expenses. Overseers continued to be appointed after 1834; although they were no longer responsible for administering relief, rates were still assessed and collected on a parochial basis. In places where the new poor law was not implemented for some years, the overseers continued to operate under the older legislation.

Under the Act of 1662 the poor were supposed only to be relieved in the parish in which they had a legal 'settlement', most commonly that in which they were born, had lived for some years, served an apprenticeship, paid poor rate or served a parish office. Unless a prospective recipient could establish eligibility, he (or she) was likely to be removed to another parish. The right to settlement was determined by a formal 'examination' by a JP, before whom the applicant was brought by the overseers. If the applicant admitted to a settlement elsewhere, the justice made an order, confirmed later by quarter sessions (p. 90), for the person to be removed. The overseers and constable were responsible for setting someone thus removed on his way and for delivering him to the officers of the next parish on the road towards that in which he was settled. Alternatively, the applicant might produce a settlement certificate showing that his right to relief had already been admitted. Removal orders might also be appealed to quarter sessions, which involved the overseers in further trouble and expense. Records of this system of settlement and removal survive for some places in great quantity: a large parish crossed by a busy main road might have a continual influx of strangers whom the overseers wished to move on, leaving behind them bundles of examinations and removal orders, of which the former are usually of more interest, since they contain biographical detail, while the orders are formal. The system may also be studied through quarter sessions material, chiefly the order books, or papers put into court where a case was disputed.

Two other types of loose document sometimes found among overseers' records are bastardy papers and apprenticeship indentures. The former record efforts to ensure that the fathers of illegitimate children maintained their offspring, thus 'saving the parish harmless' in the conventional phrase used in the bonds. Another technique for reducing the charge on the poor rate represented by pauper children was to bind them to serve a local master (or mistress), who took responsibility for keeping them. The overseers entered into a formal agreement (embodied in an indenture) with the master but this form of apprentice often provided only a nominal training in a trade.[25]

Pre-1834 poor law material, especially in town parishes, may also include the records of a workhouse established either for a single community or a number of parishes. Some were set up, from the late seventeenth century onwards, by local Act, others under the general legislation of 1722 (9 Geo. I, c.7) or, more commonly, 1782 (22 Geo. III, c.83). The latter, often called 'Gilbert's Act', allowed parishes to combine and erect a workhouse, in which each parish met the cost of maintaining its own poor but achieved savings by sharing premises, and thus foreshadowed the provisions of the Poor Law Amendment Act of 1834 (p. 112). Workhouse records are not common for this period, since the running of the house was often let to contractors, but occasionally there may be an admission register or list of inmates. If the workhouse was built not by the parish but by a separate corporation, there may be minutes of a governing body. Some of these remained in existence after 1834, since existing workhouses were not immediately abolished by the new Act.[26]

Boroughs and Improvement Commissions

Like the manor, the borough survived from the middle ages into modern times little changed in form (cf. p. 41). Most towns received new charters from one or more of the Tudor sovereigns, the grants often culminating in a late Elizabethan charter fully incorporating the burgesses for the first time and establishing a separate commission of the peace, either for petty sessions or quarter sessions (p. 86). In a small town, it may only be from this date that the office of mayor appears, replacing the bailiff or alderman who presided over the burgesses in the middle ages. The sequence of charters generally ends with a grant by Charles II or James II, which forms the basis of borough government until the beginning of statutory reform in 1835 (p. 101). Few, if any, charters were granted between the Revolution and the Municipal Corporations Act. Petitions for the renewal of privileges during this period would have been referred to the Privy Council, whose unpublished register and loose papers may contain a few references of this kind (p. 56). The grants themselves are normally to be found on the patent roll (p. 26), although most of the copies issued to grantees are probably still in existence locally.[27]

While many boroughs received a new charter in the second half of the sixteenth century, the main thrust of legislation was to transfer work from traditional agencies – the manor and borough – to the county and parish. The larger boroughs secured partial or, in some cases, complete exemption from county jurisdiction with their own court of quarter sessions and most retained separate parliamentary representation. Otherwise, the burgesses found themselves increasingly bereft of real responsibility, which fell instead on the vestry or, in the eighteenth century, on *ad hoc* 'improvement commissions'. Especially after 1660, when a changing political and economic climate meant that they lost the last remnants of control over local trade and industry, many small corporations withered into little more than property trusts and dining clubs.

Where borough records are reasonably well preserved, the most important documents after the charters are generally those containing minutes of corporation meetings. Some corporations worked through a rudimentary system of committees, for which there may be separate minutes. There may also be records of the civil court which existed in most of the larger towns, usually with a limited jurisdiction in cases of debt or other matters likely to arise in the course of trade. Some of these were chartered or prescriptive but many were set up by local Act during the eighteenth century. A few survived until the Local Government Act, 1972; most ceased to function after the revival of the county court in 1846 (p. 160). A third series may contain orders and other proceedings of the borough justices in quarter sessions or petty sessions. Subsidiary documents may include by-laws; lists of admissions to the corporation and mayoralty; poll-books or other papers concerned with parliamentary elections; and, possibly, a precedent book containing forms for admissions, various legal procedures and translations or abstracts of the charters. Most boroughs also obtained, often with the renewal of their privileges in the sixteenth century, the right to enrol deeds, although the extent to which this was taken advantage of by the burgesses varied from place to place.

Alongside records kept by the town clerk there may be financial material arising from the work of either a borough treasurer or, more commonly, the chamberlains, who were chosen annually from amongst members of the corporation. In their simplest form, borough accounts are merely statements of receipts and disbursements; where the corporation managed substantial property there may be more elaborate accounting and estate records, including rentals, surveys and leases. The acquisition of the property, some of which may in fact have been entrusted to the burgeses for charitable uses, rather than owned by them outright, may be recorded in surviving deeds. Apart from rent, the burgesses' income was derived from a borough rate, for which assessments may survive, and, in some towns, market tolls.

The craft gilds and fraternities to be found in all but the smallest medieval boroughs (p. 42) either disappeared at the Reformation or survived as purely social organisations, except for a few merchant companies in the largest provincial centres and, of course, the London livery companies. Occasionally, these societies are still in existence and retain their own muniments; more commonly, where material survives, it will be amongst the borough records. The same may be true of trusts established to administer benefactions received by the burgesses. In some towns, the corporation administered all such gifts, often failing to keep rent from charity estate separate from other income, a common source of complaint by reformers in the early nineteenth century. Elsewhere, especially if the benefaction led to the construction of an almshouse, school or other building, separate trustees were appointed, usually including representatives of the corporation. After the establishment of the Charity Commission in 1853 (p. 178) and the Endowed Schools Commission in 1869 (p. 143), the management of charities was separated from corporations. Early records, however, may have remained with the burgesses, whose archives may contain deeds, leases and other estate material relating to a hospital or grammar school. In exceptional cases there may be records of the admission of almspeople or pupils, the latter predating anything now in the hands of the school itself (p. 155).

The decay of borough government was arrested by the Municipal Corporations Act, 1835, which reformed the constitution of towns scheduled in the Act and provided for the incorporation of others.[28] The procedure remained the same: ratepayers petitioned the Privy Council and the crown made a grant enrolled on the patent roll, a copy of which was presented to the burgesses. The 1835 Act reformed the conduct of corporations, rather than their powers and duties, and it was only through separate legislation relating to police (p. 156) and, more important, public health (p. 129) that the older bodies were brought into the mainstream of Victorian local government. The law was consolidated afresh in 1882 (45 & 46 Vict., c.50), while another Act the following year (46 & 47 Vict., c.18) abolished corporations in a number of small places not covered by the earlier legislation, transferring any property to charitable trusts, which were not local authorities. Other corporations either became county boroughs in 1888 (p. 130) or remained non-county boroughs until the sweeping changes of 1974 (p. 109).

The present whereabouts of borough records, like those of other authorities abolished by the 1972 Act, varies from place to place. The successors of municipal corporations (and more especially county boroughs) have shown a marked reluctance to transfer charters to record offices, preferring to keep them hanging behind glass on town hall or museum walls as a reminder of former glories. Other records are more likely to be in archival custody but a considerable quantity appear to have been retained by district, parish or 'town' councils. In other cases, material may have reached record offices from solicitors whose predecessors acted as clerk to small boroughs on a part-time basis.

The lack of vitality of most municipal corporations in the eighteenth century coincided in many towns with an increase in population, an extension of the built-up area and the arrival of new industry. These changes created problems of public health, highway maintenance and the like with which the traditional corporation was entirely unfitted to deal. The same was normally true of the parish vestry and, where it remained a living institution, the manor court leet. In some towns, nothing was done until the Public Health Act, 1848, provided a framework within which local authorities could be set up (p. 129). Elsewhere, the eighteenth-century response was for each community to seek a local Act establishing a statutory commission alongside the corporation, vestry or leet. The powers of these commissions varied, depending on local needs, but in general they were charged with paving and lighting the streets, building new ones where needed, controlling building, improving drainage and, in some cases, watching and policing. To carry out these functions, the commission was empowered to levy a rate.[29]

Improvement commission records generally consist of minutes and possibly also rate-books and building plans. Although usually more active than corporations, they were early instances of the 'statutory authority for special purposes', which became more common in the nineteenth century (pp. 110-111) and their records are accordingly more limited in range, since they reflect the discharge of functions defined by statute. Some commissions were wound up after 1835 or with the adoption locally of the 1848 Public Health Act or 1858 Local Government Act, under either of which improvement commission districts could form the basis of sanitary districts. A few survived to become urban sanitary authorities under the Public Health Act of 1872 (pp. 129-30) and the last were absorbed into municipal corporations after 1882. Their records should have passed to the successor authority.

The early nineteenth century also saw the installation in many towns of piped water and, a little later, gas. This may have been undertaken either by improvement commissioners or by separate companies, most commonly incorporated, at least before the Joint Stock Companies Act, 1844 (p. 172), by local Act. These concerns generally passed into municipal hands later in the century; gas, water and electricity have since been taken into public ownership on a national basis (p. 159).

Turnpike Trusts

The other characteristic statutory authority of the late eighteenth century and early nineteenth was the trust established to maintain a stretch of main road. The idea originated in a scheme of 1663 (15 Ch. II, c.1) to take over part of the Great North Road; by the 1830s most of the major routes in England and Wales had been turnpiked. Some trusts controlled all or most of the main road mileage in their county, especially in Wales, others were responsible for only a single length. Many main roads came under several different trusts of varying efficiency. Each was established by local Act; its members were empowered to mortgage prospective income from tolls to provide a capital sum for improvement or rebuilding, which was intended to be repaid over 21 years. The trust would then be liquidated and the road returned to the parish (p. 97). This hope was rarely, if ever, realised and the trusts were renewed when their term expired, their debts becoming a permanent charge on toll income. The building of the railways ruined the trusts and the roads were gradually 'dis-turnpiked'. In South Wales this happened as early as 1844, with statutory roads boards taking their place (p. 139); elsewhere, the roads passed either to highway boards, themselves taken over by county councils in 1888, or passed directly to county councils on their establishment (p. 140). The bulk of trust records have thus been in local authority custody since 1888; a few have been deposited more recently by solicitors whose predecessors acted as clerk to a trust.[30] Papers from the trust administering the particularly important post road from London to Holyhead via Shrewsbury are (uniquely) in central custody amongst Local Government Board records at Kew (class MH 27; cf. p. 128).

The eighteenth century also saw the construction of a small number of bridges by similar trusts. Most of these are now in the hands of county councils but a few survive, in which case trust records should be in the custody of their clerk or on deposit at the record office.

Turnpike records most commonly consist of minutes of the fairly infrequent meetings of the trustees, together, in some cases, with accounts or lists of members. None of these shed much light on the day-to-day running of the trust, much less traffic carried, since management was largely devolved to surveyors and to contractors who took leases of tolls in return for a lump sum. Only occasionally are there accounts which actually record the movement of vehicles; more commonly, there will be lists of contractors and the amounts at which each toll-gate was let. Advertisements for sales of this kind, either by auction or tender, occur frequently in local newspapers around the turn of the nineteenth century. Besides the trusts' own papers, the county record office will also have (from 1792) plans deposited with the clerk of the peace showing the line of new turnpike roads built under parliamentary authority (p. 89).

The incorporation of trustees or commissioners by local Act was a procedure used from the Restoration to the early nineteenth century for other purposes besides road improvement. Some docks and harbours were built and managed in this way and most river navigation schemes between 1660 and 1760 were also undertaken by statutory commissions, rather than individual patentees, as had been more common before the Civil War. Surviving records may be in local custody, or in the PRO at Kew, if the undertaking was nationalised after the second world war (p. 176). In either case, minutes and accounts, possibly accompanied by engineers' reports, plans and specifications, may exist. After 1760 interest in river improvement waned as schemes for deadwater canals were promoted instead. The projectors of one of the first of these, the Grand Trunk Canal linking the Trent and Mersey, rejected the idea of establishing a trust similar to those for roads and rivers and instead secured incorporation as a joint-stock company in 1766 (6 Geo. III, c.xcvi).[31] This decision influenced the entire course of canal building over the following half-century, virtually all of which was undertaken by similar concerns, and provided the model for both early horse-operated railway companies, of which the first was incorporated in 1801 (41 Geo. III, c.xxxiii), and, more important, the later main line network. Canal and railway records, as well as those of other transport undertakings incorporated on joint-stock principles, are thus somewhat different in character from those of earlier bodies and have mostly ended up in central custody (p. 177).

Church Records

The growth of record keeping by the parish from the mid-sixteenth century has already been mentioned (p. 94), as have the records of some of the central institutions of the early modern church (p. 80). The same period also saw changes at diocesan level, partly as a result of the creation of several sees by Henry VIII and the re-foundation of monastic cathedrals with secular chapters.[32] In the old dioceses as well as those established in the sixteenth century the medieval practice of entering administrative acts in a single series of general registers (p. 48) gave way to a division of material between several sets of books and the filing of loose documents in support of the registers. Thus, in most diocesan archives, there are papers relating to the ordination of the clergy, the consecration of new churches and the licensing not only of unbeneficed curates but also certain classes of laity, for example schoolmasters. Licences were also required for marriages not preceded by the calling of banns.[33] Two other types of document, faculties and glebe terriers, have already been mentioned (pp. 95-6), since, although both were in origin diocesan records, copies relating to individual churches and livings are often to be found in parish collections.

Other documents dating from the sixteenth century and later stem from the increasing regulation of the Church by statute, such as the requirement for both incumbents and others (including, again, schoolmasters) to subscribe to the supremacy of the crown, the Book of Common Prayer and the Thirty-Nine Articles, first introduced in 1558 (1 Eliz., c.1) and consoled by the Act of Uniformity of 1662 (14 Charles II, c.4), from which latter date, if not before, subscription books should survive. The return of parish register transcripts to the diocesan registry (p. 95), generally from 1597, is another instance of the same process. So also is the compilation of lists of conformists, nonconformists and recusants, notably in 1563, 1603 and 1676, from which returns by parish and diocese, mostly preserved centrally rather than locally, are a valuable source for population history.[34] When the Toleration Act of 1688 (1 Wm & Mary, c.18) allowed protestant dissenters to establish meeting-houses, such buildings had to be registered with the bishop in whose diocese they stood. Such registers, together with those kept by quarter sessions (p. 88), often provide the only clue to the first appearance of dissent in a particular community, since the congregation may have no early records of their own. Registration in this way continued until the mid-nineteenth century, when it was taken over by the Registrar General (p. 122).[35]

Episcopal visitations (p. 48) continued from the middle ages into modern times with the basic procedure unchanged, although a wider range of documents generally survives from the sixteenth century onwards. A newly enthroned bishop normally made (and makes) a primary visitation of his diocese within twelve months of his appointment and thereafter at intervals of three or four years. Between these visitations the archdeacons made similar annual visits to parishes within their jurisdiction. In both cases, parishes were required to return answers to articles of enquiry, some of which were routine, others, especially those issued on the instructions of energetic nineteenth-century reforming bishops, were more penetrating and the replies correspondingly more interesting. Besides the general condition of the church fabric, the number of worshippers and services and the income of the living, visitation articles might also ask about the extent of dissent and Roman Catholicism in the parishes, the existence of schools and charities and other more general topics.[36]

Episcopal and archidiaconal jurisdiction over the clergy and, to a lesser extent, laity, likewise continued. For some dioceses, but not all, considerable quantities of court papers have survived, which throw light not only on the nature of ecclesiastical jurisdiction in the sixteenth and seventeenth centuries but also on morality, allegiance to the established church and other aspects of life in local communities. The records, although complex in structure and not usually arranged to facilitate the location of cases relating to a particular parish, have formed the basis of some important case studies.[37]

Far better known and more easily accessible are the records of the church's exclusive retention of jurisdiction over probate until 1858. Grants of probate and administration might be made by provincial (pp. 81-83), diocesan or archidiaconal courts, depending on the size of the estate and its whereabouts; in addition, numerous small areas formed 'peculiar' jurisdictions outside the general pattern.[38] A comparatively small number of medieval wills are to be found either in bishops' registers or elsewhere, but from the sixteenth century the material becomes voluminous, consisting generally both of original filed wills and registered copies, together with act books recording grants. Important subsidiary documents, which may either be attached to wills or filed separately, include inventories of personal estate, executors' and administrators' accounts and bonds entered into by those responsible for the affairs of the deceased, whether or not he left a will. Few classes of material have been so extensively exploited by local historians in recent years (besides their traditional use by genealogists) and many editions of probate inventories, sometimes accompanied by abstracts of wills, have been published, as have indexes to grants. There remains, however, no general study of early modern wills and willmaking or of the working of the probate courts. The sheer bulk of material available for even a small parish, coupled with the detail both wills and inventories shed on so many aspects of early modern society, still tends to obscure the problems surrounding the material. We do not know precisely who made wills, whether certain families consistently did so from one generation to the next, why families sought probate in the provincial court instead of locally, why relatives of men and women who died intestate sometimes obtained grants of administration and sometimes did not, and what exactly appraisers were seeking to do when they compiled an inventory. No local historian interested in his community between about 1550 and 1750 can ignore wills and, more especially, inventories as a major source of information but, equally, he should try to consider some of the unanswered questions.[39]

Besides the administrative and judicial classes, diocesan record offices also have material, often of considerable local interest, relating to the estates held by the diocese or, more commonly, the dean and chapter, including, for example, long runs of manor court records, leases, rentals, surveys other material, which will generally be relatively well preserved because of the continuity of ownership and administration typically found on church estates. The chapter act books, recording the administrative work of the dean and his colleagues, will usually be of less interest, except for the building history of the cathedral itself and its furnishings.[40]

From the late eighteenth century changes in the church and in its relations with the state are reflected in the pattern of record keeping.[41] The building of new churches and the restoration and enlargement of old ones; the creation of new parishes and the appointment of additional incumbents and assistant clergy; the establishment of church schools and later teacher training colleges all produce new categories of material in diocesan archives or greatly increase the bulk of existing series (e.g. faculties). On the other hand, the same period saw the gradual withering of ecclesiastical jurisdiction over the laity, a process completed by the removal of divorce and probate in 1858 (pp. 179-80), and, less important, the abandonment of parish register transcripts after the civil registration of birth, marriage and death was introduced in 1837 (p. 117). The establishment of the Ecclesiastical Commissioners in 1835, who took over the administration of the landed possessions of the church, was a further major reform.[42] In other respects, however, church administration at local level changed much less in the nineteenth century than, for example, did local government, and some classes of record continue to accrue to the present day, including most of those relating to church buildings and the clergy, as well as visitation. A number of new dioceses have been established since the mid-nineteenth century and both archdeaconry and parish boundaries have been much altered, but the basic three-tier structure has survived.

Since the concept of diocesan record offices was first enunciated in a Measure of the Church Assembly in 1929 (19 & 20 Geo. V, No 1), which in practice amounted to the recognition of an existing local authority office as an approved repository, most older material from diocesan registries has been transferred. All the English bishops have now appointed a record office, not merely for their own but also for capitular, archidiaconal and parochial records. Two classes of material have reached offices indirectly. During the nineteenth century estate muniments were handed over to the Ecclesiastical Commissioners, whose successors, the Church Commissioners (set up in 1948), have since re-distributed them to appropriate local offices, in some cases re-uniting material with closely related documents which had remained in diocesan or capitular custody. The Church Commissioners themselves retain a great quantity of modern material concerning their properties, which is reasonably accessible to enquirers.[43] Secondly, the probate records were transferred after 1858 to the new lay court, in whose hands they languished, either at Somerset House or in a district registry, in unsatisfactory conditions with poor facilities for searchers. These have now also been placed in local record offices alongside the other judicial records of the dioceses and archdeaconries.

The provincial records of the Church of England are in some

respects similar to those of the constituent dioceses; some of the judicial records of the southern province, relating to the whole of England and Wales, were mentioned in the previous chapter (p. 80). Other material is divided between Lambeth Palace Library and the Kent Archives Office, while the whole of the records of the northern province remain at York at the Borthwick Institute of Historical Research.[44]

In 1920 the Church in Wales (i.e. the dioceses of Bangor, Llandaff, St Asaph and St Davids, all of which lay in the province of Canterbury) was disestablished and disendowed. Wales has since formed a separate province of the Anglican communion, with an archbishop and five diocesans.[45] The Church in Wales is a statutory corporation, with a Governing Body, whose title is self-explanatory, and a Representative Body, which holds its property. Record keeping at all levels is similar to that in the modern Church of England, while the Church in Wales has, of course, inherited the older records of the dioceses, chapters, archdeaconries and parishes which pre-date disestablishment. In 1944 an agreement was reached with the National Library under which the Department of Manuscripts and Records became the sole approved repository for the non-parochial records of the Church in Wales; parish records may (since 1976) be deposited either locally or at the Library (p. 94). After 1945 probate records from the ecclesiastical courts in Wales were also transferred to the NLW, an arrangement which is perhaps one of the most controversial aspects of the problem of where to keep Welsh local records.[46] The Library has done little towards making available modern indexes to the probate material and levies a penal charge for the supply of copies, which successfully discourages use by local historians in most parts of the country of documents which in England would be readily available in a county office. The Library also has a fine collection of estate records for Welsh dioceses and chapters, deposited by the Welsh Church Commission which carried out the provisions of the Acts of 1914 (4 & 5 Geo. V, c.91) and 1919 (9 & 10 Geo. V, c.65) concerning disendowment. The property itself was in part returned to the Church in Wales (in the case of churches, churchyards and parsonages) and in part handed either to the county councils (who acquired parochial glebeland) or to the University of Wales (who had the diocesan and capitular estates). The modern history of these properties must therefore be pursued either with county record offices or estates departments or with the University Registry.

Chapter Five
THE MODERN LOCAL GOVERNMENT SYSTEM

The present pattern of local government in England and Wales is essentially the product of statutory reform in 1972, which has itself already been substantially revised.[1] Despite the semblance of continuity in many areas outside the major cities between the authorities which existed before 1 April 1974 (and the reality of continuity of policy in many cases) the Local Government Act 1972 forms a convenient terminal date in this account of local government records. Although most non-metropolitan counties in England (but not in Wales) retained the same names as those borne by county councils before 1974, all were modified as a result of boundary changes under the Act, if only through the abolition of the county boroughs and their absorption back into the counties to which they had generally belonged before 1888. In the major conurbations, changes were more sweeping if, as it has proved, shorter-lived, with the disappearance of unitary authorities – the county boroughs – and the substitution of a clumsy and unsatisfactory dual system of metropolitan counties and metropolitan districts. Here there was anything but continuity. Outside these areas, three types of authority created in 1888-94 – the county borough, urban district and rural district – were abolished, as were municipal corporations, and the whole of England and Wales outside Greater London and the metropolitan counties divided into 'districts', with uniform powers (except for four in South Wales which remain library authorities). The number of second-tier councils was greatly reduced and their relationship with the counties changed; for the former county boroughs which failed to become metropolitan districts the changes were especially marked. Finally, the third tier of local government created in 1894, the rural civil parish with its parish meeting or parish council or both, was retained, in an attenuated form, with its name in Wales changed to 'community'. Since 1974 it has even been possible to establish parish councils for areas which were already urban in 1894 and therefore not subject to the earlier Act, but where now a representative body is deemed desirable.

Although the system established in 1972 is much neater than its predecessor, this is partly disguised by the retention of older names for authorities which are now simply districts or civil parishes. A number of new councils, especially those which succeeded a former county or municipal borough, went to considerable trouble and expense to ensure that their authority was still known as a 'city council' or 'borough council', and to secure from the crown a 'borough charter' (in fact letters patent whose sole purpose was to confer a new title on the district council), even though incorporation in this manner was now abolished. The motives behind this appeared to stem partly from a snobbish association of the term 'district' with the old urban district councils, from which municipal boroughs assiduously distinguished themselves, even when their powers were identical, and partly from a misunderstood sense of history which can be traced in most towns back to the late nineteenth century. Much the same was true, in a less marked form, of parish councils which sought the title 'town council' and have designated their chairman 'town mayor' since 1974 in a determined effort to keep alive the memory of a former municipal corporation (or even a UDC) which functioned within similar boundaries.

The irony of these attempts to hold on to the past was that the system which many councillors and their officers viewed with such affection lacked the deep roots which in 1972-4 were claimed for it. While it was appreciated that urban and rural district councils lacked any antiquity (or, in most cases, any other desirable quality), those concerned with the effect of local government reorganisation ignored the fact that the authorities being abolished were themselves the product of nineteenth-century statutory reform. The system swept away in 1974 was essentially that created by a series of Acts between 1834 and 1894, with a number of later modifications, of which the Education Act of 1902, the Local Government Act of 1929 and the National Health Service Act of 1946 were probably the most important. In part, the authorities set up in the nineteenth century were grafted on to the system described in the previous chapter and therefore older names were retained, such as county, borough and parish. In other respects there was no continunity. The mere survival of nomenclature, however, especially in towns where the local authority was a county or municipal borough, was enough for a later generation to claim in 1974 that their new authorities should preserve the names, if not the boundaries or powers, of their predecessors. This phenomenon is itself an interesting aspect of local government history but its unsound basis should be appreciated by anyone seeking to understand the evolution of the system and the records thus created centrally and locally.

The twin starting-points for any account of statutory reform are the Poor Law Amendment Act of 1834, whose importance extends well beyond the (admittedly large) area of social policy with which it sought to deal, and the Municipal Corporations Act, 1835. Apart from reforming the administration of poor relief the Act of 1834 established principles that were to guide local government reform for the following two generations, while the administrative geography of poor relief under the Act survived in places until 1974. Following the precedent of the Poor Law Amendment Act, local authorities were henceforth established by statute, normally for the discharge of a single function, although this doctrine was the first to be questioned and the reforms of 1888 and 1894 marked its abandonment. Other principles stemmed from the reform of municipal corporations in 1835: the new authorities were to be made up of members elected by a franchise that was at least as liberal as the parliamentary franchise of the day and generally more so. Meetings of members were to be open to the press and public and their financial operations subject to independent audit. Their funds were to be drawn from a rate levied, at least in the early days, for a particular purpose. Members' decisions were to be executed by paid officers, admittedly to begin with part-time officers remunerated by fee rather than salary, but who by the end of the nineteenth century would advise members on policy and formulate details, rather than merely carry out instructions. Perhaps most important, not least for its archival consequences, was the principle of close control of local authorities by central government, coupled with the doctrine of *ultra vires,* under which an authority might take a particular action only if specifically required or allowed to do so by statute.[2]

The enforcement of this policy and the generally tight discipline imposed on local authorities by central government up to 1939 was largely the responsibility of new departments of state. Although the Home Secretary retained some duties in connection with local government, chiefly concerning the maintenance of order (p. 162), most reforms entailed the creation of a department charged with the supervision of a new type of local authority. The modernisation of local government thus led to changes in the machinery of central government. There was also a change in approach, in which the traditional role of the secretary of state as a final arbiter to be consulted only occasionally gave way to detailed intervention by the central departments. Initially, this control was largely negative; increasingly, however, the central departments tried to lead local authorities towards a more positive view of their role, sometimes by extending their statutory powers or duties but more often by encouraging the more enterprising and holding them up as examples to their less enlightened brethren. This interplay between centre and localities is an important aspect of nineteenth-century local government; its overall effect is that after 1834 central government records shed more light on local government than at any time since the Restoration, as the long period in which the localities (especially the counties) were left largely to their own devices came to an end.

The major areas in which the expansion of activity led to the establishment of new local authorities were poor relief, public health and education, which, coupled with the creation of a modern police force, gradually fused to form the basis of a unified system of local government. The process by which authorities set up for a single purpose merged into others with multiple functions was comparatively slow and not always smooth. The main lines of the system were defined by the Local Government Acts of 1888 and 1894 but education was not absorbed until 1902 and poor relief not until 1929. At the centre there was a parallel process of amalgamation which was never so complete. Thus education has remained the province of a separate department to the present day, while only since 1970 have most other activities of local government come under the supervision of a single secretary of state. Responsibility for personal and public health, unified in 1919 with the establishment of the Ministry of Health, was separated from planning in 1942. In turn, the creation of the National Health Service in 1948 partly removed the personal health services from local government while leaving them under the supervision of the Minister of Health, whose control of public health, still at that date a dominant concern of local government, passed to the Ministry of Housing and Local Government. In this situation, there is no wholly satisfactory way of describing what records should be available and where they are likely to be found. The approach here is mostly functional, taking each major activity in turn, identifying the local authority responsible at different dates and relating local sources to material in the PRO. The transition from the single-purpose authorities of the nineteenth century to the modern unified system is described mainly in the section concerned with public health, since most of the local authorities (apart from civil parishes) which existed on the eve of reorganisation in 1974 were in origin sanitary authorities. The modernisation of local government at county and parish level was outlined in the previous chapter (pp. 87, 93); here we shall see how the work of county councils developed after 1889.

Poor Relief and Medical Services

The Poor Law Amendment Act of 1834 (4 & 5 William IV, c.76) appointed commissioners to carry out its provisions, principally the establishment throughout the country of unions of parishes which would henceforth be responsible for the local administration of poor relief, in place of individual parishes and townships (p. 98).[3] The commissioners were continued in office until 1847, when a Poor Law Board was set up (10 & 11 Vict., c.109), initially as a temporary department but made permanent in 1867 (30 & 31 Vict. c.106). Four years later the Local Government Board Act (34 & 35 Vict. c.70) created a single department to take responsibility for both poor relief and public health, replacing the Poor Law Board and the Local Government Act Office of the Home Office (pp. 127-8). Between 1871 and 1919 the Local Government Board remained the department responsible for most of central government's dealings with local government, until the Ministry of Health was established (9 & 10 Geo. V, c.21), which took over the functions of the Local Government Board and also those of the Insurance Commissioners and the Welsh Insurance Commissioners, set up in 1911 (1 & 2 Geo.

V, c.55) to administer the first national insurance scheme. Although some of the Ministry of Health's powers concerning the supervision of local authority planning were transferred to the Ministry of Works and Planning in 1942 (the predecessor of the Ministry of Housing and Local Government), responsibility for the personal health services remained with the former department until the last remnants of the poor law were abolished with the setting up of the National Health Service in 1948 (9 & 10 Geo. VI, c.81). The records transferred to the PRO by the Ministry of Health and its successor, the Department of Health and Social Security, include many dating from the period after 1871, when the administration of the poor law was merged, both centrally and, in some cases, locally, with public health. As far as possible, the classes mentioned here are concerned purely with the poor law and the medical services which evolved from it; public health material is described below (p. 128).

The major class of local interest is MH 12, consisting of over 16,000 volumes of correspondence between the Poor Law Commission, the Poor Law Board and Local Government Board on the one hand, and the poor law unions on the other. For each union there should be correspondence with the clerk to the guardians from whenever a particular union was set up down to 1900, the counterpart of which is unlikely to be preserved locally. Most papers after 1900 were destroyed during the second world war but such as have survived now form MH 68, which continues until the guardians were abolished in 1929. Two other series (MH 48 and MH 52) contain files of correspondence between the central department and local authorities from about 1900 to the 1960s concerning both poor law (including hospitals before 1948) and public health. For the Ministry of Health's dealings with hospitals since 1948 three classes are worth checking, MH 87, 88 and 89, which are concerned with hospital management committees, regional hospital boards and the governors of teaching hospitals respectively (cf. p. 115). The group also contains a set of files (MH 102), originally created by the Home Office, for institutions such as industrial and approved schools and reformatories for young offenders, some of which were established under the poor law and some under prisons legislation (cf. p. 158); since 1972 all have come under DHSS supervision.

Several subsidiary classes also contain local material. MH 9 consists of registers of paid officers employed by unions between 1837 and 1921, listing every officer employed in whatever capacity (from clerk to the guardians or workhouse master down to porters and rate collectors), the dates of their appointment and departure (with reason for leaving) and their salary. Much of this information can also be found in the minutes of the guardians for each union, but some of the entries have policy comments added by civil servants. MH 14 is a class of plans of poor law unions, while MH 34 contains registers of authorisations of expenditure, arranged alphabetically by union (1834-1902), again probably mainly summarising information that could be obtained more laboriously from individual guardians' minutes. Finally, MH 54 contains schemes drawn up by county and county borough councils under the Local Government Act 1929 (19 & 20 Geo. V, c.17), showing how they proposed to replace the guardians as the local authority for poor relief. Two volumes of the List & Index Society (96 and 99) provide a class-list for the group as far as MH 83, while three others (56, 64 and 77) form a more detailed guide to MH 12.

Under the Poor Law Amendment Act of 1834 the whole of England and Wales was to be divided into unions of parishes, in each of which an elected board of guardians was to administer poor relief. As far as possible, unions were arranged so as to contain a market town that was already the natural centre of the district but their areas did not always respect county boundaries. Parochial responsibility for poor relief thus disappeared, although individual parishes (or townships) continued to assess and collect their own poor rate. In the years following 1834, assistant commissioners strove to implement the act, sometimes with comparative ease but in the north of England especially in the face of considerable opposition. Some towns continued to administer poor relief under local acts well into the mid-nineteenth century. The essential feature of the new poor law was the building in each union of a workhouse in which, as far as possible, those in receipt of relief were to be housed. In practice, not all unions built workhouses at once and some merely took over those erected by parishes or unions formed under the Act of 1782 (22 Geo. III c.83; cf. p. 99). More important, a great deal of out-relief continued to be administered, leaving the workhouses gradually to evolve into orphanages and hospitals, especially for the feeble-minded, aged and infirm. Two main themes of recent work on the new poor law have been the degree of continuity from the old system and the way in which medical services soon (and quite unexpectedly) came to bulk very large in the work of the guardians. By the end of the nineteenth century a rudimentary 'national health service' for the poor had grown up in this way.[4] Besides the aged poor, it was children who received a great deal of attention. During the middle decades of the nineteenth century unions established schools for children in their care (gradually given up as state provision for elementary education grew from 1870; cf. p. 147), and towards the end of the century there was a trend towards establishing separate 'cottage' or 'scattered' homes for children, before the Children Act of 1908 (8 Edw. VII, c.67) finally removed them from the workhouse.

As the only elected local authority which covered England and Wales uniformly before 1888, the guardians were adopted as the vehicle for the administration of several other services, chiefly the registration of birth, marriage and death from 1837 and the decennial census from 1841 (p. 122). In 1846 they were given limited public health powers in rural areas under the first of several

Nuisance Removal Acts (9 & 10 Vict. c.96; 11 & 12 Vict., c.123; 18 & 19 Vict., c.121), which were renewed on a larger scale by the Public Health Act of 1872 (35 & 36 Vict., c.79). The guardians now became 'rural sanitary authorities' in all parishes where there was no urban sanitary authority (pp. 129-30), a development which foreshadowed the setting up of rural district councils under the Local Government Act of 1894, consisting of the rural parishes in each union. The 1894 Act, however, marked the end of direct elections to the boards of guardians: henceforth, members of RDCs were to sit as guardians for their respective parishes, whereas before the guardians had, without further election, formed a rural sanitary authority. The guardians' responsibility for poor relief was not altered by this legislation, nor was the recommendation of the Minority Report on the Poor Laws of 1909 that the guardians be abolished acted upon for another twenty years. Only with the Local Government Act 1929 (19 & 20 Geo. V. c.17) and the Poor Law Act 1930 (20 & 21 Geo. V. c.17) were unions swept away and responsibility for the poor law, including many hospitals, transferred to the county and county borough councils established under the Local Government Act of 1888. This is the origin of the counties' (and since 1974 the metropolitan districts') responsibilities for social services, which have grown in importance enormously in recent years.

The counties' responsibility for hospital services, however, lasted only until the setting up of the National Health Service in 1948, under which all the former poor law and voluntary hospitals (except those which became old people's homes run by county councils) were vested in the Ministry of Health. Local administration was divided between hospital governors (in the case of teaching hospitals) and regional hospital boards (all others), while general practice and dental, ophthalmic and pharmaceutical services were administered in each county or county borough by a local executive council, a non-elected body responsible directly to the minister. The counties remained local health authorities for a variety of non-hospital services, including ambulances, vaccination and immunisation, health visiting and home nursing, antenatal and child welfare clinics and midwifery.[5]

The local records of poor relief since 1834, including the provision of medical services, consist chiefly of the archives of the boards of guardians from whatever date a particular board was established down to 1929, and those of public assistance (later welfare or social services) committees of county and county borough councils from then until 1974. For some places there may also be material from parishes or unions which remained poor law authorities after 1834. In all three cases, there were two levels of record creation: the supervising authority and the institution (whether workhouse, hospital, orphanage or whatever). Surviving union records should have passed to county and county borough councils and therefore now be in county record offices or repositories maintained by district or metropolitan district councils, who should also have any poor law material from pre-1834 authorities that remained in existence. The amount of later material transferred by social services departments may vary considerably between authorities but should include committee minutes and officers' reports, even if files have either been destroyed or retained. National Health Service records, including inherited documents dating from before 1948, are public records but are in local rather than central custody. Some NHS material has been transferred to record offices, either from regional hospital boards or executive councils, but much appears still to be in administrative custody.

Most of the records described here are open to public inspection 30 years after their creation, although those containing medical information relating to individuals may be closed for 100 years.

As with all local authorities, the quantity and character of surviving records of boards of guardians vary considerably between different unions, although because of the close supervision of the central department and the detailed statutory definition of their powers and duties, guardians' records are possibly more homogeneous than some. At the heart of the general administration of the union were the board meetings themselves, frequently held weekly in unions of any size, whose minutes were kept by the guardians' principal adviser, the clerk, an office normally held part-time by a local solicitor.[6] Flanking the main series of minutes there may be draft minute books and the minutes of standing and ad hoc committees, including (between 1872 and 1894) those of meetings of the guardians sitting as the rural sanitary authority. Other records kept by the clerk (which survive much less commonly) include correspondence, either loose or entered in volumes; papers concerned with guardians' elections; and (if the union became involved in litigation) case-papers. The clerk's archives may also include copies of a number of regular or occasional returns required either by the guardians or the central department, most often summarising the numbers of those receiving relief within different categories. The other major group of material is normally financial, including treasurers' and guardians' ledgers, parochial ledgers and a series for the RSA. There may also be records of payments and receipts made by relieving officers employed by the union and the overseers of the poor from each vestry.[7]

The other record-creating officers in the union were those in charge of the workhouse and any other institutions administered by the guardians, which by the end of the nineteenth century might include cottage homes for children, a separate infirmary and 'industrial schools', in which children received practical training for a trade. Much of this material continues unchanged after the reform of 1929-30 until 1948. For the workhouse itself, the longest series is generally that of admission and discharge registers (with separate series for vagrants and casual paupers later in the century), which record the entry and departure of inmates, including their name, date of birth, parish, former occupation, marital status and reason for seeking relief, as well as the circumstances of their departure and possibly observations as to their general character.[8] Where the guardians maintained a separate school for pauper children there would be a register for that also. The master of a workhouse was required to keep accounts, principally of domestic expenditure and of wages for staff, and also records of the weekly diet in the house. The latter are perhaps the best known workhouse records, although other material provides more information about the running of the institution and the various registers more personal detail.

Workhouses were renamed 'public assistance institutions' after the guardians were replaced by the counties but some of the records of internal administration continue to 1948 with little or no change. Guardians' records, however, end in 1929 and are replaced by those of the appropriate committee of the county or county borough council. After the separation of health and social services in 1948 the administrative history of hospitals previously maintained by the guardians or the counties must be traced through the records of the local health authority, which may be in a county record office or still in the hands of the NHS, while hospital records themselves may also have been transferred by management committees or may still be in official custody.[9]

Registration of Birth, Marriage and Death and the Census

Although marriage registration was reformed by an Act of 1753 (26 Geo. II, c.33) and that of baptism and burial by another of 1812 (52 Geo. III, c.146), both of which introduced printed forms so as to ensure that at least a minimum of information was recorded (p. 94), it was clear by the 1820s that further changes were needed. In particular, Anglican baptism and burial registration fell far short of a complete record of births and deaths, while the Marriage Act 1753, which allowed only Jews and Quakers to marry outside the Church of England, restricted the civil liberties of Roman Catholic and Protestant dissenters. Further pressure came from the medical profession, who sought better statistics of both birth and death, especially as to the cause of death. In 1833 a Select Committee was appointed, whose recommendations formed the basis of two Acts of 1836 (6 & 7 William IV cc. 85, 86), marriage registration being dealt with separately as it had in 1753. The delay in introducing legislation may have been due partly to the lack of suitable officials who could operate a system of civil registration locally. The Poor Law Amendment Act of 1834 provided the administrative framework and the registration service remained essentially linked with the poor law until 1948.

Under the registration Acts the whole of England and Wales was divided into registration districts, in each of which a superintendent registrar of births, deaths and marriages was appointed. In practice, the registration districts were co-terminous with the poor law unions and the superintendents normally the clerks to the guardians. Indeed, the assistant poor law commissioners, struggling in many parts of the country to introduce the new poor law, used the registration Acts, to which there was little opposition, to establish unions which might at least work that legislation, even if they refused to take any action under the Poor Law Amendment Act. Each registration district was divided into several sub-districts, in each of which there was a registrar of births and deaths, who might (at the discretion of the superintendent) also be a registrar of marriages. In practice, the sub-districts were those into which the union was divided for the administration of poor relief and the registrars were the union relieving officers.

The central authority under the Acts of 1836 was a new department, the General Register Office, presided over by the Registrar General, a civil servant for whom, until 1871, the Home Secretary took parliamentary responsibility. He then came under the Local Government Board until its absorption into the Ministry of Health in 1919 (p. 128). In 1970 the department was remodelled as the Office of Population Censuses and Surveys, whose director retains the statutory title of Registrar General. Although a number of classes have been transferred to both branches of the PRO, where they form the RG group, some of the earlier records of the General Register Office will be found among the Home Office papers, while the best known classes, the copy certificates of birth, marriage and death, remain in the department's own custody and are not directly accessible to the public.

Since 1 July 1837 it has been a requirement of the law that all live births in England and Wales be registered within 42 days of the event. Until 1874 (37 & 38 Vict., c.88) there was no penalty for non-compliance, nor with the rule that deaths had to be registered within five days, and during the early years of civil registration there was much discussion as to the completeness of the registers, especially of birth. There is, of course, no easy way of establishing the extent of non-registration, although anyone searching for a certificate, especially before 1874, should be aware that not all events were registered. Both the superintendent registrar and his registrars kept their own registers of births and deaths, but when the registrars' books were full they were forwarded to the superintendent and preserved in his office, rather than in the sub-district, where, at least in the nineteenth century, the registrar often worked merely from a private house. Most superintendent registrars' offices were on workhouse premises; even today, many are still in the grounds of hospitals once owned by the guardians. Every three months a copy of all birth and death entries is forwarded to the Registrar General.

This system, which has changed remarkably little since 1837, is too well known, as is the information provided by the certificates, to warrant detailed exposition here, although its origin as part of the poor law reform of 1834 is perhaps not always fully appreciated.[10] The unsatisfactory access at present allowed to registration records is also well known. Neither the Registrar General, nor a superintendent registrar, is able to supply information from registers in his custody except in the form of a certified copy, an arrangement originally devised on the assumption that an enquirer would want a copy of an entry for some official purpose rather than historical research. A fee is charged for the certificate which reflects the full economic cost of providing the copy and deters academic use of the service. The only access allowed is to indexes compiled by both the Registrar General and superintendent registrars to books in their custody. In the former case, the indexes cover the whole of England and Wales in a single alphabetical sequence for a period of three months at a time; they may be consulted without charge at the headquarters of OPCS at St Catherine's House, 10 Kingsway WC2. Fees are charged for searches commissioned by postal enquiry. Superintendent registrars will make limited searches in local indexes in response to personal or postal enquiries, if given a reasonable amount of information as to the entry being sought. The public may also make a 'general search' in a superintendent's indexes (whether of birth, death or marriage) for a period of six consecutive hours on payment of a fee, an arrangement of limited value at offices open for less than six hours a day, as is the case with many in rural districts. The indexes to the copy certificates in the custody of the Registrar General were microfilmed some years ago and copies of these films have recently been offered to local libraries and record offices. It is not clear as yet how widely these will now be available but the facility may slightly relieve pressure on St Catherine's House, where conditions for search are invariably uncomfortable and often intolerable. Nothing has yet come of plans to make the copy certificates available on microfilm in premises administered by the Public Record Office, or to transfer superintendent registrars' certificates to local record offices.

It is generally preferable to apply to a superintendent registrar for both searches and certificates, assuming one knows where an event took place, since the cost will be less. The department's charges are revised annually but a superintendent's fees are normally half those of the Registrar General. Any superintendent's office will supply the address of any other in England and Wales and will identify the registration district within which a particular place lies.

The system of marriage registration introduced in 1837 was more complicated than that for births and deaths. The Church of England, together with the Society of Friends (the Quakers) and the Jews, were allowed, as they had been since 1754, to take responsibility for marriage registration themselves. Henceforth, marriages in these denominations were to be registered in duplicate; when the books were full one was to be sent to the superintendent registrar of the district in which the church, meeting-house or synagogue was situated. The superintendent was required to make a third copy, which was sent to the Registrar General. Only a limited concession was made to other denominations, who previously had been unable to celebrate lawful marriages at all under the Act of 1753. Weddings might now be held at nonconformist chapels or Roman Catholic churches but the event was registered either by the superintendent registrar of the district (or, where one was appointed, the registrar of marriages of the sub-district) in which the church or chapel stood. In either case, the entry was made in a book kept by the registrar, not the church or chapel, and, once again, a copy was sent to the Registrar General. The most fundamental change introduced by the 1836 Act, however, was the creation of a form of 'civil marriage', solemnised by a registrar at a register office, not a place of worship.

The main modification to marriage registration in the nineteenth century was introduced by the Marriage Act, 1898 (61 & 62 Vict., c.58), by which 'authorised persons' could be appointed to register marriages in places of worship other than those mentioned in the 1836 Act. This enabled nonconformist congregations or Roman Catholic churches to apply for a minister, priest or lay official to be appointed to keep duplicate marriage registers on the same lines as the Church of England, Society of Friends and Jews had since 1837, forwarding one book when full to the local superintendent, who would in turn send a copy to the Registrar General. Since 1898 a number of places have applied for 'AP' status, but others have not, so that marriages outside the Church of England, the Society of Friends or the Jewish faith may be registered in a book kept either by a superintendent registrar, a registrar of marriages or an authorised person. In all three cases, there will be copies of the entry both at St Catherine's House and in the custody of the local superintendent, but whereas the indexes in London cover the whole of England and Wales in a single alphabetical sequence for each quarterly period, most superintendents have indexes only to individual books, so that unless an enquirer knows at which place of worship a marriage took place (as well as roughly when) it may be impossible for a superintendent to locate the event. He may be able to check whether it was registered in a book kept by one of his predecessors but to make a search in all the registers kept in his district by individual places of worship, especially after 1898, is normally impracticable.

The disestablishment of the Church in Wales in 1920 (4 & 5 Geo. V, c.91) had no effect on marriage registration, which is conducted on the same lines as in the Church of England, apart from the introduction in recent years (as with birth and death certificates in Wales) of bilingual certificate forms on which entries may be made in either Welsh or English.

There are various ways in which the expense of obtaining certified copies and the general inconvenience of the present regime may be circumvented. The most obvious, and for many purposes sufficient, means of establishing an approximate date of birth is to locate a baptism entry in a register kept either by an Anglican incumbent or the minister of another denomination which practises infant baptism (pp. 94, 122). Similarly, an entry in a burial register will provide an approximate date of death. A notice of birth, death, engagement or marriage in local newspapers, or an obituary or funeral report, may also serve as a substitute for a certificate. Some burial board records include registers of interments in civil cemeteries, which account for an increasing proportion of nineteenth-century burials and which were not necessarily entered in the burial register of the place of worship where a preceeding funeral service took place; more recently registers have been kept of cremations in the same way. Local authorities of several kinds could (and did) adopt the Burial Acts during the nineteenth century, acquiring powers now exercised by district councils, who may retain earlier records or may have passed them to the county record office. Less well known is the provision of the Vaccination Act, 1871 (34 & 35 Vict., c.98), requiring duplicate birth certificates to be forwarded to vaccination officers; where these have survived they should now be among the records of the boards of guardians in county record offices (p. 116). Workhouse records may also include registers of births and deaths which took place in the institution, which supply less information than certificates but may be an acceptable substitute.

In the case of marriages conducted by the Church of England and, since 1920, the Church in Wales, the books of certificates kept by the clergy should, for earlier years, now be in archival custody. The fate of duplicate marriage registers kept by authorised persons under the Act of 1898 (together with registers kept by Quaker or Jewish congregations since 1837) is more varied, but many are now in local record offices. For marriages entered in books kept only by registrars, which includes those solemnised at register offices; places of worship other than those of the Established Church, the Society of Friends or the Jews before 1898; places of worship which did not have authorised persons; and (exceptionally) places that did but where a registrar was asked to be present on a particular occasion, direct access to the entry remains impossible. A necessary preliminary to such marriages, however, was the giving of 'Notice of Intention to Marry', the counterpart of banns in the Church. These were entered in books, some of which were transferred to record offices with other guardians' records; alternatively, original notices may survive. They were also read out at three successive meetings of the guardians for the union in which the marriage was to take place (again parallelling banns) and may occasionally be entered in the minutes of the meeting. The notices are not evidence that a marriage took place but serve to locate civil marriages and those held in nonconformist chapels, which, although comparatively few in number, may be the hardest to track down.

For the history of the registration service at local level (which has attracted little attention from historians) the only available material is that which has reached record offices as part of guardians' records, since the personnel of the service was identical with that of the poor law. Apart from the minutes and correspondence already mentioned (p. 116) and documents ancillary to the main series of birth, death and marriage registers retained by superintendents, little seems to have survived. Much the same is true of transfers to the PRO. Class RG 21 is concerned with the local registration service, but consists of only a dozen files, eight of them for districts whose names begin with W, suggesting that they are the rump of a class otherwise destroyed. The appointment of authorised persons under the Marriage Act, 1898, is recorded in registers which now form RG 42, in which entries are arranged chronologically rather than by locality. Both these classes are at the Kew; most of the rest of the group is at Chancery Lane, including a large number of non-parochial registers of baptism and burial (occasionally also birth) surrendered by nonconformist congregations to the Registrar General under the provisions of the Non-Parochial Registers Act, 1840 (3 & 4 Vict., c.92), or the Registration of Births and Deaths Act, 1858 (21 & 22 Vict., c.25). These are now divided between several classes (RG 4 to RG 8); for RG 4 and RG 6 a list was printed in 1859 as a non-Parliamentary official publication; the search-room copy of this, annotated with corrections and piece-numbers, has been reproduced as List & Index Society 42. Many other nonconformist registers are, of course, elsewhere, notably county record offices or the headquarters of some of the denominations.[11]

Besides registration, the major function of the General Register Office since 1841 has been the conduct of the decennial census, the importance of which is now reflected in new title of the department. A census of population was first proposed in parliament in 1753 but only in 1800 was an Act passed authorising a count to be made the following year; a census has been taken every tenth year since then, except in 1941.[9] Between 1801 and 1831 the enumeration was made locally by the overseer of the poor in each parish or township for which a separate overseer was appointed; only a very simple count of the number of households and their occupants (divided by sex, with a simple occupational breakdown) was required. In addition, incumbents were asked to extract numbers of baptisms, marriages and burials from parish registers; for 1831 the original returns from this enquiry now form HO 71 but for earlier years are evidently lost.[12] All the statistical material thus collected was published by parliament but no archive material (apart from HO 71) survives centrally from the early censuses. In recent years, however, a number of schedules compiled by the overseers, presumably as the basis of copies sent to London, have come to light in parish collections in local record offices, which illustrate more fully how the census was taken. These normally name each head of household and supply details of household size.

In 1841 the census was conducted for the first time by the Registrar General, whose local officials supervised a far more detailed enumeration of the population. In each sub-district a number of 'enumerators' were appointed, who issued a form to each household asking for the names of all occupants, their approximate ages, marital status, occupation and whether or not they had been born in the county in which they were now being enumerated. The census was taken on a specific night (instead of being spread over several days) and enumerators had to collect completed forms the following day. They were then copied into books ruled in the same way as the forms, checked and a statistical summary tabulated before the books were handed back to the registrar. He and his superintendent made further checks before transmitting all the books for the district to London. In general, each enumerator in a rural area was responsible for a single parish or township, while towns were divided into several districts, so that the information continued to be collected within the same units as before. It was also presented, however, by registration county, district and sub-district.

The success of the 1841 census led to the same procedure being adopted in 1851 and subsequent years, with improvements to the form to produce more accurate reporting of age and birth-place. There was no major change in the taking of the census until 1911, when for the first time data was analysed directly from householders' schedules using punched cards. For the censuses between 1841 and 1901 the original schedules were destroyed in 1904, apparently completely, so that there is no means of checking the reliability of the transcripts made by the enumerators or establishing which householders were unable to complete the forms themselves. In view of the immense value of the census for almost any kind of nineteenth-century local history and the extensive use to which the material has been put, it is important to remember that the enumerators' books are not, strictly speaking, 'raw data', but fair copies made by officials whose general standard of education was probably rather higher than the average in the community which they were enumerating. Incomplete or misunderstood forms may have been silently 'improved' to a degree that cannot now be estimated.

Because of the personal information they contain enumerators' books are closed for 100 years; at present, therefore, only those for 1841-81 are available, although the Registrar General will release a limited amount of information from the 1891 and 1901 schedules to direct descendants if supplied with a precise address and the appropriate fee. The schedules for 1841 and 1851 form HO 107 at the PRO (the secretary of state then being parliamentary head of the General Register Office); those for 1861, 1871 and 1881 are RG 9, RG 10 and RG 11. The books are produced, normally on microfilm, at a branch of the PRO in the Land Registry Building (Portugal Street, WC2) maintained especially for the purpose, where there are a number of topographical finding-aids, including street indexes for the larger towns. Mainly because of their value for genealogy, the enumerators' books for each county are now available on microfilm locally, either at the county library or record office or both. The accessibility of the material has encouraged family history societies and others to compile name-indexes to some of the books, chiefly those for 1851, which for some counties have now been published. The PRO does not have any name indexes.[13]

In 1851 two supplementary surveys were undertaken; neither has ever been repeated. One was a census of educational provision, for which returns were supposed to be made by the head of every day, Sunday or evening school, as well as mechanics' institutes and the like, supplying details of date of establishment, religious affiliation, income and expenditure, the number of teachers, their pay and qualifications, and the number of pupils and subjects taught. There were many gaps in the returns, which were published in summary form as part of the report on the 1851 census. The original forms, however, are lost and may have been destroyed with other records of the Committee of the Privy Council on Education (p. 146). More useful is what is generally known as the 'religious census', strictly a census of accommodation and attendance, in which returns were to be made for every place of worship. Again, summary data was presented to parliament and published officially, but the original returns, arranged by registration county, district and sub-district, survive to form HO 129 at Chancery Lane. Those for Wales have been published in full in a valuable edition, close analysis of which illustates some of the problems, noted at the time by the authorities, of producing reliable returns on a controversial subject on the basis of attendance at worship on a single Sunday.[14]

Mental Health Care

Public responsibility for the mentally ill and mentally handicapped has evolved on somewhat different lines from the other personal health services but may conveniently be mentioned here.[15] Until the early nineteenth century the only institutions for the care of the mentally ill or handicapped were private establishments, run for profit, together with a few charitable hospitals and parish or union workhouses. Pauper lunatics might also receive outdoor relief from the overseers. Under an Act of 1828 (9 Geo. IV, c.40), which consolidated earlier legislation, the justices of the peace were empowered to erect and maintain asylums from the county rates, but were only required to do so in 1845, under an Act (8 & 9 Vict., c.126) which laid a duty on the magistrates of both counties and the larger boroughs (those with their own quarter sessions, clerk of the peace and recorder) to provide suitable accommodation for pauper lunatics. In 1888 this duty was transferred to county and county borough councils, who might combine through joint committees or act alone through a mental hospital visiting committee, which replaced the visiting committees of magistrates. Local authorities' obligations were consolidated afresh by the Lunacy Act, 1890 (53 Vict., c.5), which, as amended the following year (54 & 55 Vict., c.65), remained the principal statute until the Mental Health Act of 1959 (7 & 8 Eliz. II, c.72), and in 1913 were augmented by the Mental Deficiency Act (3 & 4 Geo. V, c.28), which required them to make similar provision for the care of the mentally handicapped. Their responsibilities for mental health, including the maintenance of what were often very large long-stay hospitals, ended with the setting up of the National Health Service in 1948, to which all hospitals were transferred (p. 115).

The local sources for publicly provided mental health care will thus be found among the records of quarter sessions prior to 1888 and county and county borough councils from 1889 to 1948. In the former case, surviving material may include returns to the clerk of the peace under the Act of 1828 (or sometimes an earlier Act of 1815, 55 Geo. III c.46) and reports to the justices by committees of visitors required by the Act of 1845 to supervise the running of county asylums; these reports will begin at an earlier date if the justices built an asylum under the permissive legislation of 1815 and 1828. There may also be correspondence relating to lunacy amongst the clerk's records and accounts amongst those of the county treasurer, plus plans and specifications for asylum buildings prepared by the county surveyor. After 1889 similar classes should survive among county and county borough council records, including the minutes of either the visiting committee or a joint committee, typically made up of the county and county boroughs within the geographical county. From 1913 there should also be minutes of a mental deficiency committee appointed under the Act of that year. All these classes normally end in 1948 and for the subsequent period there may be nothing available, unless the local health authority has transferred material to the county record office.

Besides administrative records, documents should have accumulated at institutional level, which would in general have passed to the National Health Service in 1948 and may have been transferred to record offices. Since, however, many asylums are still in use, added to which there has always been considerable public sensitivity concerning mental illness, transfers of this kind are probably rather limited and material identifying individuals may either have been destroyed or closed for 100 years. For example, the 1845 Act prescribed forms for admission and discharge registers for asylums giving personal details of patients, including the nature of their illness, but few seem to have reached record offices. It is characteristic of contemporary attitudes that whereas inmates of workhouses and gaols are enumerated in full in the mid-nineteenth-century censuses (p. 123), those in asylums are identified by initials only. Alternative sources may be found among guardians' records, either in the minutes or in separate registers and returns of pauper lunatics, since the duty of making returns to the clerk of the peace, laid on the overseers in 1828, was transferred to the guardians in 1842. The other possibility, worth considering in a search for a particular patient whose approximate date of admission is known, is to use the series of registers compiled chronologically for the whole of England and Wales between 1846 and 1960 by the Lunacy Commissioners and later the Board of Control. These are now MH 94 at Kew and identify the name of each patient, date and place of admission, and the treatment administered.

The Act of 1845 established, for the whole of England and Wales, a body of Commissioners in Lunacy as the central authority for the supervision of the insane, enlarging the work in earlier years of the Metropolitan Commissioners in Lunacy. Control was divided between the Lord Chancellor, who was responsible for judicial aspects of lunacy, and (after 1871) the President of the Local Government Board, who answered in parliament for the commission. The Mental Deficiency Act of 1913 merged the commission into the Board of Control responsible for mental handicap, while the National Health Service Act of 1946 transferred the board's powers to the Minister of Health. Minutes of both commissioners and board have been transferred to the PRO as MH 50 but more useful for local studies are the correspondence and papers in MH 51, which include files on individual asylums as well as gaols with insane prisoners. The building of asylums under the 1845 Act is the subject of another class (MH 83), which is arranged by county and county borough council.

Alongside asylums maintained by local authorities there were (and on a reduced scale, still are) private houses for the insane, which from 1774 (14 Geo. III, c.49) came under increasingly close public contol. Acts of 1828 and 1845 gave magistrates considerable powers of licensing and inspection which they retained under the National Health Service Act of 1946. Only under the Mental Health Act of 1959 were counties and county boroughs made responsible for registering private mental nursing homes. Since little archive material appears to survive from private institutions the main sources for their history are to be found among quarter sessions records, including enrolled licences, the minutes of visitors' committees and returns of patients admitted and discharged. Private houses were supervised by the same central authority as county asylums but an important source pre-dating the setting up of commissioners in 1845 is a register of houses outside London for the period 1798-1812 (MH 51/735), which is the only survivor of two series of books compiled under the 1774 Act for metropolitan and provincial mad-houses.[16] The later registers in MH 94 include admissions to private establishments as well as county asylums.

Public Health

The evolution of local authorities concerned with the welfare of the community as a whole rather than the health of individuals is the second major strand, alongside poor relief, in the evolution of modern local government. Between the setting up of town improvement commissions in the eighteenth century (p. 102) and the legislation of 1871-75, a unified organisation slowly emerged, which from 1894 formed the basis of all local government below county level. Areas originally chosen for their suitability for a single purpose were taken over for others, although such was the influence of the administrative geography of 1834 that union boundaries continued to determine the size and shape of sanitary districts.

At the beginning of the nineteenth century local responsibility for public health was divided between vestries, manorial courts, boroughs and improvement commissioners established by local Act. There was no central authority specifically charged with the duty, although in 1805-6 and 1831-2 outbreaks of yellow fever and cholera led to temporary boards of health being established as committees of the Privy Council. Minutes and papers of both these bodies survive in PC 1 at the PRO, but in the case of the epidemic of 1805-6 there was no local administration. In 1831-2, however, some 800 local boards were established in England and Wales (plus 400 in Scotland), regulated by the Cholera Act, 1832 (2 & 3 William IV, c.10). The local boards worked alongside, and often in conflict with, vestries and improvement commissioners, and were subject to control by the justices, who might order expenses to be met from poor rates. The central board was dissolved at the end of 1832, although the Privy Council Office continued to deal with routine matters until early in 1834. No list appears to survive of local bodies set up in this period and any records should now be in local offices.[17]

The idea of a central authority concerned with public health was not revived until an Act of 1848 (11 & 12 Vict., c.63), which followed the model of the Poor Law Amendment Act in establishing a small body of officials, not directly answerable to parliament, to supervise local authorities constituted on uniform lines. The General Board of Health, however, proved less durable than the Poor Law Board. Remodelled in 1854 (17 & 18 Vict., c.95), it was abolished four years later, when its functions were divided between the Privy Council, which took over its medical work (21 & 22 Vict., c.97), and the Home Office, who took responsibility for local authorities established under either the 1848 Act or the amending statute of 1858 (21 & 22 Vict., c.98). The Privy Council set up a medical committee to discharge its duties under the new

Act, while at the Home Office a separate Local Government Act Office was established, to which local boards had to report annually and which was responsible for setting up new boards and amending boundaries.[18]

A single authority was re-established in 1871 (34 & 35 Vict., c.70), when the Local Government Board took over the powers and duties of the Poor Law Board, the Medical Committee of the Privy Council, the Local Government Act Office and the General Register Office, thus uniting under one department, whose head sat in parliament, all central government responsibility for poor relief, public health and local government generally. In 1919 the LGB became the main constituent of the Ministry of Health, whose title emphasised how far local government was still concerned with public health. In 1942, however, the Ministry of Health's planning powers under the Town and Country Planning Act of 1932 were transferred to the Ministry of Works, which now became the Ministry of Works and Planning. In 1943 a Minister of Town and Country Planning was appointed, to whom were transferred the planning powers of the Minister of Works. Further reorganisation followed in 1951, with the transfer of responsibility for housing, environmental health and the general oversight of local government from the Ministry of Health to what now became the Ministry of Local Government and Planning, which later the same year was renamed the Ministry of Housing and Local Government. This survived until the creation of the Department of the Environment in 1970, which re-united the Ministry of Works with the various responsibilities detached from the Ministry of Health between 1942 and 1951.[19]

Because of successive rearrangements of central responsibility for public health, material of local interest has been transferred to the PRO by both the Ministry of Health and the Ministry of Housing and Local Government. In general, classes concerned with public health as more narrowly defined by legislation up to 1875 are to be found in the MH group, while those relating to housing and planning, functions which only evolved from this date, now form part of the HLG group. Surviving records of the General Board of Health and Local Government Act Office are, in fact, rather limited, consisting, apart from the minutes of the Board (MH 5), of one series of correspondence and papers relating to dealings with local authorities (MH 13). These volumes cover the period 1848-71 and are arranged according to the local sanitary areas established under the Public Health Act, 1872 (pp. 129-30). Later papers of the same kind are incorporated into the parallel poor law union series (MH 12, cf. p. 113), which go down to about 1900.[20] Most later material was destroyed in the second world war, with surviving documents divided between MH 68 (further correspondence with poor law unions down to to their abolition in 1929), MH 48 and MH 52 (concerned with both public health and poor law services), and HLG 1, to which papers relating to environmental health services were transferred. For the period 1872-1904 there is a separate series of correspondence between the LGB and county authorities (quarter sessions before 1889, county councils thereafter) in MH 30, concerned with all aspects of local government and public health. More recent Ministry of Health classes deal mainly with personal health services but the results of a public health survey conducted under the Local Government Act, 1929, arranged by counties, with separate series for boroughs and urban districts, form MH 66.

The evolution of local sanitary authorities in the mid-nineteenth century was piecemeal, especially when compared with the poor law unions, but proved ultimately to be the key to a comprehensive system of local government in both urban and rural areas. Under the Public Health Act of 1848 a municipal corporation (scheduled as such by the Act of 1835 or subsequently established thereunder) might, by resolution of its members, seek to become a local board of health within its boundaries. Any other area might adopt the Act by a lengthy procedure involving a petition of ratepayers, an enquiry by the General Board, a report and finally an Order in Council, which led to the election of a local board.[21] In towns which had improvement commissioners under a local Act public health might remain in their hands and in general only the larger corporate boroughs and parishes which contained towns lacking any administrative structure other than a vestry adopted the Act. Local boards of health had to appoint a surveyor and inspector of nuisances, as well as a clerk and treasurer, and might appoint a medical officer. They were given powers to dealt with sewers, drains, street-cleansing, nuisances, slaughter-houses, lodging-houses and 'cellar dwellings'; they might provide public parks, a clean water supply and burial grounds. They also became the surveyor of highways in place of the parish surveyor (p. 97).

The Local Government Act of 1858 strengthened the powers of local boards (which now adopted this shorter name) and encouraged the adoption of the act by far more places, many of them comparatively small towns which felt the need for more effective control of public health. Local authorities under the Act included corporate boroughs which had not adopted the 1848 Act, improvement commission districts, and any other place 'having a known boundary', including townships assessed separately to the poor rate as well as ecclesiastical parishes. In boroughs and improvement commission districts the existing authority was to form the local board, elsewhere a separate body was to be elected. Adoption was by provisional order confirmed by Act. The fragmentation of responsibility for public health among very small local boards was arrested by an Act of 1863 (26 & 27 Vict., c.17), which prevented the setting up of new boards in places with a population of less than 3,000; finally, the Public Health Act, 1872, divided the whole country into sanitary districts, which henceforth were to be of two kinds only, even if both varied greatly in size. In corporate boroughs the municipal corporation was to be the urban sanitary authority, while local boards constituted under the Acts of 1848 and 1858 also became USAs. The rest of England and Wales was divided into rural sanitary districts, which were to consist of those parts of each poor law union not within an urban sanitary district and in which the authority was to be the board of guardians, who had possessed elementary public health powers since 1846 under the Nuisance Removal Acts (pp. 114-115). Improvement commissions acting under local statutes were absorbed by municipal corporations, which were further reformed by the Municipal Corporations Act, 1882 (45 & 46 Vict., c.50), under which they obtained additional powers over public health, drains and sewers, parks and baths, gas and water supply and other matters, which were more extensive than those enjoyed by other USAs.

The final stages in the creation of the modern system were marked by the Local Government Acts of 1888 (51 & 52 Vict., c.41) and 1894 (56 & 57 Vict., c.73). The former transferred all administrative functions of quarter sessions (p. 87) to an elected council in each 'administrative county' (with the partial exception of the county police, which became the responsibility of a standing joint committee of quarter sessions and the county council), while towns with a population of 50,000 or more became 'county boroughs',[22] whose councils were entrusted with all local government functions in their areas, including those of urban sanitary authority. The county councils were also empowered by the 1888 Act to appoint a medical officer, although outside county boroughs public health remained largely in the hands of urban and rural sanitary authorities. Under the Act of 1894 these were renamed urban and rural district councils (often later known, together with the non-county boroughs, as 'county districts'), of which the latter became elected authorities for the first time (p. 115). Their boundaries, powers and duties were not affected by the Act.

With the passing of the 1894 Act a unified, if not uniform, system was completed. Subsequent structural reform mainly affected the county and county borough councils, who absorbed the functions of school boards in 1902 (with some responsibility for elementary education reserved to the larger non-county boroughs and urban districts) and the boards of guardians in 1929 (pp. 115, 144). From 1890 county districts acquired housing and later planning powers, of which the latter were progressively transferred to county councils from 1932 (pp. 134-5). The era of the single-purpose authority, however, had passed and as the scope of local government widened it was existing authorities which assumed new powers and duties. Local authority boundaries were revised at various dates after 1894, as county boroughs and municipal boroughs grew larger, generally at the expense of small urban districts on their outskirts, while there was a parallel process of aggrandisement by which municipal boroughs tried to become county boroughs and urban districts tried to become boroughs, which not only retained greater prestige but also wider powers. The unifying characteristic of the three second-tier authorities between 1894 and 1972, however, was their origin as sanitary authorities, which gives some homogeneity to their records, despite great differences in size of authority.

Any enquiry into the local sources for the history of public health must begin by establishing the name and type of authority responsible for the service in the area and period in question. Local circumstances can often be established most easily from a contemporary directory; there are also several officially published lists of local authorities at different dates.[23] Where one authority was absorbed into another the records of the defunct body should have passed to its successor; in practice no records appear to survive for a number of local boards or some district councils which went out of existence fairly soon after 1894. The guardians sometimes retained their rural sanitary authority records in 1894 and did not pass them to rural district councils, in which case they will now be in county record offices amongst poor law material (p. 116). Otherwise, surviving documents should, on the eve of reorganisation in 1974, have been in the hands of county boroughs, municipal boroughs and urban and rural district councils. Outside the metropolitan counties, the provision of archive services was reserved in the Local Government Act, 1972, to county councils, and on a strict interpretation of the Act all documents inherited by the new district councils not required for current administrative use should have been transferred to county record offices; in some counties considerable quantities of borough and district council records had already been taken on deposit before 1974. In the event, some district councils have provided archive services since reorganisation, especially those whose predecessors included a county borough, as have both metropolitan districts and former metropolitan counties. The metropolitan districts, together with four non-metropolitan districts in South Wales (Merthyr Tydfil, Cynon Valley and Rhondda in Mid Glamorgan; Llanelli in Dyfed), are also library authorities, and the former borough and county borough libraries which they took over had long been favoured resting-places in some authorities for older administrative records. It is therefore impossible to state precisely where surviving pre-1974 county borough, municipal borough and urban and rural district council records may now be, even outside the metropolitan counties. The majority are probably in county record offices, but others are still in the hands of district councils (including many that do not provide an archive service) or even a 'town' (i.e. parish) council.

The quantity and nature of sanitary authority records varies greatly, partly through the hazards of survival, but also depending on the size of the authority and its exact powers. The most important documents, and the ones most likely to have been preserved, are the minutes of meetings of the authority from whatever date it was established down to 1894 in the case of local boards, and from 1894 for urban and rural districts, or municipal boroughs acting as UDCs. There will also be minutes of standing and *ad hoc* committees and by-laws. The earliest minutes will usually contain officers' annual reports, of which those of the medical officer will often be the most interesting, shedding light on the problems faced by the authority and urging action to remedy them. Later reports were usually printed and distributed separately. The clerk's archives may also include correspondence, either loose or in letterbooks, of which the earlier material may be the counterpart of letters preserved in MH 13 (p. 128). Financial records kept by the treasurer may include a series of general ledgers and others for specific purposes. Ratebooks survive less commonly and tend to be retained by archivists only for selected years because of their bulk, repetitive nature and limited interest.[24]

The various officers of a sanitary authority (medical officer, inspector of nuisances (later public health inspector) and surveyor as a minimum besides clerk and treasurer) were required to keep a number of statutory registers, ranging from those of hackney carriages and their drivers to cow-keepers and slaughter-houses. Those of canal boats and their occupiers can sometimes be a useful ancillary source for the history of a local waterway. Rather more interesting, where they survive, are applications under the Public Health Act, 1875 (or, where an earlier board existed, that of 1848), for the erection of new buildings, since the application had to be accompanied by a plan of the proposed works. In many cases, presumably because of their bulk, no building plans survive or, if they do, there are no registers or other finding-aids for thousands of drawings, but for a few towns there are nearly complete series from 1875 or before, which provide a superb picture of the development of the physical environment.[25]

Once a unified system of local government had been created, further functions developed from the original concern for public health, while others were transferred from older authorities. Some of these have been described already, the others occupy the remainder of this chapter.

Housing and Planning

Public interest in housing derived essentially from concern about the sanitary condition of towns; interest in planning evolved in turn from the need to control new housing developments.[26] At the same time as the Public Health Act, 1875, empowered local authorities to make by-laws governing the building of new houses and streets, two other statutes of 1868 (31 & 32 Vict., c.130) and 1875 (38 & 39 Vict., c.36) gave local authorities more extensive powers over existing property. Under the Artizans and Labourers Dwellings Act

(1868) they could require owners to make necessary repairs; if they refused, the authority might close or demolish the premises or do repairs themselves and recover the cost from the owner. The 1875 Act extended these powers to whole areas, not merely individual properties, the first recognition of the need to plan redevelopment, rather than merely demolish insanitary houses. Under the 1868 Act any borough governed by the Municipal Corporations Act, 1835 (5 & 6 Will. IV, c.76), or any local board established under the Public Health Act, 1848, or Local Government Act, 1858, might take action. The more extensive powers of 1875 were confined (outside London) to urban sanitary districts (as established under the Public Health Act, 1872) with a population of 25,000 or more, i.e. comparatively large towns.

Legislation was consolidated by the Housing of the Working Classes Act, 1890 (53 & 54 Vict., c.70), which not only confirmed local authorities' powers to close or demolish insanitary premises but also to build new houses to let to working class tenants. Although a few authorities had built such property before 1890, either under general powers or a local Act, it is from this date that 'council houses' began to appear in any number. They remained mainly a urban phenomenon, since although the 1890 Act extended powers to all urban sanitary authorities, RSAs (after 1894, RDCs) could adopt Part III, which allowed new building, only with the consent of the county countil and had to make a separate application on each occasion. Local authorities were permitted, but not required, to appoint a housing committee and so the subsequent history of housing provision by an authority may be traced either in the records of that committee of the appropriate local authority (chiefly a county borough, municipal borough or urban district council) or those of a public health committee. Separate officers responsible for housing were not appointed until much later and the work of authorities under the Act was divided between the medical officer and public health inspector (as regards the closure or repair of existing property) and the engineer or surveyor (as regards new building). Few urban authorities outside London appointed staff architects in this period; if the borough engineer did not design new works an architect in private practice would be engaged. Besides minutes and reports, one may therefore find plans, specifications and other papers relating to early council housing schemes among borough (or district) engineer's or surveyor's records.

It was the Housing, Town Planning Etc Act of 1909 (9 Edw. VII, c.44) that first gave the concept of planning statutory recognition. As well as consolidating the Housing Acts, local authorities could now prepare schemes for land in the course of development, 'with the general object of securing proper sanitary conditions, amenity, and convenience in connexion with the laying out and use of the land, and of any neighbouring lands'. The powers were permissive and were not widely used outside the county boroughs. Most municipal boroughs and urban district councils were too small and lacked the income or expertise to make effective use of the Act, while in rural areas housing, rather than planning, remained the chief problem. RDCs were now permitted to make use of Part III of the 1890 Act without specific authority from the county councils, who could, on application to the Local Government Board, exercise housing powers in rural districts, but neither did much to tackle a widely recognised shortage of cottages available to let at rents which agricultural workers could afford.

After the first world war a succession of Housing Acts, beginning with that of 1919 (9 & 10 Geo. V, c.35), which was intended to provide for the building of 500,000 'homes fit for heroes' but in practice produced less than half that number, continued to attack the problem of overcrowded and insanitary working class accommodation.[27] Local authorities built far more houses after the war than before, mostly on large estates which, together with suburban private house-building, transformed the appearance of many towns. Local source material remains similar to that for schemes before 1914: the minutes of the appropriate committee, officers' reports and architects' and engineers' plans and specifications. Although schemes under the 1919 Act were exempt from by-law regulation under the Public Health Act, 1875, plans for council houses may be found either in the department which designed them (engineer, surveyor or architect) or that which approved their construction (public health or public works). The idea of having a separate housing department responsible for managing, as well as designing and building, council schemes only evolved from the 1930s and was never adopted by the smaller districts. The overriding concern with public health was emphasised once more in the 1935 Housing Act (25 & 26 Geo. V, c.40), which required local authorities to conduct 'overcrowding surveys', involving a detailed examination of the privately owned housing stock. Where it has survived, the original data from these house-by-house surveys provides a very full picture of accommodation in working-class areas.

Throughout this period, and later, housing remained almost wholly the responsibility (outside London and the county boroughs) of district councils. The counties were not local authorities under the Housing Acts and their own stock did not normally extend beyond houses for employees, mainly police in rural areas and possibly nursing staff at remote mental hospitals.

The association of town planning with housing, which in turn was linked with public health and thus with sanitary authorities rather than county councils, proved to be a major weakness in the development of effective planning after 1909. Both the Act of that year and others down to 1932 (22 & 23 Geo. V, c.48) made county boroughs and county districts responsible for the preparation of planning schemes. Only slowly was it realised that the minor authorities lacked the vision necessary for proper planning; in most cases their areas were too small for schemes to be more than generalised 'zoning' of land on maps for purposes to which it was already being put on the ground. The Local Government Act, 1929 (19 & 20 Geo. V, c.17), allowed county councils to take part in planning and the 1932 Planning Act allowed any county district, urban or rural, to relinquish its powers to the county council. The Restriction of Ribbon Development Act, 1935 (25 & 26 Geo. V, c.47), made county and county borough councils local authorities for the control of unsightly urban sprawl, largely because they were already highway authorities and the two functions were obviously linked; as under the Highway Acts, however, county councils could delegate powers to districts. Only with the Town and Country Planning Act of 1947 (10 & 11 Geo. VI, c.51) was planning clearly identified as the concern of the counties and county boroughs who might, if they wished (few did), act through joint boards. Powers of delegation continued to be used in some counties, while others operated through area planning sub-committees.

The evolution of planning since 1909 must be traced through the records of both major and minor authorities. In the former county boroughs, who were engaged in planning long before 1947, the officer responsible tended to remain the borough (or city) engineer or architect, rather than a 'planning officer'. The same was true of county districts. The county councils, however, who only became fully involved under the 1947 Act, generally appointed planning officers from the start, since they were charged under the Act with the preparation of county development plans as well as extensive development control. County record offices may have, besides minutes and reports from the appropriate committee, material from former county boroughs as well as their own planning department relating to work under the 1947 Act. On the other hand, since the 1972 Local Government Act, in one of its less inspired provisions, divided planning between counties and districts, thus enabling both to establish departments in 1974, county borough material may be in the custody of a district planning officer in the same area.[28]

The academic enthusiasm for regional planning expressed during the period of post-war reconstruction was not shared by local authorities, nor did central government make use of its powers under the 1947 Act to set up joint planning boards for combined areas. The National Parks and Access to the Countryside Act of 1949 (12, 13 & 14 Geo. VI, c.97) did, however, lead to the establishment of special authorities in areas designated under the Act. Some of these were merely committees of a single county council (where a park lay entirely within one county) or a joint advisory committee representing several counties, each of which had its own national park committee, but in two of the most important areas, the Peak and the Lake District, the scene of much of the inter-war struggle for the national parks, joint boards were established, made up of local authority members and independent experts appointed by the minister.[29] No archive material has yet been transferred from the Peak Park JPB but the Cumbria Record Office has some files, not yet open to inspection, from the Lake District authority. Policy was initially co-ordinated by the National Parks Commission, now merged into the more broadly based Countryside Commission, whose records include those of the older body, which are now COU 1 and COU 2 at the PRO. Departmental supervision of the parks can be followed through files in HLG 92.

In each of the 'new towns' designated after the war a separate development corporation was responsible for some services in place of existing authorities.[30] The new town corporations do not have elected members and are funded entirely by the Exchequer, not from rates. The New Towns Act, 1959, set up a New Towns Commission to which local corporations are progressively transferring their functions; the commission's records have recently been deemed public records but have yet to reach the PRO. There is, however, a good deal of material on the English new towns and, until responsibility was transferred to the Welsh Office in 1965, on Cwmbran in South Wales, in HLG 84, 90, 91, 115 and 116, which have come from the New Towns Division of the Ministry of Housing and Local Government.

Central control of the housing and planning activities of local authorities was exercised from 1871 by the Local Government Board and after 1919 by the Ministry of Health. The stages by which responsibility for housing, planning and other local government services were transferred to a separate ministry have already been outlined (p. 128); most material at the PRO relating to these topics has thus come from the Ministry of Housing and Local Government and a few classes have already been mentioned. The oldest series, however, are a set of local authority files (HLG 1), which in part continue the public health and poor law files in the MH group (pp. 128-9) and are themselves continued into the post-war period in HLG 51.[31] Flanking the general files are those concerned with Treasury approval of certain types of local authority expenditure (HLG 2 and HLG 53), the accounts of local authorities (HLG 31), their audit (HLG 57), rating (HLG 56), by-laws, (HLG 25) and the promotion of parliamentary bills by authorities (HLG 54). Two of the less glamorous but nonetheless important functions of modern local government, water supply (including sewerage) and the provision of burial grounds, are the subject of other series of local authority files (HLG 50 and 113 for the first and HLG 45 for the second; before 1900 burial was a Home Office responsibility: cf. p. 163). During the years after 1945 the department operated through a regional structure in the English provinces, which was wound down in the 1950s. Files from these offices now form HLG 107; those from the Welsh regional office are merged with post-1964 Welsh Office records (p. 138).

Central government supervision of local authority housing schemes can be studied through several classes, including HLG 47, the main series of local authority files, HLG 48 (housing finance) and HLG 49 (local authority proposals). HLG 96 is a 'Record of Progress' by authorities under the pre-war Housing Acts, while formal consent to housing schemes was given through sealed orders, with accompanying plans, which now form several classes (including registers) from HLG 13 to HLG 21. Rehousing schemes by what were termed 'statutory undertakers', which included railway companies as well as local authorities, resulting from demolition of working-class housing were also approved by the department and are now HLG 24, covering the period 1890-1939. Parallel material on early planning schemes can be found in HLG 4, with associated maps in HLG 5; for planning by local authorities under the 1947 Act several classes should be searched: HLG 71 (general files, but with some local authority material included), HLG 79 (the main series of local authority files), and HLG 119, which deals with development plans drawn up by local planning authorities. The compulsory purchase of land by local authorities is the subject of files in HLG 67. Two other classes (HLG 82 and 83), although not arranged by local authority, are worth looking at for the evolution of planning policy towards the end of the second world war and immediately afterwards. Finally, the ministry inherited a quantity of plans, orders and other papers relating to various works undertaken by local authorities before the 1909 Planning Act, chiefly concerned with gas, water and sewerage, which are now HLG 6, 23, 26 and 66.

The ministry's work in supervising local government generally between 1951 and 1970 is reflected in several other classes, some originally created by the Ministry of Health, of local interest. These include a set of local authority files on the review of areas and boundaries under the 1929 Local Government Act (HLG 43), with accompanying maps (HLG 44). The papers of the royal commission whose report formed the basis of the 1929 Act are themselves in HLG 8, while those on local government in Merthyr Tydfil (HLG 12) and Tyneside (HLG 11), both of which sat in 1935-7, form two smaller classes. The second of these was appointed on the recommendation of the Commissioner for the Special Areas, a post established in 1934 (25 Geo. V, c.1), whose work can also be studied through files in HLG 30, MH 61, LAB 4 and T 187, all of which contain local detail. The continued search for a successful regional policy led to the appointment of a Royal Commission on the Distribution of the Industrial Population, which sat between 1937 and 1940, whose files (HLG 27) include some submissions from local authorities. Finally, the background to more recent changes in local government can be studied from the papers of the royal commission of 1966-9, on which the 1972 Act was in part based, in HLG 69. The records of the Local Government Boundary Commission of 1946-9, on the other hand, are in the Treasury group (T 107).

In view of the amount of material of local interest in the HLG group it is unfortunate that none of the detailed lists arranged by local authority available at the PRO have yet been issued by the List & Index Society.

Material on local government in Wales will be found partly in the classes already mentioned in this section and partly in the records of the predecessors of the Welsh Office, itself established in 1964, which have now reached the PRO at Kew (whereas many earlier Welsh public records are at Aberystwyth, cf. p. 72). The nucleus of the present department is the Welsh National Insurance Commission of 1911, which in 1919 became the Welsh Board of Health, some of whose records are now MH 96 and MH 97. Between 1951 and 1964 there was a Minister for Welsh Affairs, whose office was a branch of the Ministry of Housing and Local Government.[32] The main series of local authority files are in BD 11, which also covers water undertakers and has some general files on topics of local interest. Post-war planning under the 1947 Act is covered by BD 28, again arranged by local authority; Welsh roads are the subject of BD 30. Boundary files, similar to HLG 43 (p. 137), form BD 5 and there is a series of research papers by the Welsh branch of MHLG, arranged by local authority, in BD 29. Of less direct interest but worth checking are the records of the Council for Wales and Monmouthshire, set up in 1949 (BD 23) and private office papers for the 1951-64 period in BD 24.

Roads and Bridges

In the early nineteenth century the maintenance of roads remained, as it had since 1555, the responsibility of the parish (p. 97). The turnpiking of roads in the eighteenth and early nineteenth centuries created a new kind of *ad hoc* authority for main routes without removing the common law liability on the parish to maintain all the highways in its area (p. 103). The same was true of the setting-up of improvement commissions in some towns, which normally took over road maintenance without relieving the parish of its obligations (p. 102).

The growth of road traffic led to repeated calls for statutory reform. Eventually the General Highway Act of 1835 (5 & 6 Will. IV, c.50) repealed most earlier legislation and reaffirmed that the local highway authority was the parish in vestry assembled; in parishes with a population of 5,000 or more a board of management might be elected, but few were. The parish surveyor might now be a salaried official and had power to levy a rate. A year after the autonomy of the parish in the field of poor relief had been curtailed (p. 112), it was restated for the other major duty laid on local communities three hundred years earlier. A parish failing to maintain its highways might still be indicted at quarter sessions

(p. 88), which remained the justices' only supervisory power over local surveyors.[33]

Subsequent reform came mainly as a consequence of the growth of local sanitary authorities (pp. 127-30). Under the Public Health Act, 1848, and the Local Government Act, 1858, a local board became the surveyor of highways in its area in place of the parish; the later legislation of 1872-5 contained more extensive provisions of the same kind. Urban sanitary authorities (municipal corporations, improvement commissions and local boards) became responsible for all roads in their area; in rural sanitary districts, administered by the guardians sitting as the RSA, the existing highway authority might be either the parish under the 1835 Act or a district highway board constituted under the Highways Act, 1862 (25 & 26 Vict., c.61). This empowered quarter sessions compulsorily to combine parishes into highway districts, with a board made up of local justices and parish surveyors, the latter henceforth being responsible solely for raising the highway rate in each parish, not the actual repair of roads, a procedure analogous to the grouping of parishes into poor law unions but far less effective, since its use was permissive, not mandatory. Some counties combined parishes more energetically than others; some parishes which wished to remain outside highway districts rapidly adopted the Local Government Act, 1858, thus securing a local board which was exempt from inclusion in a district under the 1862 Act. This process of fragmentation of sanitary administration was arrested by the Local Government Amendment Act, 1863 (26 & 27 Vict., c.17), which restricted the adoption of the 1858 Act to places with a population of 3,000 or more. The grouping of parishes outside urban sanitary districts was accelerated and modified by the Highways and Locomotives Act of 1878 (41 & 42 Vict., c.77), which directed that quarter sessions, when forming or altering districts, should make them coincide as far as possible with rural sanitary districts. Where the two coincided the justices could dissolve the highway board and transfer its powers to the RSA. The final death-blow to the old system came with the Local Government Act, 1894 (56 & 57 Vict., c.73), which abolished highway districts and highway parishes, merging them with RSAs, although in some areas both survived until the end of the century.

Events took a somewhat different course in the six counties of South Wales (Brecknock, Cardigan, Carmarthen, Glamorgan, Pembroke and Radnor), where all turnpike trusts were abolished in 1844 (7 & 8 Vict., c.91) following the Rebecca Riots, their powers being transferred to a roads board in each county. The Highways (South Wales) Act, 1860 (23 & 24 Vict., c.68), extended this system to parish roads, establishing boards in each district to administer local roads. The district highway surveyor, however, was responsible to the county board, not the local body, thus establishing, outside urban areas, a unified system based on the county.[34]

Further reform in the rest of England and Wales also arose from the increasing financial difficulties and unpopularity of the turnpike trusts, whose revenue declined as the railway network expanded. After 1871 all bills to renew trusts were sent to a Turnpike Trust Committee which aimed to wind up as many as possible and return the roads to local authorities. This added to the burden borne by highway boards and parishes, since much of the mileage consisted of rural main roads; the Highways and Locomotives Act of 1878 sought to mitigate this problem by allowing quarter sessions to contribute to the maintenance of disturnpiked roads from the county fund. This principle was extended by the Local Government Act of 1888 (51 & 52 Vict., c.41), which made county councils responsible for all main roads formerly administered by turnpike trusts and gave them power to take over parish roads. The county boroughs became responsible for all roads in their area, and both authorities inherited the maintenance of county bridges from quarter sessions. Under the Local Government Act of 1894 urban and rural sanitary authorities became urban and rural district councils. The former remained highway authorities for parish roads in their area, while in rural districts main roads were administered by the county council and others by the RDC.

In some cases, county councils continued to administer highways on traditional lines after 1888, delegating the actual maintenance of main roads to minor authorities, much as quarter sessions had worked through highway boards. This was curtailed by the Local Government Act, 1929, which allowed only municipal boroughs and urban districts with a population of 20,000 or more to maintain county roads in their areas, recovering the cost from the county council. In rural areas, the county replaced the RDC as highway authority for all roads. The other major change before the war came with the Trunk Roads Act, 1936 (1 Edw. VIII & 1 Geo. VI, c.5), which made the Minister of Transport responsible for those main roads (scheduled in the Act) 'constituting the national system of routes for through traffic', except in London and the county boroughs. In practice, county councils continued to maintain trunk roads as the minister's agent. The building of the motorways since the 1950s has led to a considerable extension of central control of main roads, since this was undertaken from the start by the Ministry (now Department) of Transport through a regional structure.

The piecemeal reform of highways administration during the nineteenth century has left a complex archival legacy which can vary in character between counties, depending on the extent to which permissive Acts were adopted before 1888 and the policy of the county council thereafter. In some parishes, records described in the previous chapter (pp. 97-8, 103-4) may continue long after 1835. Elsewhere, parochial administration will give way to control by a local board or municipal corporation under the Acts of 1848 and 1858, and highway administration can be traced through urban sanitary records (p. 131). In most counties, however, there will be some records surviving from highway boards established under the Act of 1862 or in South Wales those of 1844 and 1860. Some of these may be abolished after 1878 and their powers taken over by rural sanitary authorities (p. 139), others will continue to 1894. Thereafter, the minutes of the appropriate committee of the UDC, RDC or municipal borough will be the main source, supplemented (from 1888) by those of the roads and bridges committee of the county council. In county boroughs, the highways committee alone was responsible for roads in the area.

Besides committee minutes, the archives of all responsible local authorities should also include some financial records, correspond- ence and reports by the surveyor. After the reforms of 1888-94, surveyor's department material from counties, county boroughs and the larger county districts may be more plentiful, possibly including plans and specifications for new works and files on particular schemes. All surviving records of highway boards (including county road boards in South Wales) should have passed to county councils in 1894, as should those of RDCs in 1929. County borough, municipal borough and UDC highways records may also have reached the record office or may be elsewhere (p. 131).

Until 1871 central responsibility for roads and bridges lay with the Home Office, since local supervision was entrusted to the justices, whose work as a whole was overseen by the secretary of state. There is therefore some material relating to highways in both the registered papers (HO 45) and the entry books of outgoing letters (p. 162). The department's role was essentially passive, however, and direction from the centre only began after the Local Government Board took over. Correspondence and papers concerning the LGB's dealings with highway boards between 1879 and 1900 can now be found in MH 21, with registers in MH 22; a parallel class (MH 28) relates to the winding up of turnpike trusts in the same period, but this is arranged by date rather than county or trust and there are no registers. Nothing appears to survive in this class or elsewhere from the commissioners established by the Turnpike Trusts (South Wales) Act of 1844 charged with winding up the trusts and handing their assets to the county road boards.

In 1919 the Ministry of Transport took over all central government responsibility in this field (9 & 10 Geo. V, c.50), which grew in importance between the wars because of the increase in road traffic and the introduction of civil aviation. Material transferred to the PRO relating to roads is mainly arranged by subject, making it difficult to locate items of local interest. There are no local authority files, as there are in the Health, Education or Local Goverment groups.

Education

The stages by which education has come to bulk so large in local government are sufficiently well known to need only a brief summary here.[35] Together with poor relief and public health, education forms one of the three cornerstones on which the modern structure rests, although the process of evolution has been slightly different. Whereas local authorities established to deal with poor relief and public health had other functions grafted on to them, education was itself removed at a comparatively early date from single-purpose authorities and given chiefly to county and county borough councils, whose work it soon came to dominate. At central level, education, alone of the major functions of local government, has remained the concern of a separate department. In general, both central and local authorities have preserved more material relating to education than to any other local government activity, which, together with the extensive sources for the modern history of education elsewhere, has formed the basis of innumerable local studies.

The state began to support elementary eduction in 1833, when grants were made to the two major bodies in the field, the National Society of the Church of England and the British and Foreign School Society, nominally non-denominational but in practice representing protestant nonconformity. In 1839 the administration of this grant was entrusted to a Committee of the Privy Council on Education, made up of the Lord President, Lord Privy Seal, Chancellor of the Exchequer and Home Secretary. The work of the committee expanded greatly in the middle decades of the century, as the grant regulations were made more rigorous, inspection of schools began, and some attempt was made at the training of teachers. In 1856 a Vice-President was appointed (19 & 20 Vict., c.116), who spoke for the committee in the Commons, while remaining nominally subordinate to the Lord President. At the same time the Department of Science and Art of the Board of Trade, set up in 1853 as the successor to other bodies concerned with the promotion of design and elementary science, was placed under the Vice-President's control, although it continued to function autonomously in giving grants to local science and art classes. The two bodies, one in Whitehall, the other in South Kensington, now became known together as the Education Department.

The department's work was transformed by the Elementary Education Act of 1870 (33 & 34 Vict., c.75), which divided England and Wales into 'school districts', consisting of boroughs, parishes or groups of parishes. In those districts where existing voluntary provision was deficient, an elected, rate-supported school board was to be established, charged with providing a sufficient number of elementary school places. The new system was closely supervised by the department, which henceforth was actively concerned to promote education, rather than merely subsidise voluntary effort. An Act of 1876 permitted the appointment of school attendance committees in districts where there was no school board, with powers similar to those enjoyed by the boards to make by-laws to enforce attendance; four years later a duty was imposed on all boards and committees to frame and enforce by-laws compelling attendance. The committees were appointed either by municipal corporations (in towns which did not have school boards) or elsewhere by the guardians, who in 1876 acquired the additional duty of paying school fees for children whose parents could not afford them. As a source of funding, fees rapidly declined and in 1891 were abolished, leaving elementary schools supported from charitable endowments, rates or government grant. The abolition of fees and the wider establishment of school boards led to a sharp decline in the number of voluntary schools supported by the churches, which were unable to compete with rate-supported schools.

The same period also saw efforts to modernise public schools and grammar schools. Seven of the largest foundations were reformed by the Public Schools Act, 1868 (31 & 32 Vict., c.118); most others were subject to the Endowed Schools Act, 1869 (32 & 33 Vict., c.56), the main exception being those less than 50 years old, i.e. modern public schools. An Endowed Schools Commission was set up to reform the charitable trusts under which the schools functioned, but its work was hampered by a lack of local authorities responsible for secondary education and thus the impossibility of reform on a district basis. An amending Act of 1873 (36 & 37 Vict., c.87) took schools with an annual income of less than £100 outside the scope of the commission and allowed them to deal with the Education Department, who became responsible for a large number of endowed schools in which an elementary, rather than grammar school, curriculum was taught. Another Act the following year (37 & 38 Vict., c.87) abolished the commission and transferred its work to the older established Charity Commission, whose approach was primarily legal, rather than educational, so that reform of the grammar schools was considerably slowed down.

Two statutes of 1889 complicated the administration of secondary education. The Technical Instruction Act allowed the newly established county and county borough councils to set up committees to promote a variety of teaching from elementary work to post-school training for trades and crafts. Funded by income from a Local Taxation Act of 1890 the technical instruction committees worked either through existing schools, chiefly the grammar schools, or special centres, some of which evolved into technical colleges. Secondly, the Welsh Intermediate Act allowed county and county borough councils to establish schools to fill the gap left by the shortage of endowed schools in Wales. These measures marked the beginning of the counties' involvement in education, a process which was also extended after 1888 by the Charity Commission's policy of including county council representatives on the governing bodies of reformed grammar schools.

The confusion of authorities, both centrally and locally, led to the major reforms of 1899 and 1902. The Board of Education Act, 1899 (62 & 63 Vict., c.33), created a new central authority, whose president was normally a member of the cabinet, to replace the Education Department, the Science and Art Department and the educational work of the Charity Commission. This change became fully effective only after the Education Act, 1902, abolished school boards and transferred their powers and duties to county and county borough councils, except in non-county boroughs with a population of 10,000 or more at the 1901 census and urban districts with a population of 20,000 or more, where the minor authorities were responsible for elementary education, becoming known as 'Part III authorities' from the section of the Act conferring the power. No provision was made to create new Part III authorities in areas where the population grew or remove powers from places where it fell. For all non-elementary education the local authorities were the county and county borough councils, whose technical instruction committees (where such existed) formed the nucleus of the new education committees which they were now required to establish.

At the centre, the Board of Education was initially organised into three branches, elementary, secondary and technical, reflecting the tripartite origins of its work, although the main burden fell on the elementary branch, since secondary and technical education were not at first compulsory and most children spent their entire school career under the elementary code. In 1907 a medical branch was set up following the passing of the Education (Administrative Provisions) Act, which laid a duty of medical inspection on LEAs; the branch was also responsible for the school meals service and the Board's obligations under the Mental Deficiency Act, 1913. In 1910 a universities branch was established, although from 1919 the administration of government grant to university institutions was returned to the Treasury, working through the University Grants Committee, which remains a separate department. Also in 1907, for political rather than administrative or educational reasons, a separate Welsh Department was set up, whose secretary reported directly to the president, not the permanent secretary; Wales also acquired its own inspectorate. Elementary and secondary, although not immediately technical, education were transferred to the new department, which in 1970 was absorbed into the Welsh Office.

After 1902 there were few changes in organisation until the Education Act, 1944, replaced the board with a Ministry of Education, whose head was now charged with the promotion of education, a positive role never laid on the president. At local level, in an attempt to deal with the problem of Part III authorities, only non-county boroughs and urban districts with a population of 60,000 or more in 1939, or at least 7,000 children in elementary schools, had the right to claim 'excepted district' status and remain responsible for what now became known as primary education, generally to the age of 11. Most of the rest of England and Wales outside the county boroughs (which remained unitary authorities for all non-university education) was divided into 'divisional executives' within each county, which were supposed to be areas with a population of around 60,000, a natural community of interest and a convenient administrative centre; in practice, divisions varied in population between 20,000 and 200,000, and in some counties the system was never adopted. The excepted districts were also divisional executives and their officers, although typically known as 'borough education officers' and treated as chief officers of the authority on whose premises they worked, were in fact officers of the county education committees.

The 1944 Act laid down an administrative framework within which the quantity and quality of publicly provided education expanded enormously. The only major changes since have been the abolition of the excepted districts in 1974, leaving the counties and metropolitan districts as local authorities for all non-university education, and the establishment in 1964 of the Department of Education and Science as the central authority, combining the Ministry of Education with the government's responsibilities for civil science.[36]

The intricacies of educational development since the 1830s have left a correspondingly complex archival legacy, created mainly at three levels: the central department, the local authority and the institution.[37] Centrally preserved records available for study are in the PRO at Kew; those of local authorities are chiefly in hands of county record offices, subject to the qualifications mentioned already (p. 131). Material from schools and colleges may either be in archival custody or in the hands of headteachers and principals; the latter tends to be the case with the older secondary schools and in further and higher education establishments maintained by local authorities. All university institutions in England and Wales have retained their own records, either in official custody or, where they exist, in archive departments of their libraries. The one minor exception to this is the collection of dissertations submitted for higher degrees in the University of Wales deposited in the National Library, which are formally part of the university's archives.

The quantity of material in the PRO is sufficient for the printed class-list to fill eight List & Index Society volumes (21, 48, 55, 71, 78, 94, 102 and 111), which nonetheless omit several classes of files on individual schools, the lists for which are available only at the PRO, as are those for classes numbered ED 144 onwards. The overall arrangement of the earlier classes reflects the organisation of the

Board of Education after 1902, with the material broadly divided into elementary, secondary and technical education; medical and other special services; and universities and training colleges. This pattern changes with the restructuring of education after 1944, as more recent transfers to the PRO demonstrate. Survivals from the pre-1870 period are limited: most of the records of the Privy Council Committee on Education have been destroyed, apart from a series of printed minutes (ED 17), which are also available as parliamentary papers, and applications for building grants between 1833 and 1870. (ED 103). The latter series is arranged chronologically and an index, which forms part of the class, has to be sent for as a finding-aid for papers on individual schools. Similar records survive from the Science and Art Department's period as a separate body: there are minutes in ED 28 and grant papers in ED 29. Building grant plans have been transferred to local repositories.

To locate material relating to a school after 1870 will involve searching several classes. A file was opened for each district set up under the Elementary Education Act (ED 2), containing returns by the board, inspectors' reports, correspondence and other papers, including the formal notices issued by the department as to school accommodation in the district, of which a separate series forms ED 1. The parish files, however, do not extend to London, which was served by a single board that dealt separately with the central authority; or to boroughs, where equivalent material has been incorporated into later LEA files (ED 16); or to districts with only one school (as opposed to none or more than one), where the documents have been put on the school files (ED 21). The latter class should in any case be checked for additional papers on a particular school, including proposed schools. Before a school could be added to the annual list for grant a 'preliminary statement' had to be received by the department, providing basic information as to date of erection, buildings, staff and finances. These make up ED 7, which go down to 1924; later statements are on school files. The earlier papers are arranged by LEAs under the 1902 Act, i.e. counties, county boroughs and Part III authorities. A smaller class, arranged by county, deals with compulsory purchases of land by boards and LEAs (ED 5); this ends in 1922, with later documents placed on school files. The main LEA files (ED 16), although created after 1902, incorporate earlier papers relating to the department's dealings with boards in county boroughs and what later became Part III authorities, while from 1903 to 1946 there are files for county councils also. ED 16 should be used in conjunction with ED 88, elementary branch 'grant scrutiny' files for the period 1920-42; and ED 99, the 'premises survey' files from the same period, in which the department was placing pressure on LEAs to improve school buildings. This included the compilation of black lists of defective schools from which grant might in extreme cases be withdrawn, or the LEA threatened with this as an inducement to rebuild.

Files opened for school attendance committees established under the 1876 Act in districts where there was no school board now form ED 6, arranged by county and poor law union, since most committees were appointed by the guardians. Only specimen files for a few unions have been retained. There is also a class of LEA attendance files, beginning in 1871 and continuing to 1945, which include copies of by-laws and other papers, some dealing with problems of delinquency, non-attendance and evacuation during the second world war.

In the years before 1902, some school boards were in practice providing post-elementary education, a development recognised by a board minute of 1901 but declared *ultra vires* by the courts later the same year. The situation was regularised by the 1902 Act and between then and 1944 many Part III authorities provided post-elementary education, either in elementary schools or, after the Education Act, 1918, in 'central' schools. A small class, arranged by county and school, survives to illustrate this development (ED 20), although more will be found about some of the schools in other classes, including ED 7 and ED 21. The reorganisation of elementary education following the recommendations of the Hadow Report (1926), which encouraged the establishment of separate 'senior' schools, can also be followed from ED 97.

Other elementary school material include files on 'institution schools' between 1873 and 1921, chiefly those held in orphanages (ED 30); and a series on practical instruction centres in elementary schools (1903-35), which is now ED 70. Initially, practical instruction mainly meant teaching cookery and other domestic subjects to girls, although the scope later widened; the classes were held under the elementary code and were distinct from technical education (p. 150). The parallel LEA files are in ED 96. Several classes deal with what is now called 'special education', the earliest being ED 32, files on schools established under the Elementary Education (Blind and Deaf Children) Act, 1893, which go down to 1921. Files relating to the endowment of schools for the physically and mentally handicapped are in ED 38, while the LEA files for special education before 1945 are in ED 133. LEA files on adult training centres for handicapped persons for the same period are now in ED 62. Schools in poor law institutions were the responsibility at various dates of the Poor Law Board, Local Government Board and Board of Education; in the latter group there are a couple of dozen files for individual schools in ED 132 for the period 1904-33, after the schools were handed over from the LGB and before the Local Government Act, 1929, transferred their local management from the guardians to counties. These are complemented by ED 95, which contains a file for each county and county borough dealing with the assimilation of poor law schools into the general pattern of elementary education in the decade after 1929.

A few other classes may be useful for particular topics. Surviving files on school board premises (1884-1911) form ED 57; many of these offices were also used as pupil-teacher centres. Files on children attending elementary schools outside their own area are in ED 89 (1904-45); another series (ED 106) deals with the teaching of religious education in elementary schools in the same period. Some files in ED 108 on teachers' salaries in the inter-war period deal with local issues, although most are general; problems of staffing may also be studied from ED 60 and ED 67, which deal with the same period but are arranged by LEA. Finally, miscellaneous papers on elementary education which defy classification have been put into ED 111, which is arranged by county, with some indication of the contents of each piece in the printed list.

Throughout the period in which publicly provided elementary education was becoming universal, voluntary schools survived in diminishing numbers. Information about those which received grant will be found in several of the classes already described; in addition there are a handful of files in ED 48 from a series opened for associations set up to administer an additional grant under the Voluntary Schools Act, 1897. These were mostly Anglican and were organised by diocese, but only files for those whose names begin with S or a later letter survive. The class continues to 1916; although the grant arrangements were changed in 1902 the associations continued and their history can also also be traced from their own records (p. 107). For elementary schools which lay outside the system of state inspection and grant material in the PRO is obviously limited, but for those recognised as 'efficient' under varying definitions of the term there may be files for the period 1870-1921 in ED 33. Under the Education Acts of 1918 and 1921 attempts were made to obtain a census of private schools, the returns from which now form ED 15. Reports by HMI on independent schools from 1944 onwards are in ED 172, although much of this class is at present closed.

Nursery schools developed rather later than other work under the elementary code but there are a few individual school files for the inter-war period in ED 69 and corresponding LEA files in ED 66. Another class (ED 65) contains files, arranged by LEA (although not all are represented) on 'evening play centres', organised mainly in large towns to occupy children after school hours, again between the wars.

Material relating to secondary education is arranged on lines similar to that from the elementary branch of the department. For individual schools the main class is ED 35, which contains files on all institutions providing secondary education, including public schools as well as grammar schools later taken over by LEAs, orphanages and cathedral schools. Although there are some documents in the class going back to the early nineteenth century, most date from after 1902. Two allied classes should also be checked:

ED 27 consists of former Charity Commission files on educational foundations, chiefly endowed grammar and public schools, passed to the board after the 1902 Act transferred such charities from the commission, while ED 43 contains files on the management of endowed school estates, mostly in the early part of this century.

Until 1902 there were no local authorities for secondary education, apart from the technical instruction committees (p. 143). After that date secondary schools were the concern of county and county borough councils, which simplifies the arrangement of the records. ED 53 is made up of files on each LEA after 1902 regarding all post-elementary education. This included teacher training, which in this period evolved on to modern lines from its origins as a system of pupil-teacher apprenticeship. The class covers the years in which secondary education became more widely available, as counties supported free places at grammar schools and built new county schools; it ends with the 1944 Education Act, which made secondary education a universal experience for the first time. Flanking the main files are those in ED 59, concerned with the board's grant to authorities in the inter-war period, and ED 55, which deals with the effect of the financial crisis of 1931 on the provision of 'scholarship' places at secondary schools. ED 63 and ED 107 have other files on payments to pupils for post-elementary education under the 1902 Act; ED 110 has further material on fees and free places at secondary schools. Under both the 1918 and 1921 Education Acts, LEAs had to draw up 'schemes' for the reorganisation of both elementary and secondary education: files for counties and county boroughs on this subject now form ED 120, but very little survives from Part III authorities. Earlier plans submitted under the 1902 Act, again including the minor authorities, are now in ED 139.

After 1944, the department's dealings with both primary (previously elementary) and secondary schools and LEAs were re-structured and the records change accordingly. The main series of local authority files for this period are in ED 147, flanked by others on development plans prepared by LEAs under the Butler Act in ED 152 (for England only, cf. p. 152 for Wales); on building schemes (ED 154); on the divisional executive organisation (ED 151; cf. p. 145); and on county scholarships for higher education (ED 153). The school files are split between ED 161 for primary schools (continuing ED 21) and ED 162, which includes secondary schools in counties near the beginning of the alphabet (Bedfordshire to the Isle of Ely), plus six county boroughs, as a continuation of ED 35. What has happened to the rest is not clear.

A series of more specialised interest is ED 56, files on physical training and recreation for each major authority, with which may also be mentioned ED 101, which is concerned with LEA provision for 'social and physical training', which included visits to theatres and concerts, school camps and journeys, as well as playing fields, and has files for Part III authorities as well as counties. The Education group also contain the surviving records of the National Fitness Council (1937-47), which form ED 113 and include some local files. The council was set up to encourage wider physical training and the provision of better facilities; it was partly funded by a parliamentary grant. Files of somewhat similar interest in ED 126 are concerned with 'youth welfare' during the last war. For 'adult welfare' after the war there are some LEA files in ED 169.

Finally, the group has two series of LEA files on important special services provided by authorities since the 1906 Act, school meals (ED 133) and school health services (ED 137), which, like some of the other more esoteric material, are worth checking in any thorough local study, especially for the 1902-44 period. Two ancillary services can also be investigated from LEA files in the group. Under the Public Libraries Act, 1919, the Board of Education was responsible for supervising the provision of libraries by LEAs, including Part III authorities; county library committees were formally sub-committees of the education committee and ED 64 is concerned with the board's dealings with them before the war. Secondly, the counties and county boroughs established under the 1918 Education Act what were originally 'juvenile unemployment centres', later junior instruction centres, their work in this field (the predecessor of the modern LEA careers service) coming initially under the Board of Education. Files on this subject form ED 45 (1918-40); later material, after central responsibility had been transferred to the Ministry of Labour, is in LAB 18 and LAB 19.

A variety of activities are today embraced under the term 'further education'. The main series of LEA files in this field is ED 51, which cover the period 1921-51 and include proposals by authorities, reports by HMI and details of individual schools and colleges. More general files in ED 46 have some local material, for example on regional art centres in the 1930s. The main LEA files for further education work under the 1944 Act is ED 155, with a subsidiary series on building projects in ED 160. For junior technical schools, some of which developed from earlier practical instruction centres (p. 147), there are files in ED 98; for technical schools, some of which became colleges of technology after 1944, the equivalent series is ED 82; and for the larger institutions, known as technical colleges before the war, some of which are now colleges of technology while others have formed the nucleus of polytechnics, there are files in ED 90; post-1944 files covering the same area are in ED 166 and ED 168. The parallel series for art schools, most of which are now absorbed into larger institutions, is ED 83, which takes over from ED 28 and ED 29 (p. 146) for the period before 1900, and is in turn succeeded by ED 167 after the 1944 Act. A series of endowment files, similar to those for secondary schools, form ED 37, transferred from the Charity Commission after 1902; reports by HMI on further education establishments are in ED 114. A rather different approach to teaching a similar age-group was reflected in the provision of 'day continuation schools', providing part-time education for children aged between 14 and 16 under the 1918 and 1921 Acts, for which there are LEA files in ED 75. For the period since 1944 only, the ministry's involvement in agricultural education can be followed through files in ED 174.

The other main thrust of FE work since the late nineteenth century has been the 'evening institute', a term brought into use by the board in 1926 for a type of activity that was already well established and could be supported by the major LEAs under the 1902 Act. ED 41 contains material on the institutes; other papers are on the FE authority files (ED 51). During the 1930s, as today, the LEAs also provided free classes in practical subjects for unemployed adults, a topic covered by files in ED 58. For the adult education work of universities and the Workers' Educational Association there are files for the 1920s and 1930s in ED 73, earlier material having been destroyed, while files on vacation courses for adults are in ED 76. Residential adult colleges, such as Ruskin College, Oxford, Coleg Harlech and a few others, are the subject of ED 68, covering the years 1911-35.

Higher education today is customarily divided into three branches: universities, polytechnics and institutes of higher education. The third group consists mainly of former colleges of education, previously known by the more precise name of teacher training colleges; other colleges have been absorbed into polytechnics, which are themselves often an amalgam of several technical colleges and art schools. Material on the early history of what are now polytechnics will generally be found in classes on technical education (p. 150); for teacher training colleges, which originated either as LEA establishments after 1902 (some having previously been pupil-teacher centres) or were set up earlier as religious foundations, the main files are in ED 78, which covers the period 1924-35. Older material for some colleges is in ED 40, a series of endowment files going back to the mid-nineteenth century. A handful of building grant files for LEA colleges make up ED 87, the residue of what was once a much larger class. Reports by HMI on training colleges between 1907 and 1939 are in ED 115. There are no LEA files at this level, the board dealing direct with the institution, although there are LEA files on short courses for in-service teachers between the wars in ED 61. For what were then called 'university training departments', the precursors of the modern departments, schools or faculties of education, a few files from the 1930s form ED 81.

Material relating to universities is limited, reflecting the autonomy they have retained, despite increasing dependence on state grants. Files for the older provincial universities which have grown out of civic university colleges, together with the University of Wales and its constituents, will be found in ED 119, which runs from the 1880s to 1935. Later material forms part of the records of the University Grants Committee. For the University of Durham, including Armstrong College, Newcastle (now the University of Newcastle upon Tyne), papers from a royal commission of 1926-37 are in ED 112. Endowment files for the universities from the mid-nineteenth century (which, unlike ED 119, include Oxford and Cambridge) are in ED 39. For the technological universities which have evolved from older institutions, there may be material in some of the further education classes (p. 150). Otherwise, university material in the Education group is mainly concerned with either state scholarships for undergraduates (ED 71, which contains only 16 pieces) or the school certificate examinations conducted by universities before 1944 (ED 72, which has a file for each board). There are also files (ED 105) for joint examining boards set up by universities and training colleges between the wars.

From this outline, it should be clear that for almost any aspect of the local history of education since 1870, or at least 1902, and sometimes from an earlier date, the records of the central department will provide material of interest. Apart from its sheer bulk, one of the attractions of the Education group is the arrangement of many classes by LEA or county; in addition there are some others worth searching for local material, since they are listed in reasonable detail. The class of private office papers (ED 24) contains files on local issues, while many of the 'special reports' by HMI in ED 77 are concerned with a particular authority. Also worth checking are the 'bill files' (ED 31), which include a number on local authority boundary extensions or improvement schemes, with comments by officials on the educational implications. For those interested in the work of the Welsh Department from 1907 (p. 144), the 'General Wales' files (ED 91, ED 92, ED 93) may be disappointing, since many of the department's records were lost in floods in Cardiff in 1960. Surviving papers include reports on education in different parts of the principality, on the university and its colleges, and on the teaching of Welsh. The losses of 1960 also affected Welsh files in many of the other classes. In 1970 the Welsh Department was transferred to the Welsh Office (p. 138) and one class in the latter group (BD 7) relates to development plans drawn up by LEAs in the principality under the 1944 Education Act, analogous to ED 152 for England (p. 149).

Turning to records preserved at local level, the oldest series are normally those of school boards elected under the Act of 1870, generally including minutes from their establishment until 1902, although for many small boards nothing survives. Where there are minutes, it should be possible to trace the process by which the board implemented the succession of Acts after 1870, either by building a new school (or schools) or, occasionally, by leasing existing school premises from managers unable to compete with the board. Where new schools were erected the minutes should supply the name of the architect; some local firms seem to have specialised in board schools, presumably having mastered the grant regulations of the Education Department and the wishes of a board anxious to minimise the burden on rates. Most new schools were built with money borrowed from the Public Works Loan Board and the second class of material most likely to survive is financial, including ledgers, cash-books and mortgage registers. There may also be letterbooks or, less commonly, original correspondence. After 1880, if not before, boards made by-laws compelling attendance: these may either be written into the minutes or a separate print tabbed into the book. In large towns, boards worked through committees, whose minutes should also survive; the most important of these was normally the attendance committee set up under the 1876 Act. Where there was no school board, the committee was appointed by the guardians, municipal corporation or urban sanitary authority (where a USD had a population of 5,000 or more). In these cases, attendance committee minutes may be preserved with other records of that authority.

School board records, like those of any local authority, may also include miscellaneous papers impossible to describe briefly. In particular, the clerk may have kept the preliminary notices issued by the Education Department prior to the election of the board and possibly also a census of school accommodation under the 1876 Act. Alternatively, both may be available at the PRO (p. 146).

Board schools were controlled directly by the elected authorities, with no separate bodies of managers, nor did heads deal themselves with the Education Department. Conversely, voluntary schools were usually run by managers appointed under a trust deed. Most of those which survived into the late nineteenth century were Anglican and therefore managers' minutes may now be amongst parish records. Alternatively, if the school was absorbed into the maintained system after 1902 the records may have followed suit and be with later minutes kept by managers appointed by the education committee. Church school managers corresponded directly with the Education Department and also with the National Society, whose records include files on most schools to which it has made grants.[37]

In tracing the history of an elementary school after 1902 it is essential to establish whether it lay within the area of a county borough or Part III authority or whether it came under the county education committee (p. 144). The Act did not require Part III authorities to appoint education committees, although most did; their records may continue after 1944 if the authority remained an excepted district (p. 145). Indeed, they may still be in the custody of a district council (p. 131). County and county borough councils were required to set up education committees in 1902; in most cases they had previously appointed technical instruction committees (p. 143). The county authorities, who were now responsible for all secondary and most elementary education, worked through numerous sub-committees, whose minutes are likely to be of more interest than those of the main committee, which tended merely to receive reports.

Such was its importance that the education committee functioned virtually as an autonomous authority, going to the main council only to raise money. A large staff soon grew up under the early directors of education, whose successors may have transferred departmental records to the county archivist. The files most likely to be available are series arranged by school, mirroring the pattern at central level (pp. 148-9). There may also be some on broader policy issues or the requirements of a particular Act. Principal officers also generated departmental material and may have reported to their own sub-committees, thus creating separate archives. In rural authorities, the county architect may originally have been located in the education department, since most of his work would have been for that committee, although this was not true of county boroughs. In Part III authorities, the arrangement of records (and their survival) may vary considerably, but most borough education departments were probably organised as miniature versions of those in county boroughs, except that they dealt only with elementary work.

An important structural change in 1902 was the requirement that elementary schools were henceforth to have managers, appointed solely by the LEA in the case of provided schools and jointly for non-provided (i.e. church) schools. Minutes of church school managers may be a continuation of others going back well before 1902 and may, where a school has shut or was handed over wholly to the LEA after 1944, have remained among parish records. Before 1944 provided elementary schools were usually grouped under a single body of managers; arrangements of this kind can be traced from local directories. After this date each school will generally have its own managers. The 1944 Act introduced (and that of 1972 abolished) an intermediate layer of LEA administration, the divisional executive covering part of a county, whose divisional officer reported to an education sub-committee. Divisional records (in counties which adopted this system) should have been returned to LEA headquarters in 1974 (as should those of excepted districts) and older material may have been passed to the county archivist.

The main records kept at school level under the elementary code are well known. Headteachers were required by the Education Department to keep a log-book from 1862, although by no means all board schools have them from the start, nor voluntary schools in receipt of grant. They should record the daily life of the school in reasonable detail, including special events, reasons for abnormally low attendance, and the arrival and departure of staff. The inspectors' reports should also be entered. Some heads have obviously been more conscientious than others in making entries and some have been more careful to ensure that the books are preserved. Secondly, schools may have preserved admission registers, recording the date each child entered school, his date of birth, date of passing each 'standard' under the code, and date of leaving. Well kept registers also give the first destination of each child, typically, in a country parish before 1914, a record of girls going into service and boys becoming farm labourers. As with log-books, most heads like to keep old admission registers but both should, with luck, reach record offices after a school is closed. In some counties, material has been called in from schools still open to avoid further losses.

For secondary schools and colleges maintained by LEAs there may be proportionately more in the hands of headteachers and less with the authority. It is perhaps not always fully appreciated today that many secondary schools were not provided, but merely assisted, by LEAs before 1944; the older grammar schools contrived to retain considerable autonomy after that date. Former grammar schools occasionally have trust or title deeds, wills and other endowment papers from as early as the seventeenth century or they have been kept by a local solicitor as clerk to the foundation and may now be in the record office. Schools of this kind may also have comparatively early admission registers, although their printed registers are often retrospective compilations based on university records, rather than editions of surviving documents.[39] There may also be a run of school magazines from the late nineteenth century, or at least a collection of ephemera and old photographs, and perhaps minute books of school clubs. Schools established by LEAs after 1902 (or in Wales under the Act of 1889) may have rather less of this kind. For all secondary schools, however, there should be governors' minutes, either from the school's establishment if it is a modern foundation or, for older endowed schools remodelled in the late nineteenth century, from whenever a new instrument of government was drawn up. Maintained secondary schools also keep log-books (possibly with separate punishment books) and may have a card index of pupils.

Records of the smaller independent schools, again normally retained by the schools themselves, are similar to those of former grammar schools but may be more extensive; those of the major public schools may be far richer but less local in character. For independent (including former direct grant) schools which are part of a wider grouping (e.g. the Woodard Corporation or the Girls' Public Day School Trust) the records of the parent body may supplement what is available at an individual school. Equally, for secondary schools which were (and may still be) church foundations, diocesan records may be useful in both the Church of England and the Roman Catholic church. Records of private secondary schools which no longer exist are generally not well preserved: there may be a little at the PRO either in the Education group (p. 148) or from the Board of Trade in the case of those run by limited companies (p. 172). Occasionally, material may have been deposited by an owner's descendant or solicitor. Proprietors of existing schools appear to share the general reluctance of businessmen to allow investigators access to records.

Finally, in public sector further and higher education, all colleges of any age should have preserved some records and will normally retain them until closure. The reorganisation of teaching training has led to some deposits in local record offices; other material may have been destroyed or retained by a successor polytechnic or institute. Although such colleges now operate at least in part on a national basis, both these and the older provincial universities were originally mainly concerned to extend local educational opportunity. The major classes of record that should now be available to researchers, at least up to 1900, include minutes of the governing body and its committees, admission registers, lists of graduates (in the case of university institutions), correspondence and accounts. Less formal material should normally include printed prospectuses and calendars, photographs and records of student organisations. In larger colleges and in universities files may also have been preserved in individual academic and administrative departments, depending on how much interest has been shown in the past and how many moves of site there have been. Several provincial universities have recently celebrated their centenary, which has led both to the publication of books to mark the event and, one hopes, a stronger sense of record preservation, if not record management. It has not led to deposits in local authority record offices.

Police, Prisons and Fire Service

At the beginning of the nineteenth century the only police outside London available to deal with the problems of maintaining order in an industrialising society were the petty constables appointed for each township by the manor court leet or vestry (p. 92), or in some towns by the corporation or improvement commissioners (p. 102). Attempts were made to improve policing in rural communities by Acts of 1833 (3 & 4 Will. IV, c.90), 1842 (5 & 6 Vict., c.109) and 1850 (13 & 14 Vict., c.20), which provided for the payment of parish constables and the appointment of inspectors and superintendents to take charge in each petty sessional division. The County Police Act of 1839 (2 & 3 Vict., c.93) first allowed the justices to establish forces on modern lines but was only adopted wholeheartedly in a few counties; elsewhere it was applied only to a single division or simply ignored, the justices continuing to rely on parish constables.[40]

The Municipal Corporations Act, 1835 (5 & 6 Will. IV, c.76) required boroughs subject to the Act to appoint a sufficient number of constables and enjoined improvement commissions to hand over police powers to them. The Town Police Clauses Act, 1847 (10 & 11

Vict., c.89) codified local statutes and made police powers available not merely to improvement commissions but also boards of guardians and vestries. Finally, the Local Government Act, 1858 (21 & 22 Vict., c.98) enabled any local board (p. 129) to become a police authority, a measure which considerably increased the number of separate forces in small towns.

It was against this background that the County and Borough Police Act, 1856 (19 & 20 Vict., c.69) sought to establish some degree of uniformity and impose direction from the centre. All counties were required to set up a force whose authority would extend to all parishes outside boroughs with their own police. All county and most borough forces were subject to Home Office inspection and were to be partly funded by Exchequer grants, the size of grant depending on the results of inspection, an arrangement that continues to the present day. Borough forces in places with a population of under 5,000 were excluded from the Act in the hope that they would merge with county forces; in the event, many forces in towns larger than this remained too small to be efficient and were progressively brought into the county system later in the nineteenth century.

In 1888, when local government in the counties was finally modernised, control of the police proved one of the most difficult matters to resolve and a compromise was agreed, by which county forces were made responsible to a standing joint committee of quarter sessions and the county council. The county boroughs were allowed to retain or establish their own forces, answerable to watch committees; other boroughs gradually ceased to be police authorities. The administrative structure then changed comparatively little until the 1960s, when the number of forces was reduced by amalgamation. The standing joint committees disappeared with the abolition of quarter sessions under the Courts Act, 1971, leaving committees of county councils (or joint committees, where amalgamations have crossed county boundaries) responsible for local forces. In practice, because of the close supervision exercised by the Home Office and the operational freedom demanded by modern chief constables, the powers of police committees are limited.

The history of county forces between 1856 (or in a few cases 1839) and 1888 can be traced from quarter sessions records (p. 87), which will generally include the minutes of a police committee and possibly some accounting records and correspondence. Some, but by no means all, forces have preserved establishment records from this period, which make it possible to say a good deal about the men recruited into the service; scraps of similar information may also be gleaned from census enumerators' books (p. 123). After 1888, the minutes of the standing joint committee and chief constables' reports are the main sources for the administrative history of the force, supplemented by any other papers which have survived and which chief constables have passed into archival custody. Minute books and reports should be in county record offices, although subsidiary material may be in the museums maintained by many forces. Some of these were established in the wake of celebrations marking the centenary of most forces in 1956-7, an occasion which also prompted the publication of commemorative histories.

The development of borough and county borough forces can be followed through the minutes of the watch committee and the annual reports of the chief constables. These should be with the other minutes of the authority, which from the late nineteenth century will be printed and available in libraries. Early manuscript volumes may be more elusive, especially in conurbations where administrative boundaries have changed a good deal (p. 131). Establishment records and other material on the day-to-day work of the police probably survives less commonly for the smaller forces, not least because of losses during the mergers of the 1960s.

Home Office supervision of provincial police forces can be studied in several classes, including HO 45, the main series of registered papers (p. 163), entry books of out-letters (HO 65) and annual returns (HO 63, 1858-69).

Alongside their responsibility for the police, the justices also maintained county gaols, for which some material should survive among quarter sessions for the nineteenth century and possibly before (pp. 88-9). Home Office inspection of county gaols and direct responsibility for convict prisons (mostly in London) and hulks began in the early nineteenth century and is reflected in several series of correspondence, entry books and registers, of which the most useful are probably the registers of prisoners in county gaols, with details of individual inmates (1847-66) in HO 23, and statistical returns for local prisons for the 1860s in HO 24. A later series of registers (HO 140) continues to 1909. The Prisons Act, 1877 (40 & 41 Vict., c.21) removed gaols from local control and placed all penal establishments in the hands of a Prison Commission, a subdepartment of the Home Office whose records form a separate group at Kew (PCOM). The include some prisoners' registers, licences and other material relating to individuals, but mainly for the former convict prisons rather than local gaols. In some counties the justices established reformatory schools for young offenders in the mid-nineteenth century, which were not taken over by central government and whose records should also be in quarter sessions. Supervision of such institutions was transferred from the Home Office to the Department of Health and Social Security in 1972, which has transferred a set of old Home Office files to become MH 102.

Like the police, the fire service has developed as a local authority function subject to Home Office supervision, indeed, in many towns both were originally administered by the same committee. The history of the service can thus be traced through local authority minutes and reports, supplemented by material in HO 45, the general series of registered papers (p. 163). The files in HO 187, which deal with the National Fire Service set up during the second word war, are general rather than local in character.[41]

Municipal Trading

The establishment of water and gas undertakings in many towns during the first half of the nineteenth century, either by improvement commissions or companies incorporated by local Act has already been mentioned (pp. 102-3). These early ventures were later joined by others registered under the joint-stock legislation (p. 172). Towards the end of the century many concerns passed into the hands of revitalised municipal corporations, which either initiated or took over other enterprises, such as the running of open and covered markets, the generation and supply of electricity and the building and operation of horse or electric tramways. This activity came to be known as municipal trading and its growth may be followed through minutes of the various committees of a borough or county borough council responsible for each operation, plus the annual reports of chief officers or managers. In some cases, where a corporation took over a private company, there may be inherited records. The later history of these enterprises varies. Many towns still manage markets and provide bus services: here the records should continue to the present day. Gas and electricity, however, have passed into public ownership on a national basis, as has virtually the whole of the water industry. Pre-nationalization archive material may have remained in municipal hands and thus now be in local record offices; alternatively, documents may have been deposited by successor boards, as is the case with the gas industry. Most electricity records, however, are held centrally.[42]

None of the utilities' modern records come within the scope of the Public Records Act, although all were the subject of Board of Trade regulation in the nineteenth century, exercised (somewhat incongruously) by the Railway Department, which also controlled the running of municipal tramways (p. 175). After the Railway Department became the nucleus of the Ministry of Transport in 1919, the other industries formerly under its supervision stayed with the Board of Trade until the Ministry of Power, the predecessor of the Department of Energy, was established (p. 174).

Licensing and the Administration of Justice

There were comparatively few changes in the local administration of justice during the nineteenth century and many of the records described in the previous chapter continued to accrue. Thus quarter sessions, although stripped of its administrative work in 1888 (p. 130), sat as a criminal court until 1971, when the assize courts

(p. 70) were also abolished. The justices' summary jurisdiction was likewise still exercised in each borough or county division (p. 90), a system from which the present network of magistrates' courts has evolved.[43] Petty sessional records, which consist mainly of minute books containing a brief note of each case heard, generally survive only from the second half of the nineteenth century and later. The documents were regarded as the private papers of the clerk of the division until 1958, when they were deemed public records. Since then, older material has been transferred from many court offices to approved local repositories, although often more can be learnt of petty sessional hearings from the local press than the formal record.

On the civil side, some borough courts of record, especially in the larger towns which had their own recorder, remained in existence until the Local Government Act, 1972. Many others ceased to sit after the establishment of the modern county court in 1846 (9 & 10 Vict., c.95). While opinion differed as to whether this was a new court or a revival of the medieval sheriff's court (p. 40), there was no doubt as to the success of the reform.[44] The whole of England and Wales was divided into county court districts, with a full-time judge appointed to each, who sat in different towns at least once a month, hearing and determining small debt and other civil cases quickly and cheaply, unencumbered by a jury or, for the most part, the pleadings of counsel. The courts were gradually given wider jurisdiction, including, for example, personal injury claims and proceedings under the employers' liability Acts. By the end of the century their accessibility and efficiency had drawn much business away from the divisional court, to which successful appeals were remarkably few. Surviving county court records consist mainly of registers, which list brief details of the parties, claims and finding in each case; because the courts were popular the registers are bulky but provide only limited information. Some registrars have made transfers to the AK group at the PRO; elsewhere the volumes remain in court custody or have been destroyed. County court cases are not normally found in the law reports and only the more important will be mentioned in the local press. Little use appears to have been made of the material by local historians, although they would presumably be of some value for the study of small-scale business or the consequences of changes in the law relating to personal injury at work in favour of the employee.

Other developments, notably the establishment of lay courts to deal with probate and divorce (p. 179), are dealt with in the next chapter, since most records are preserved centrally. The reformed high court after 1873 established district registries and on occasion sat outside London; records thus created, however, are also in central custody (p. 180).

Besides retaining their criminal jurisdiction, the justices remained responsible for most local licensing, both of public houses (p. 89) and various other institutions, for example private mental homes

(p. 125). On the other hand, when the registration of motor vehicles and the licensing of drivers was introduced in 1903, it was entrusted to the clerks of county and county borough councils, with whom it remained until the Vehicle and Driver Licensing Act, 1969, centralised the work at the Driver and Vehicle Licensing Centre, Swansea, an out-station (now) of the Department of Transport. Although the operative date under the Act was 1 April 1971, there was a lengthy transitional period (lasting until 1978) during which the local authorities acted as agents. The older registers were not called in and those that survive should now be in county record offices or, possibly, with district councils which are the successors of county boroughs.[45]

Finally, the oldest of the county officials to remain a living part of modern judicial administration, the coroner, has continued to flourish with his powers and duties little changed over the past two centuries.[46] Under the Local Government Act, 1888, the appointment of coroners was transferred from the freeholders of the county (i.e. the medieval shire court, which had long ceased to sit and whose duty in this respect was in practice discharged by the justices) to the county councils, where it remains today. Coroners' records only became public records under the 1958 Act and should now be transferred regularly to approved local repositories. Since, however, they consist of files on every case referred to them, the papers are too bulky for most archivists to retain in full, a disappointment for genealogists whose ancestors had suicidal tendencies or suffered sudden or mysterious deaths. They are in any case closed for 75 years.

Chapter Six

LOCAL MATERIAL AMONGST THE MODERN RECORDS OF CENTRAL GOVERNMENT

Although the greatest proportion of modern central government records of local interest have been created by departments set up to supervise the work of local government, material of value has also been transferred to the PRO from a number of other ministries, boards and subsidiary organisations. This chapter seeks to outline what is available, generally at Kew, amongst records dating mostly from after 1800. As far as possible, departments have been grouped under broad subject headings, although the work of the Home Office defies classification in this way. The nineteenth-century revolution in government was paralleled by reforms in the administration of justice, the implications of which for local studies are explained in the final section.

Home Office and Privy Council

The creation of the Home Office in 1782, the consequence of dividing the work of the two secretaries of state so that henceforth one dealt exclusively with domestic and the other with foreign affairs, did not greatly alter the nature of their duties. Home secretaries continued to discharge functions stemming from their position as adviser on the exercise of the royal prerogative and as the medium of communication between sovereign and subject and sovereign and local peace officers, as their predecessors had since the sixteenth century (p. 52). In addition, parliament assigned new tasks to the office, either because the work fitted appropriately with existing duties (such as responsibility for police and prisons, closely linked with the prerogative function of maintaining the peace) or because there was, at the time, no other department to take on the work. In turn, Home Office activities have been hived off to separate departments, including the Ministry of Labour, the Board of Agriculture and those dealt with in the previous chapter. Even today, however, the office retains two historic characteristics in that some of its work derives from prerogative rather than statutory powers and it remains responsible for any domestic government function not assigned to another ministry.[1]

Early Home Office papers are a continuation of the older State Papers (Domestic), of which there are published calendars for part of George III's reign but not later (p. 54). The incoming papers between 1782 and 1820 form HO 42, those for 1820-61 are HO 44. A parallel series of entry books containing outgoing letters is HO 43

(1782-1898). Papers relating to 'disturbances' in the localities, mainly in the troubled period after the end of the Napoleonic War in 1815, are bound separately as HO 40, with entry books in HO 41, while correspondence, again chiefly with lieutenants and magistrates, relating to the militia and local volunteer forces in the early nineteenth century is in HO 50. A subsidiary series of 'municipal and provincial' correspondence (HO 52), covers the period 1820-50.

From the mid-nineteenth century, most Home Office material on general topics is either filed as 'registered papers' (HO 45) or to be found in sets of out-letter entry books divided by subject. There is no published finding-aid for these volumes, beyond the list printed in the *Guide* (vol. II, pp.187-9), although some have their own internal indexes and some series are comparatively short. For HO 45 there is a list arranged by subject for the period 1879-1924 (List & Index Society 22, 23, 30, 39, 50, 84, 89, 90), which lacks a topographical index but can be searched without too much effort. Subject-headings likely to yield items of interest include local government, borough charters, markets and fairs, administration of justice, prostitution, burials, lunacy and law and order, to take a random selection of the problems which Victorian home secretaries had to deal with. The list gives a brief indication of the contents of each file and the covering dates but not its bulk: some promising entries may contain only a handful of papers. The HO 45 lists for 1841-79 and after 1924 are arranged in the same way as the published volumes but are available only at the PRO. This is also true of HO 144, a supplementary class of files closed for 100 years for security reasons, although little of this material appears to be of local interest.

Home Office supervision of police and prisons has already been mentioned (p. 158); the other work for which the nineteenth-century department is best remembered is probably that of its inspectorates, small groups of men charged with enforcing, generally by persuasion rather than prosecution, parliament's wish to regulate the running of mines and factories, burial grounds and reformatory schools, salmon fisheries and cruelty to animals, explosives and anatomy dissection. Important as this was in the development of modern government, the archival legacy is disappointing and, apart from entry books, the main source for the work of, say, the mines and factories inspectors, are the officers' annual reports, which were presented to parliament and printed as sessional papers. These contain a wealth of statistical information, much of it local in character, together with details of individual works, their owners and employees, but are outside the scope of this guide.[2]

The Home Office group incorporates the surviving records of the Ministry of Home Security, a temporary department established during the second world war which operated in the provinces through a network of regional commissioners, whose papers now form HO 207. Other classes possibly of interest include HO 199, which contains reports on bomb damage, mainly in London and the south east, and HO 215, concerned with internment camps for enemy aliens and others.[3]

Alongside the Home Office, the other older element in the central executive which survived into modern times was the Privy Council (p. 55). The unprinted Council register is difficult to use for local studies but the 4,500 bundles of unbound papers from the Council Office include much of interest and are reasonably accessible through a published list (List & Index Society 36). Some of the subject entries there, such as borough charters or burial boards, are similar to those for the Home Office papers, while others reflect the work of the Council in the fields of public health and education, responsibility for which was transferred in the mid-nineteenth century to separate departments (pp. 127, 142).

Agriculture and the Land

The present Ministry of Agriculture, Fisheries and Food was established in 1955, the successor of the Board of Agriculture set up in 1889 (52 & 53 Vict., c.30). The latter department had no connection with the older Board of Agriculture, a chartered society which existed between 1793 and 1822 and is best remembered for its series of published reports on the agriculture and economy of each county. This body was revived in 1838 as the forerunner of the Royal Agricultural Society of England; its records, together with those of the RASE and several other national organisations in this field, are now at Reading University. The modern department, which became a ministry in 1919 (9 & 10 Geo. V, c.91), did, however, inherit the functions and, in some cases, the records of commissions set up by the Tithe Act, 1836 (6 & 7 Will. IV, c.71), the Copyhold Act, 1841 (4 & 5 Vict., c.35), and the General Inclosure Act, 1845 (8 & 9 Vict., c.118); conversely, its own responsibilities were remodelled several times after 1889, notably in 1911 (1 & 2 Geo. V, c.49), with the transfer of most Scottish business to a department of the Scottish Office; in 1919 (9 & 10 Geo. V, c.58), with the setting up of the Forestry Commission; and in 1936 (26 Geo. V & 1 Edw. VIII, c.43), with the transfer of tithe business to a separate office, later absorbed by the Inland Revenue. For most of the last hundred years, the president of the board (or minister) has also taken parliamentary responsibility for the Ordnance Survey.[4]

The records of the Tithe Commission established under the Act of 1836 and of its successor, the Tithe Redemption Commission of 1936, are divided between classes transferred to the PRO some years ago and others which have arrived more recently from the Inland Revenue, following the closure of the commission's office. The 1836 Act provided for the commutation of tithe payments into a rent-charge, where this had not already been done, with arrangements for each parish being embodied in an agreement (or, where local agreement proved impossible, an imposed award), drawn up by assistant commissioners and approved by the commission in London. The best known legacy of this process was the production of a large-scale plan of each parish subject to the Act, with an accompanying schedule, showing the tithe rent-charge payable on each parcel, plus the ownership, occupation and use of land in the parish. The tithe surveys are too familiar to need further description here: their value for almost any kind of topographical enquiry has been emphasised on numerous occasions.[5] The original maps and schedules now form IR 29 and IR 30; a list by county and 'tithe district' is in List & Index Society 68 and 83. A tithe district was generally a parish, although in some upland areas each township was dealt with separately; the list includes cross-references from ecclesiastical parishes. Two copies were made of the survey, one of which was placed in the custody of the diocesan registrar, the other in the hands of the parish (or township) to which it related. Under the Tithe Act of 1936 most diocesan copies have been transferred to local record offices, as have the parish copies. Diocesan copies in Wales are at the National Library; parish copies are generally in county offices. In practice, in both England and Wales, local historians interested in a particular place will find it more convenient to use a copy in local custody, but the existence of a complete set centrally has advantages, as does a published list for the whole country.

Other material relating to the long and contentious history of tithe can be found locally in family and estate papers, parish records, the proceedings of church courts and elsewhere; at the PRO the most important series after the surveys themselves are the parish 'tithe files' of 1836-70 (IR 18), while subsidiary classes, again arranged topographically, include awards by assistant commissioners settling boundary disputes between parishes (TITH 1), agreements prior to final apportionments (TITH 2) and papers recording the merger of tithe and tithe rent-charge where the landowner also owned the tithe (TITH 3). More recent transfers by the Inland Revenue include several classes of maps and plans concerned with tithe redemption under the 1936 Act, including IR 90 and IR 94, which show plots subject to redemption; IR 93, which are 1:10,560 maps used to establish parish boundaries in connection with tithe disputes; and IR 105, marked-up 1:63,360 maps with additional information inserted by the commission. The papers of the Royal Commission on Tithe Rentcharge (1934), whose report formed the basis of the legislation two years later, are now IR 101 and IR 102. A thorough study of tithe in a particular parish should include checks on all this material, for none of which, unfortunately, are there published lists. The documents themselves are mostly kept at Hayes, where (unlike most such material) they can be seen by readers on the spot, rather than requisitioned to Chancery Lane.

In 1882 the Tithe Commission was merged with the Copyhold and Enclosure commissions to form the Land Commission, which in turn was absorbed into the Board of Agriculture seven years later. Several of the older MAF classes are inheritances from these bodies, including enclosure awards drawn up under the Acts of 1845 and later (MAF 1). For a century prior to this date, enclosure had most commonly been authorised by local Act; the procedure was now simplified but the requirement to enrol a copy of the award with the clerk of the peace of the county in which the enclosure took place was retained. These copies are now in county record offices (p. 89) and are generally more accessible for local studies than those in the PRO.[6] Deeds and awards enfranchising copyhold land from 1864 are now MAF 9 and are listed by county in the (unpublished) class-list; similar documents extinguishing manorial incidents under legislation of 1922-24 are in MAF 13. Other manorial documents, including deeds, will be found in MAF 5 and MAF 6, with files on individual manors in the nineteenth century in MAF 20. There are also several classes concerned with the administration of common land under the Commons Act, 1899, and other legislation, including orders in MAF 3 and correspondence and papers (arranged by county) in MAF 25 and MAF 48. Counterpart series for Welsh common land are in BD 1 and BD 3 amongst Welsh Office records.[7]

Much of the more recent material is arranged in subject files, so that it is difficult to find items of local interest without a prolonged search, especially as none of the classes has a published list. There are, however, files on land drainage and water supply for each local drainage authority in MAF 49 (cf. p. 91), with maps and plans in MAF 77, and files on local cattle markets in MAF 91. Other maps, concerned with freshwater fisheries, are in MAF 71. Minutes of local committees of the Wheat Commission set up under an Act of 1932 (22 & 23 Geo. V, c.24) are in MAF 61, those of local Agricultural Wages Committees in MAF 64 and of Food Control Committees in MAF 67. For the second world war (but not the first, for which there are only general files) the history of the Women's Land Army may be traced from county files in MAF 59. Regional office papers form several classes from MAF 105 for England and MAF 112 for Wales; files from the Welsh Department of the ministry are in MAF 70.

Of greater interest for local work are three statistical classes, of which the oldest and best known is HO 67, the 'crop returns' of 1801, containing reports to the Home Secretary from incumbents as to the crops grown in certain parishes and, in some cases, agricultural conditions generally. The original material is arranged by diocese but a modern digest by Michael Turner (List & Index Society 189, 190, 195, indexed in 196) presents the data by county, while retaining all the detail of the original, reference to which is probably now unnecessary for most purposes. Some other early returns are in HO 42 (p. 162). Modern agricultural statistics date from 1866, since when volumes have been published annually either as sessional papers or official non-parliamentary publications. Somewhat unusually with material of this kind, the department has preserved information not used in the printed tables; although the original returns from individual farmers have been destroyed, there are parish summaries from 1866 in MAF 68. Finally, MAF 10 contains corn price series from selected markets from the early nineteenth century.[8]

Surviving Ordnance Survey records, of which many were destroyed by enemy action in the second world war, are divided between the department's headquarters at Southampton and the Kew branch of the PRO. Classes of local interest include parish acreage lists (OS 4), detailing the total of land, water etc in each parish, which form the basis of all official statistics involving land areas, and parish 'name books', containing notes on the spelling of names, boundaries and other information (OS 23). Details of the triangulation stations in each county are given in volumes which now form OS 2. Among the various specialist maps produced by the Survey is a series marking commons and open spaces within 25 miles of London in 1865 (OS 25); other miscellaneous maps are in OS 5. Archive material retained by the department includes a set of 'boundary remark books' and other papers relating to disputed boundaries, covering most of England and Wales in the mid-nineteenth century.[9]

The Forestry Commission was set up in 1919 (9 & 10 Geo. V, c.58) to make good the losses to native woodland of the first world war and generally restore a declining industry; today the department administers some three million acres of land, about two million of which are planted. Crown woodland was transferred to the commission in 1924 (13 & 14 Geo. V, c.21), as a consequence of which their records include material on the recent history of the royal forests which complements earlier documents elsewhere (pp. 32, 64-7, 168). A series of classes (F 3 to F 13) contain files on each forest from the mid-nineteenth century, of which those on New Forest (F 10, cf. also F 2) and Dean (F 3) are the largest, while F 37 is a set of 'forest histories', begun in 1951, including details of how the wood from each estate has been used. Records of woodland censuses taken in 1924, 1938 and 1942 form F 22, F 23 and F 30, with information on hedgerows, parks and private timber. There are maps and plans, especially for New Forest and Dean, in F 17, while for Dean alone manorial documents of the eighteenth and nineteenth centuries may be found in F 14, deeds in F 15 and verderers' court records from the seventeenth century in F 16. There are other court papers in family collections in the Gloucestershire Record Office.[10]

Three more important groups for the recent history of crown lands are the records of the Office of Land Revenue Records and Enrolments, the Crown Estate Commissioners and the Ministry of

Works. The first of these was established in 1832 (2 & 3 Will. IV, c.1), when the office of Auditor of the Land Revenue was finally abolished (p. 65), and placed under the supervision of the Commissioners of Woods, Forests and Land Revenues, who administered the crown estates under an Act of 1810 (50 Geo. III, c.65), as successors to the Surveyors General of Land Revenue and Surveyors General of Woods, Forests, Parks and Chases, between whom administration had been shared since the mid-sixteenth century. In 1832 the commissioners also absorbed the office of Surveyor General of Works and Public Buildings, a unity that was broken in 1851 (14 & 15 Vict., c.42), when public buildings, royal palaces and parks were placed under a separate Office of Works and the remaining crown estate taken over by an Office of Woods and Forests. In 1923 the Commissioners of Woods and Forests were renamed the Commissioners of Crown Lands and in 1956 became the Crown Estate Commissioners.[11] Meanwhile, the Office of Works, an institution with a continuous history since at least the sixteenth century, was remodelled into the Ministry of Works in 1940 and continued, as the Ministry of Public Building and Works, until 1970, when it formed, with the Ministry of Housing and Local Government (with which it had been briefly linked during the war), one of the main constituents of the Department of the Environment. Since then, a Property Services Agency within the department has discharged many of the old Ministry of Works functions.[12]

The Office of Land Revenue Records and Enrolments is essentially a registry in which deeds and other documents relating to crown estate are either enrolled or, as is now the practice, registered by the deposit of duplicates. All enrolments and deposits are closed for 100 years and there is thus only a limited amount of material in the main series (LRRO 13 to LRRO 18) available to searchers, much of which is accessible through indexes in LRRO 66 or registers in LRRO 64, of which the latter are themselves indexed. The finding-aids give brief details of each document registered or enrolled, its date and the estate to which it relates. The deeds are concerned only with crown land in the narrow sense of the term, i.e. the remaining royal estate that has survived earlier alienations (p. 64), plus property acquired in recent centuries. They do not include the main run of government estate administered by the Office of Works and its successors (p. 169). The other class in this group which may be of interest is LRRO 12, containing some 2,000 rentals of crown lands from 1832, indexed in LRRO 65.

Most documents relating to the actual management of crown estates since the Restoration are now separately grouped as records of the modern commissioners. There is no published list of the CRES group but several classes are either arranged topographically or indexed, including the general series of in-letters (CRES 2); out-going correspondence was entered in volumes, most of which have internal indexes. The oldest of these are the Constat Books

(CRES 6), beginning in 1661, which contain detailed reports and drafts preliminary to the granting of leases. For the later nineteenth century there are separate entry books for estates in the north, south and Scotland. Other modern records are in registered files, which are listed by county, with a brief note of their contents (CRES 34 and CRES 35), while the group also contains nineteenth-century manor court rolls (CRES 5), estate surveys (CRES 39), deeds (CRES 38), and photographs (CRES 43, mainly of London property). The miscellaneous books (CRES 40) are sufficiently fully listed to be worth checking. The commissioners are not responsible for the crown's holdings in right of the Duchy of Lancaster, for which modern material will be found in the DL classes at Chancery Lane, nor the Duchy of Cornwall estates (pp. 38-9).

Ministry of Works records are mainly of interest to local historians insofar as they relate to individual properties, rather than the adminstration of the department as a whole. There is a published class-list for the group (LIS 59, 65, 79). Two general series of correspondence and papers are concerned with public buildings (WORK 12 and WORK 17), which have topographical indexes, and several others deal with particular parts of the government estate, such as the royal palaces (WORK 19) or statues and memorials (WORK 20); or individual properties, e.g. Osborne on the Isle of Wight (WORK 15); or a particular class of property, as in the case of WORK 26, on the royal ordnance factories. These are parallelled by maps and plans divided into similar categories, of which WORK 30 is the general series, to which again there is an index by place. WORK 41 to WORK 44 consist of maps and plans of estates occupied by the armed forces and naval dockyards, while WORK 14 and WORK 31 are respectively the papers and maps relating to ancient monuments in the care of the state. It may be worth adding that reports by the ancient monuments laboratory on structures and archaeological sites since 1950 have been put into a separate group (AT 1) at the other end of the alphabet. For both ancient monuments and historic buildings (of which the latter are protected under the planning Acts rather than antiquities legislation) it is worth looking at HLG 126, which contains files on individual properties.

Four classes are listed as 'Deeds', which is to some extent misleading. WORK 7 and WORK 8 do contain conveyances, mainly relating to London, while WORK 24 is a small class of oddments. WORK 13, however, which mostly relates to property in the provinces, consists largely of contracts and specifications for the erection of new buildings, chiefly between the wars when the government estate in many places was expanding to accommodate, for example, telephone exchanges for the Post Office, employment exchanges for the Ministry of Labour, and local offices for the Inland Revenue. For anyone interested in public building in this period the class contains superbly detailed architects' drawings; it will not, on the other hand, supply information on the history of the site which one normally obtains from deeds. This appears to be recorded in the series of Government Property Registers (WORK 50), which are said to contain a description and map of each estate – civil and military – owned by the government, together with a list of deeds relating to the property, information of considerable value to anyone working on the detailed topography of their community. It is therefore unfortunate that the class is closed for considerably longer than the usual 30 years and that the Property Services Agency refuses to relax this rule in response to individual requests. Even more regrettable is PSA's refusal to allow access to the prior deeds acquired with purchases, which are kept at their Lambeth Bridge House offices (Albert Embankment, SE1). These are apparently not subject to the Public Records Act and are regarded, irrespective of age, as being current records accessible only to PSA staff or the Treasury Solicitor, who acts as the government's conveyancer. This attitude, now happily rare among departments that find it necessary to retain documents of historical interest, means that local historians reconstructing the history of their town tenement-by-tenement cannot trace the development of plots owned by central government.[13]

Trade, Industry and Transport

Although customs duties on both imports and exports have been levied since the thirteenth century (p. 31), a separate department to administer the system was established only in the late seventeenth, while revenue continued to be accounted for at the Exchequer. During the eighteenth century two series of documents record the movement of goods in and out of the country: the Exchequer port books (p. 58) and the ledgers compiled by the Inspector General of Imports and Exports appointed in 1696. The ledgers (CUST 3) are, however, of limited value for local historians, since they were compiled primarily to show England's balance of trade with each country, not the trade of each port. For each country the quantity of goods imported and exported is listed, with their 'official' values, but the only other division is between the trade of London and that of the 'outports', i.e. the rest of England and Wales. For the trade of individual provincial ports one has no choice but to rely on the port books, unless there is an alternative source locally. After 1792 the ledgers divide into separate series for imports and exports (CUST 4 to 13) and are arranged both by countries and commodities, but still with no local information. For the limited period 1873-99 details of imports passing through individual ports are given in CUST 23, showing the quantity and value of each article and its country of origin. CUST 24 provides similar information for exports and both series are abstracted in CUST 25 and CUST 26. A more extensive source for the trade of particular ports are the 'entry lists' published as daily newspapers in some ports in the second half of the nineteenth century and later, which may be found in local libraries, at the British Newspaper Library at Colindale, or the Customs and Excise library, but not the PRO. These give full details of ships entering and clearing, their port of origin or destination, and the cargo on board.[14]

The other major source for the history of individual ports among the Customs records are the lengthy series of correspondence between the board in London and the collector in each outport, which in some cases begins in the early eighteenth century and normally continues until the late nineteenth (CUST 50 onwards). For each port there are two sets of books, one for in-letters and another for out-letters, which have been transferred from local custom houses. They are particularly valuable because of the destruction by fire of many of the records at the Custom House in London. Although much of the material is routine, the books are undoubtedly worth searching for information about both trade and shipping and commercial life generally in a port and its hinterland. For the nineteenth century the books may be supplemented by establishment records from the outports (CUST 38), staff lists (CUST 19) and a series of reports on the running of the service in each port in the 1830s and later (CUST 32).[15]

List & Index Society 20 provides a list of some, but not all, Customs classes as far as CUST 45; it would be helpful if the rest of the class-list could be put into print.

The collection of excise duties has been united with the Customs only since the establishment of the present board in 1909, although duties were first levied in 1642. Disappointingly little local material survives before modern times, either amongst Exchequer records (p. 61) or in the Customs and Excise group. CUST 43 consists of excise district office records of the eighteenth and nineteenth centuries, arranged by 'collection', the units into which the country is divided by the department. Most of the documents are letterbooks containing correspondence between the collector and central authority (Board of Excise until 1849, then Inland Revenue to 1909), or entry books concerning the collection of duties. The areas covered include at least a single county and in some cases several, so that the amount of information on particular localities is limited.

From 1621 a series of committees of the Privy Council was appointed to deal with business arising from overseas trade, especially with the American colonies. The last of these was dissolved in 1782, towards the end of the American War of Independence and their records eventually passed to the Colonial Office; they are obviously not of interest to local historians. The modern Board of Trade was established by order in council in 1784 and continued to function under another order of 1786 until its absorption into the Department of Trade and Industry in 1970, which has since been separated into two and re-united. During the nineteenth century the Board of Trade was mainly concerned with shipping and overseas trade, although it acquired supervisory powers over railways and inland waterways and was responsible for the registration of joint-stock companies and some aspects of bankruptcy, all of which has created records of local interest.[16]

Two categories of material concerned with shipping are important for the history of individual ports. Since 1786 local Customs officials have maintained, as agents for the Board of Trade and its successors, a register of ships and their owners in each port. Although some documents concerned with ship registration are at Kew (BT 107 to BT 111, plus BT 145 for fishing boats), the main series of registers, which may begin in 1786 or later, have been transferred to appropriate county record offices. The books give the name and official number of each vessel, its date of registration and details of ownership, property in ships being divided traditionally into 64 shares. Since the mid-eighteenth century, lists have also been kept of crews employed on British vessels, which again are arranged by port and use the official numbers assigned to ships in the other registers. With the expansion of British shipping and the extension of the system to ports of the overseas empire, these lists (and accompanying agreements to serve, ships' logs and other documents) have grown to a bulk disproportionate to their general interest. While older material (prior to 1863) has been retained by the PRO (BT 98), thereafter there is only a 10 per cent sample up to 1938 (BT 99), plus papers for famous ships in BT 100. The National Maritime Museum at Greenwich has a further sample, while the remainder of the pre-1913 lists were offered first to British repositories in maritime counties, who could choose to take none, a sample or all material relating to local ports, and then to Memorial University, St Johns, Newfoundland, who took what was left. A later tranche, once samples for the PRO and NMM had been removed, was disposed of entirely to Newfoundland. Current records are kept by the General Registry of Shipping and Seamen, Llantrisant Road, Cardiff CF5 2YS, an out-station of the Department of Transport, which has some material dating from before 1700 as well as a great deal from more recent years.[17]

Board of Trade regulation of joint-stock companies dates from two Acts of 1844 (7 & 8 Vict., cc.110,111), which were superseded by another of 1856 (19 & 20 Vict., c.47), under which companies had to re-register. Files relating to companies registered before 1860 under either statute, irrespective of whether they survived after that date, now form BT 41, for which there is an unpublished list at Kew arranged in two alphabetical sequences, one for general companies and the other for railways (including some canals). Files on companies registered under the 1856 Act which have gone out of existence since 1860 are in BT 31, a class notorious for having been heavily weeded but which remains a major source for the history of countless businesses whose own records have perished. The companies are listed chronologically, with a name index at Kew arranged in strict alphabetical order, so that J. Bloggs & Co will be found under J, not B. Despite this, it is fairly easy to locate files on particular companies once one has a name from a directory or some other source, while it is usually also worth looking up the place in which one is interested, since there should be some firms whose name began with that word. The register includes only joint-stock companies, identifiable after 1855 by the word 'Limited' in their title, and does not extend to partnerships, sole proprietorships or companies incorporated under Act of Parliament or royal charter. This excludes the older overseas trading companies, the larger insurance concerns, most railway and canal undertakings and a fair proportion of gas- and water-works, as well as the great bulk of mid-nineteenth-century firms, which were typically partnerships or run by one person. Companies registered under the Act of 1856 and later statutes which are still in existence may be traced through files at Companies House, Crown Way, Maindy, Cardiff CF4 3UZ, which charges search fees but provides microfiche copies which one may take away at no extra cost.[18]

Businesses not registered under the joint-stock legislation make little impression on early Board of Trade records, although for the late nineteenth century it may be worth checking classes relating to bankruptcy, of which BT 221 and BT 226 are probably most useful. Both consist of files on individuals and companies, the former dealing with non-court matters and the latter with High Court business under the Bankruptcy Act, 1883 (46 & 47 Vict., c.52). There is a name index for BT 226 between 1891 and 1914 at Kew. Other bankruptcy material is to be found amongst court records at Chancery Lane (p. 181).

Board of Trade interest in private business, apart from registration and bankruptcy work, grew up mainly after the establishment of a Companies Department in 1904, whose surviving papers (BT 58) include some files of local interest. For industry in the post-war 'development areas', the successors of the 'special areas' of the 1930s (p. 137), the board's work under the Distribution of Industry Acts of 1945 and 1950 may be followed through files in BT 177, which also has material on particular places and firms.[19]

After 1945 the government took into public ownership large areas of manufacturing industry as well as most of the transport sector. Some industries have remained in public hands since the 1940s, others have been returned to private ownership. The archival implications of these changes vary. In the original legislation, only the records of the National Coal Board, including those inherited from former colliery companies, were deemed public records. The COAL group at Kew contains not only the NCB's older files, some of which may be of interest for local studies, but also papers from the Coal Mines Reorganisation Commission set up under the Coal Mines Act, 1930, and its successor under the 1938 Coal Act, the Coal Commission, to which the board was itself partly the successor.

Both COAL 12 and COAL 17, the files of the two pre-war commissions, are worth checking for material on individual colliery companies, as are COAL 34 to COAL 40, which relate to the transfer of assets under the Coal Industry Nationalisation Act, 1946, again with files for each concern. Former Ministry of Mines files relating to the nationalisation of the collieries, including details of some individual concerns, can now be found in two Ministry of Fuel and Power classes, POWE 35 and POWE 36. Colliery company records acquired by the NCB have generally been transferred to local record offices in coalfields, although the board has a network of repositories of its own. NCB material in county offices can often be disappointing, with few local companies represented, since so much appears to have been destroyed at vesting.[20]

In the case of iron and steel, records of the British Steel Corporation, together with those of former private companies and of various employers' organisations, are in the custody of the BSC, which has three regional repositories.[21] On the other hand, most county record offices in ironmaking areas (and some elsewhere) have material from private companies, while the records of the Iron and Steel Board at Kew (BE 1) include papers on private steelmakers, mainly from the 1950s, after the industry was de-nationalised. Early material on the gas, water and electricity supply industries, all of which have local origins, has already been mentioned (p. 159); after nationalisation all came under the supervision of the Ministry of Fuel and Power, most of whose records are arranged in subject files, although some of these appear to be of local interest. There are papers on individual power stations from the 1920s in POWE 12 and POWE 14. A rather different aspect of direct public control of industry is reflected in the Ministry of Supply files on each royal ordnance factory in SUPP 5.

Since government intervention in the affairs of private business was so limited until recent times, except for temporary controls during the two world wars and efforts, on a broad scale, to reorganise some sectors between the wars, there is comparatively little for local historians interested in industry among the public records apart from the Board of Trade classes mentioned here and those relating to transport outlined below. For some companies there may be business records, or at least legal or family papers, in county record offices, but otherwise the most profitable approach may well be to pursue the individuals who owned local companies through standard biographical and genealogical sources, or to see whether the company or its proprietors were involved in litigation in one of the superior courts (especially Chancery), in which case exhibits may throw light on the firm's activities (pp. 74-6).[22]

Since the end of the nineteenth century the government has also been involved in the promotion of good industrial relations, work originally undertaken by the Board of Trade and later transferred to the Ministry of Labour. Here, however, the main series of registered papers (LAB 2) is difficult to use for local studies, since it is vast and lacks a suitable topographical index. On the other hand, anyone interested in a particular company known to have been involved in a major trade dispute in the earlier part of this century might find it worth searching the 'IC' (Industrial Conciliation) series within LAB 2, which contains files on individual companies from 1911 onwards. The series is continued in LAB 3 but here files are concerned with whole industries rather than companies. LAB 21 contains regional office papers, some of which relate to local industrial relations issues.

Government supervision of inland transport began in 1840, with the creation of the Railway Department of the Board of Trade, which also became responsible for canals, light railways, tramways, gas, water and electricity.[23] Those parts of its work strictly concerned with transport were transferred, with elements from other departments, to the Ministry of Transport on its establishment in 1919 (9 & 10 Geo. V, c.50), and the records are now divided between that department (for railways and tramways) and the Board of Trade (other functions). Some 2,600 boxes of files have been transferred from the Railway Department to the PRO, containing a mass of correspondence and papers of considerable local interest, touching practically every railway company and town in the country. There is a three-volume list of MT 6 (List & Index Society 107, 114, 123), to which another three volumes (206, 207, 208) provide a full index by place and company, including tramways and light railways. These should be searched in any work on local railway history. The other main survival from the nineteenth century is a set of reports by the railway inspectorate on accidents and other matters (1840-1930) in MT 29, indexed in MT 30, although reports on the more spectacular Victorian disasters were often published in the local press. For lines built under the light railway legislation of 1896 (59 & 60 Vict., c.48) the papers of the Light Railway Commission (MT 14 to MT 18) are worth checking, together with a set of plans of proposed lines (MT 54) and the orders under which light railways were built (as opposed to the Acts of Parliament standard railway companies were obliged to promote). In practice, the plans can usually be found more easily in county record offices, since copies had to be deposited with the clerk of the peace, as for other public works (p. 89); the clerk's law library will also generally have prints of local orders.

Responsibility for inland waterways lay with the Railway Department until 1919, when it passed to the Ministry of Transport. For the later period correspondence and papers relating to individual canals will be found in MT 52, including a good deal on proposed closures; for earlier years little seems to survive. In the case of docks and harbours the ministry inherited papers from the Admiralty (1848-63) and the Board of Trade (from 1864), which are now MT 19 and MT 10 respectively. The Admiralty material is arranged by harbour but the later files are listed chronologically, although there is a subject index (BT 19). Papers transferred from the trustees of Ramsgate Harbour are now MT 21 and MT 22; for another half-dozen ports (Cardiff, Glasgow, Hull, Newcastle upon Tyne, South Shields and Sunderland) minutes of local marine boards (1850-1910) are in MT 26. Nineteenth-century surveys of local rights to wreck in different ports (BT 212) may also be of interest, while for the 1960s and 1970s the records of the National Ports Council (DK 1) include some British Transport Docks Board files on the trade of individual ports.

The major area of growth in the Ministry of Transport's work between the wars and since has, of course, been in road transport, but here archival material is disappointing for local studies. Most papers are arranged by subject and, although some files appear to be of interest, there is no index. Local authority records thus form the main source for the modern history of the roads themselves (pp. 138-41), while for the traffic on them one is largely dependent on the limited survival of business records of private passenger and goods carriers, mostly in local record offices.[24] The nationalisation of road transport in 1947, however, brought material from some of the larger private road haulage companies into the hands of the British Transport Commission and this now forms AN 68 at Kew. For municipal bus and tram undertakings local authority records are again the main source (p. 159), plus MT 6 for tramways, whether municipal or privately owned.

For inland transport other than roads, the major archive is that assembled by the BTC after nationalisation, when virtually all railway, canal, river navigation and dock undertakings passed into public ownership, together with an immensely rich collection of administrative records. Maintained for some years by the British Railways Board at repositories in London and York, this material was later transferred to the PRO, where it is now mostly classified as the RAIL group, irrespective of the form of transport. Some documents, mostly archives of various central bodies in the railway industry prior to nationalisation, have been grouped separately (AN); these are not, except for AN 68, of any obvious interest for local studies. The RAIL group, on the other hand, are the predecessor archives of the canal and railway companies, plus a smaller number of dock, harbour, river and steamship concerns, which existed from the eighteenth century down to 1947. For most there are, as a minimum, minutes of directors' and shareholders' meetings and some financial records; for the larger railway companies there are the records of an intricate structure of committees and sub-committees; working agreements between ostensible rivals; establishment records; maps and plans; engineering, locomotive and rolling stock records; and much else, including printed brochures, timetables and other booklets, as well as photographs. With the documents came a fine library of transport history which, although no longer kept up-to-date, remains a useful resource to use alongside the archives.[25]

For the canal, dock, harbour and steamship companies there is a published class-list (LIS 142), arranged alphabetically by company, with a short note outlining the constitutional history of each concern prefacing a summary list of the records, which are now RAIL 800 to RAIL 887. As yet, class-lists have been issued for only two of the railway companies, the London & North Western and the Midland, the main constituents of the London, Midland & Scottish Railway at the 'grouping' of 1923, which are now RAIL 410 and RAIL 491 (LIS 172). Published lists for the four post-1923 companies and for the dozen or so others which before the first world war controlled most of the mileage, traffic and revenue of the system would be helpful.

Because of the comprehensive character of transport nationalis-ation, few canal and railway records remained in local custody after 1947 and there is little in most county record offices, apart from deposited plans (p. 89) and printed Acts. Since virtually all undertakings were authorised by parliament the other main central source is the House of Lords Record Office, where the passage of bills may be traced in various documents.[26] A less satisfactory aspect of this field is the way in which a good deal of semi-archival railway material, chiefly that reproduced by lithography, photography, dye-lining or similar processes, but not published or, in most cases, widely available, has been scattered between places outside the PRO. The National Railway Museum at York has a large collection of official railway photographs, plans and drawings, while British Rail have passed similar material to a joint venture with a private publisher (Railprint, 302 Holdenhurst Road, Bournemouth), from which copies may be obtained. With the contraction of the industry in recent years further quantities of civil and mechanical engineering records and photographs appear to have fallen into the hands of private collectors and enthusiasts' organisations, where conditions of storage, much less cataloguing or access, may be far from ideal.

Supervision of Voluntary Organisations

The major category of material under this heading at Kew of local interest is that transferred from the Registry of Friendly Societies. In 1828 a barrister was appointed to certify the rules of savings banks, whose duties were extended the following year to friendly societies. Under the Friendly Societies Act, 1846 (9 & 10 Vict., c.27) this officer was constituted the Registrar of Friendly Societies for England (including Wales); similar appointments were made for Scotland and Ireland. An Act of 1855 (18 & 19 Vict., c.63) required clerks of the peace, with whom friendly society rules had been deposited since 1793 (33 Geo. III, c.54) to pass these documents to the central registry, but in practice some were retained locally and are now in county record offices (p. 89). During the mid-nineteenth century the registry also assumed responsibility for building societies, trade unions and industrial and provident societies, all of which had to make annual returns.[27]

For each type of organisation there are files for each society, arranged in a single alphabetical sequence; there is no sub-division by county, nor have any of the lists been published. To search an entire class for organisations in a particular place may therefore be a lengthy task; alternatively, with a list of societies culled from directories, returns deposited with the clerk of the peace or, where they survive, the records of the organisations itself, one can locate the appropriate central files quite easily.

Material on societies registered under one of the early Acts (1793-1855) forms FS 1, while files for societies removed from the register between 1876 and 1912 are in FS 3; these classes are indexed in FS 2 and FS 4. Local societies registered under the Friendly Societies Act, 1896, have files of rules in FS 15 and annual returns in FS 16, while those which were branches of national organisations can be traced through FS 5 and (after 1912) FS 10. Files on building societies registered under Acts of 1836 and 1874 which went out of existence before 1913 form FS 6, with later material in FS 16. Files on trade unions from the 1850s, which, like building societies, were mostly local in this period, are in FS 7, FS 11 and FS 12; those on industrial and provident societies (mostly local co-operative organisations) are in FS 8, FS 17 and FS 18; and those on local local societies certified under an Act of 1840 are in FS 9, FS 19 and FS 22. Finally, FS 23 is a class of subject files, mainly concerning disputes over the management of societies.

Perhaps better known than the Registry of Friendly Societies is the Charity Commission, established on a permanent basis in 1853, following the recommendations of a royal commission in 1849; there had previously been several *ad hoc* commissions to enquire into charities whose reports are a major source for this subject.[28] In 1860 the Charitable Trusts Act gave the commission powers, previously reserved to the courts, to appoint or remove trustees and to vary the purpose of a trust by means of a scheme. Under the Board of Education Act, 1899, charities whose purpose was exclusively educational (i.e. chiefly those whose income was used to maintain endowed schools) were transferred from the commission to the board, along with records relating to them (pp. 143, 148-9). Today, the Charity Commission operates principally under the Charities Act, 1960, and maintains a central register of charities at two premises: 14 Ryder Street SW1, and Graeme House, Derby Square, Liverpool. The London office is responsible for national and overseas charities and those based in England south of a line between the Severn and Wash. The northern office looks after Welsh charities and those elsewhere in England. Documents in the central register more than 30 years old are open to inspection in the same way as other public records; the commission does not make transfers to the PRO since its own offices are approved places for deposit. The register can often provide useful information about charities supplementing anything available locally in the hands of trustees or their clerks or in record offices, where the bulk of charity material is to be found in parish collections (p. 96).

Finally, it may be worth mentioning the Development Commission, established under the Development and Road Improvement Funds Acts of 1909 and 1910 to administer an annual grant from parliament which may be used for any purpose 'calculated to benefit the rural economy of England', provided that no other statutory provision for helping a particular scheme exists. The commission has devoted most of its resources to promoting social and cultural life in the countryside, mainly working through rural community councils in each county (known in Wales since 1974 as community services councils). It has also been involved in agricultural advisory work and help for small ports and harbours. The commission's files (D 4) are open up to the 1950s and contain a good deal of local material, including a series for each RCC, which can be used in conjunction with the records of individual councils, some of which are now in local record offices. One of the commission's best known offspring is the National Council for Voluntary Organisations (formerly the National Council of Social Service), some of whose records are also in D 4, though others are retained by the council.[29] The NCSS in turned spawned the Standing Conference for Local History, which from 1948 to 1982 was the only central body for the subject and has since been remodelled as the British Association for Local History. No SCLH records have reached the PRO.

Administration of Justice

Two statutes of 1857 removed from the ecclesiastical courts the last remnants of their jurisidiction over lay persons (pp. 80, 105). The Probate Act transferred all business from the two prerogative courts and the multiplicity of local courts to a new Court of Probate, with a principal registry at Somerset House. Grants of probate or administration might be made either in London or at one of the district registries established throughout England and Wales, mostly in places where a diocesan court had previously sat. Amongst other improvements was the institution of a single annual calendar of all grants which was printed and copies distributed to local registries (although not otherwise published). Similarly, copies of grants and wills were transmitted to London, where they were registered in volumes similar to those compiled in the PCC (p. 81).

Under the Supreme Court of Judicature Act of 1873 (36 & 37 Vict., c.66), the Probate Court became part of the Probate, Divorce and Admiralty Division of the High Court, from which probate and divorce have since been removed to the present Family

Division. Any will proved in England and Wales since January 1858, except those of sovereigns and their immediate family, may be consulted at Somerset House on payment of a small fee. The annual calendars of grants, which for some purposes are a sufficient substitute for actual examination of a will, may be searched free of charge: the entries give the name and address of the testator, date of death, occupation and the approximate value of estate, as well as date of probate. The Principal Registry has copies of all wills; the local registries now retain only those proved in their own districts since 1929 (or later in some cases), together with calendars from the same date. Earlier material – both calendars and registered copy wills – has been transferred to local record offices (including some library archive departments which are approved places of deposit under the Public Records Act). The migration of modern probate records in the last few years is a complex subject, since it includes documents from some of the smaller district registries closed in 1928 whose records were subsequently kept in other districts before transfers began. Fortunately, Jeremy Gibson's guide includes post-1857 material as well as ecclesiastical court records and is frequently updated. The documents remain as valuable for all kinds of local studies as the earlier material, especially as an increasing proportion of the adult male population has made wills since the mid-nineteenth century.[30]

The Family Division has not made available, either at Somerset House or the PRO, other probate records besides the grants and registered wills. There are presumably papers analogous to earlier PCC classes (p. 83) arising from contentious causes still in the court's custody.

Another Act of 1857 (20 & 21 Vict., c.85) established the Court for Divorce and Matrimonial Causes, which in 1873 also became part of the Probate, Divorce and Admiralty Division and is now part of the Family Division. Some 3,000 divorce files between 1858 and 1934 now form J 77 at Chancery Lane, to which J 78 provides an index. The papers include minutes, pleadings and decrees.

The superior common law and equity courts, together with the High Court of Admiralty, were consolidated in 1873 (36 & 37 Vict., c.66) into the Supreme Court of Judicature. The equity courts, plus the common law side of the Chancery and the revenue jurisdiction of the Exchequer, formed a Chancery Division within the High Court, while the common law courts initially became Queen's Bench, Common Pleas and Exchequer divisions, which in 1880 were amalgamated into a single Queen's Bench Division. Several courts exercising appellate jurisdiction were consolidated into the Court of Appeal.

In some cases, especially in the Chancery Division, the records continue after 1873 with little discontinuity and some Supreme Court classes have already been mentioned (pp. 74-6). On the common law side there was a more fundamental break, as the plea rolls (p. 33) give way to judgment books. Otherwise, Supreme Court records are similar in character to those of the older courts and are of similar value for local studies. Suits between families or between members of the same family heard in the Chancery Division will generally be of more interest than most common law actions, while the most convenient way into the formidable bulk of modern high court records will often be from a stray case paper in a family collection or solicitors' deposit in a local record office. It is also worth remembering that far more cases appear in the published law reports in this period than before, or were reported in *The Times* or local press, all of which may supply more detail than surviving court records. Another point is that many modern judicial classes are out-housed at Hayes and seven days' notice is required for productions at Chancery Lane.

Among the courts absorbed into the Chancery Division was the Court of Bankruptcy established in 1831 (1 & 2 Will. IV, c.56), which sat both in London and the country. Before this date the Lord Chancellor appointed commissions under an Act of 1571 (13 Eliz., c.7) to examine the affairs of bankrupts, take depositions and make other enquiries, on the basis of which the Chancellor made orders in bankruptcy.[31] Since 1873, bankruptcy cases have been heard in the Chancery Division but most documents created under all three procedures are grouped together as the records of the Bankruptcy Court, while other material will be found in Board of Trade classes (p. 173). The main series, to which a modern index, including places and occupations as well as names, has recently been compiled, is B 3, the files of examinations, depositions and other papers, which begin in 1759. Flanking these are the order books (B 1), extending from 1710 to 1877. There are also minute books from 1714 (B 7) and registers from 1733 (B 6). Proceedings under the Acts of 1831 and later are in B 9 and those under the Joint Stock Company Acts of 1856 and 1857 in B 10. Both have been weeded, leaving only files 'of some material interest'. A more promising class may be J 13, winding-up proceedings under the Companies Act, 1862, and later legislation, which contains 19,000 files arranged alphabetically by company name.

Appendix One
CLASSES OF PUBLIC RECORDS REFERRED TO IN THE TEXT

The following table lists, in alphanumeric order, all the classes at the PRO mentioned in the preceding chapters (first column), together with page references (second column) and an indication of what published finding-aids are available in each case (third column). In the third column the abbreviation *L&I (Supp.)* refers to the PRO series of *Lists & Indexes (Supplementary)* (for which see HMSO Sectional List 24), LIS to the publications of the List & Index Society (see Chapter 1, note 22), and *DKR* to the annual reports of the Deputy Keeper of Public Records, some of which have lists and calendars printed as appendices. For other finding-aids (and, in some cases, complete transcripts or calendars) see the text at the page referred to in the second column.

AK	160	–
AN 68	176	–
ASSI	69–71	LIS 6
AT 1	169	–
B 1, 3, 6, 7, 9, 10	181	–
BD 1, 3	166	–
BD 5	138	–
BD 7	152	–
BD 11, 23, 24, 28, 29, 30	138	–
BE 1	174	–
BT 19	176	–
BT 31, 41	172–3	–
BT 58	173	–
BT 98, 99, 100, 107 to 111, 145	172	–
BT 177	173	–
BT 212	176	–
BT 221, 226	173	–
C 1	74	*L&I* 12, 16, 20, 29, 38, 43, 50, 51, 54, 55
C 2, C 3	74	*L&I* 7, 24, 30, 47; LIS 202
C 5	74–5	*L&I* 29, 42, 44, 45
C 6 to C 15	74–5	–
C 21, C 22, C 24	75	–
C 31, C 33, C 36, C 38, C 39, C 41	75	–
C 43, C 44	28	LIS 67
C 47	28–9, 32	LIS 7, 15, 26, 38, 49, 81, 105, 145
C 52 to C 56, C 60	25–7	–
C 66	26	LIS 97, 98, 109, 121, 122, 133, 134, 141, 157, 164, 167, 187, 193

ED 112	152	LIS 111
ED 113, ED 114	150	LIS 111
ED 115	151	LIS 111
ED 119	151–2	LIS 111
ED 120	149	LIS 111
ED 126	150	LIS 111
ED 132	147	LIS 111
ED 133	147, 150	LIS 111
ED 137	150	LIS 111
ED 139	149	LIS 111
ED 147	149	–
ED 151	149	–
ED 152	149, 152	–
ED 153, ED 154	149	–
ED 155, ED 160	150	–
ED 161, ED 162	149	–
ED 166, ED 167, ED 168 ED 169	150	–
ED 172	148	–
ED 174	151	–
F 3 to F 17, F 22, F 23 F 30, F 37	167	–
FS 1 to FS 23	178	–
HCA 1 et passim	80	LIS 27, 45, 46, 93, 112, 183, 184, 194
HLG 1	128–9, 136	–
HLG 2	136	–
HLG 4 to HLG 6, HLG 8, HLG 11 to 21, HLG 23, HLG 24	137	–
HLG 25	136	–
HLG 26, HLG 27, HLG 30	137	–
HLG 31	136	–
HLG 43, HLG 44	137–8	–
HLG 45	136	–
HLG 47 to HLG 49	137	–
HLG 50, HLG 53, HLG 54, HLG 56, HLG 57	136	–
HLG 67, HLG 69, HLG 71, HLG 79, HLG 82, HLG 83	137	–
HLG 84, HLG 90 to HLG 92	136	–
HLG 96	137	–
HLG 107, HLG 113, HLG 115, HLG 116	136	–
HLG 119	137	–
HLG 126	169	–
HO 23, HO 24	158	–
HO 40, HO 41	163	–
HO 42	162, 166	–
HO 43	162–3	–
HO 44	162	–
HO 45	141, 158, 159, 163	LIS 22, 23, 30, 39, 50, 84, 89, 90

Appendix Two
THE DIVISION OF RECORDS AT THE PRO

The following list, which is Crown Copyright and reproduced here by kind permission of the Keeper of Public Records and HM Stationery Office, shows the distribution of record groups between the Kew and Chancery Lane branches of the office. Local historians should note, in particular, the division of the Registrar General's records between the two and that some of the classes listed as being at Chancery Lane (i.e. the census enumerators' books, cf. p. 124) are in fact at the nearby Census Reading Room in Portugal Street. Some of the Chancery Lane classes, including material from several different groups, are stored at a repository at Hayes, Middlesex, and seven days' notice must be given to see such documents. In general, records cannot be consulted at Hayes, although some classes of maps and associated documents from the Tithe Redemption Commission (p. 165), which now form IR 90, IR 93 to IR 97 and IR 102 to IR 110 (all inclusive), may be inspected there by appointment. As far as possible, classes kept at Hayes are those for which there is little demand from readers, but it is worth noting that they include some modern judicial material of possible local interest as well as the original (as opposed to the registered copy) wills of the Prerogative Court of Canterbury (p. 81). Because storage arrangements fluctuate, the PRO felt that it would not be helpful to print details of classes at Hayes here; such lists are displayed in the search-rooms at Chancery Lane.

Records at Kew

Admiralty	(ADM)	Cabinet Office	(CAB)
Advisory Conciliation &		Captured Enemy	
Arbitration Service	(CW)	Documents	(GFM)
Agriculture, Fisheries & Food,		Central Midwives Board	(DV)
Ministry of	(MAF)	Certification Office for Trades	
Aircraft and Shipbuilding		Unions and Employers	
Industries Arbitration		Associations	(CL)
Tribunal	(BS 11)	Channel Tunnel Advisory	
Air Ministry	(AIR)	Groups	(BS 1)
Aviation, Ministry of	(AVIA)	Civil Aviation Authority	(DR)
		Civil Service Commission	(CSC)
British Council	(BW)	Civil Service Department	(BA)
British Railways Board	(AN)	Civil Service Pay, Committee	
British Transport Docks		on	(BS 15)
Board	(BR)	Civil Service Pay Research	
British Transport Historical	(RAIL)	Unit	(CSPR)
Records	(ZLIB)	Coal Industry Social Welfare	
	(ZPER)	Organisation	(BX)
	(ZSPC)	Colonial Office	(CO)

Commonwealth Relations
Office (DO)
Copyright Office (COPY)
Countryside Commission (COU)
Crown Agents for Overseas
Governments and
Administrations (CAOG)
Customs & Excise,
Board of (CUST)

Defence, Ministry of (DEFE)
Development Commission (D)
Distribution of Income and
Wealth, Royal Commission
on (BS 7)

Education & Science,
Department of (ED)
Elizabeth Garett Anderson
Hospital (CF)
Environment, Department of
the (AT)
Environmental Pollution,
Royal Commission on (CY)
Exchequer and Audit
Department (AO)
Export Credits Guarantee
Department (ECG)

Financial Institutions,
Committee to review the
functioning of (BS 9)
Foreign Office (FO)
Forestry Commission (F)
Forfeited Estates,
Commissioners of (FEC)
Friendly Societies, Registry of (FS)

Gambling, Royal Commission
on (BS 3)
General Nursing Council (DT)
General Register Office except
Census Returns (RG 9–RG
10), Non-Parochial
Registers and records (RG
4–RG 8) and certain other
registers and associated
papers (RG 18, 19, 27,
30–37, 43) (RG)
Government Actuary's
Department (ACT)

Health & Social Security,
Department of (BN)
Health, Ministry of (MH)
Health Services Board (BS 8)
Historical Manuscripts
Commission (HMC)
Home Office (except Census
Returns (HO 107)) (HO)
Housing & Local Government,
Ministry of (HLG)
Hudson's Bay Company
Microfilm. Access by
permission of the Company
only (BH)

Information, Central
Office of (INF)
Inland Revenue, Board of
except Estate Duty
Registers (IR 26 and IR 27) (IR)
International Organisations,
records of (DG)
Irish Sailors' & Soldiers' Land
Trust (AP)
Iron and Steel Board (BE)

Labour, Ministry of (LAB)
Land Registry (LAR)
Lands Tribunal (LT)
Law Commission (BC)
Local Government Boundary
Commission for England (AX)
Local Government Boundary
Commission for Wales (DD)
Location of Offices Bureau (AH)
London Gazette (ZJ)
Lord Chancellor's Office (LCO)

Meteorological Office (BJ)
Metropolitan Police Force (MEPO)
Monuments, Ancient &
Historic in Wales and
Monmouthshire, Royal
Commission on (MONW)
Monuments, Historic
(England), Royal
Commission on (AE)
Munitions, Ministry of (MUN)

National Academic Awards,
Council for (DB)
National Assistance Board (AST)

National Coal Board (COAL)
National Debt Office (NDO)
National Dock Labour Board (BK)
National Health Service, Royal
  Commission on (BS 6)
National Incomes
  Commission (NICO)
National Insurance Audit
  Department (NIA)
National Insurance
  Commissioners (CT)
National Ports Council (DK)
National Savings, Department
  for (NSC)
National Service, Ministry
  of (NATS)

Occupational Pensions Board (DM)
Operators' Licensing,
  Committee of enquiry
  into (BS 4)
Ordnance Survey Department (OS)
Ordnance Survey Review
  Committee (BS 13)
Overseas Development,
  Ministry of (OD)

Parliamentary Boundary
  Commission (AF)
Parliamentary Papers (ZHC)
 (ZHL)
Parole Board (BV)
Paymaster General's Office (PMG)
Pensions & National
  Insurance, Ministry of (PIN)
Pensions Appeal Tribunal (BF)
Personal Social Services
  Council (BS 10)
Power, Ministry of (POWE)
Press, Royal Commission on
  the (BS 2)
Price Commission (CX)
Prime Minister's Office (PREM)
Prison Commission (PCOM)
Public Building & Works,
  Ministry of (WORK)
Publich Health Laboratory
  Services Board (DN)
Public Record Office all classes
  (except transcripts (PRO
  31) and certain classes of
  gifts and deposits (PRO
  30))[1] (PRO)

Public Trustee Office (PT)
Public Works Loan Board (PWLB)

Reconstruction, Ministry
  of (RECO)
Remploy Ltd (BM)
Research Institutes (AY)
Royal Fine Art Commission (BP)
Royal Mint (MINT)

Scientific & Industrial
  Research, Department of (DSIR)
Sessional Papers,
  House of Commons, (ZHC)
  House of Lords (ZHL)
Stationery Office (STAT)
Supply, Ministry of (SUPP)

Tithe Redemption
  Commission (TITH)
Trade, Board of (BT)
Transport, Ministry of (MT)
Treasury (T)
Tribunals, Council on (BL)

United Kingdom Atomic
  Energy Authority (AB)
University Grants
  Committee (UGC)

Value Added Tax Tribunals (CV)

Wallace Collection (AR)
War Office (WO)
Welsh Office (BD)

Records at Chancery Lane[2]

Admiralty, High Court of (HCA)
Alienation Office (A)
Assize, Clerks of (ASSI)

Bankruptcy, Court of (B)

Central Criminal Court (CRIM)
Chancery (C)
Chester, Palatinate of (CHES)
Common Pleas, Court of (CP)
County Courts (AK)
Crown Estate
  Commissioners (CRES)

Delegates, Court of   (DEL)
Durham, Palatinate of   (DURH)

Exchequer   (E)
                                          (LR)

General Register Office
   Census Returns (RG 9–RG
   10), Non-Parochial
   Registers and records (RG
   4–RG 8) and certain other
   registers and associated
   papers (RG 18, 19, 27,
   30–37, 43) only   (RG)

Home Office Census Returns
   1841 and 1851 only   (HO 107)

Inland Revenue, Board of
   Estate Duty Registers   (IR 26)
   only   (IR 27)

Judicature, Supreme Court of   (J)
Justices Itinerant   (JUST)

King's Bench, Court of   (KB)
King's Bench Prison   (PRIS)
Lancaster, Duchy of   (DL)
Lancaster, Palatinate of   (PL)
Land Revenue Record
   Office   (LRRO)
Law Officers' Department   (LO)
Lord Chamberlain's
   Department   (LC)

Lord Steward's Office   (LS)

Palace Court   (PALA)
Peveril, Court of the Honour
   of   (PEV)
Prerogative Court of
   Canterbury   (PROB)
Privy Council, Judicial
   Committee of the   (PCAP)
Privy Council Office   (PC)
Privy Purse Office   (PP)
Privy Seal Office   (PSO)
Public Prosecutions, Director
   of   (DPP)
Public Record Office
   (Transcripts) and certain
   classes of gifts and deposits
   (PRO 30)[3]   (PRO 31)

Queen Anne's Bounty   (QAB)

Requests, Court of   (REQ)

Signet Office   (SO)
Special Collections   (SC)
Star Chamber, Court of   (STAC)
State Paper Office   (SP)

Treasury Solicitor   (TS)

Wales, Principality of   (WALE)
Wards & Liveries, Court
   of   (WARD)

---

[1]See footnote 3.
[2]Some classes to be seen at Chancery Lane are housed at Hayes, Middlesex, and notice of several
   working days is required
[3]PRO 30/5, 18–19, 21, 23–26, 28, 34, 38, 41, 44, 47, 49, 50, 53 and 80
   PRO 31/20 is at Kew
   PRO 30/4, 13–15, 62 are no longer held in the Public Record Office

Appendix Three
WATER RECORDS

During the preparation of this book I became aware of a lack of published references on the records of local water undertakings, the predecessors of the regional water authorities. Accordingly, I decided to conduct my own very small scale survey by writing to the ten authorities in England and Wales. The replies of the six who kindly responded to my enquiries are summarised here; no reply was received from Anglian Water, Northumbrian Water, North West Water or South West Water.

Severn Trent Water Authority (Abelson House, 2297 Coventry Road, Sheldon, Birmingham B26 3PU). The authority has recently commissioned a survey and report from Nottingham University, which will advise on what records should be preserved and how. Future policy will be determined in the light of these recommendations. To date, deposits of archival material include the following: Trent River Authority and Lower Trent Division of STWA to Nottingham University; Severn River Authority (English records) to Worcestershire Record Office and (Welsh records) to National Library of Wales; navigation on the Severn to Gloucestershire Record Office; Upper Tame Main Drainage Authority to Birmingham Reference Library. Other deposits will be identified in the forthcoming report. Deposited records may only be consulted with the consent of the authority which, however, would not normally be withheld for *bona fide* research students. More recent records remain in the authority's own custody.

Southern Water (Guildbourne House, Worthing, West Sussex BN11 1LD). The authority has not determined a specific policy with regard to any of its records which may be of interest, but reports, agenda and minutes of board and committee meetings are retained in the committee section. Older material is available for inspection at Guildbourne House during normal office hours, although current reports and minutes are not open. Some minute books belonging to predecessor authorities were at one stage offered to a local authority archive but were declined as they were not felt to be of sufficient importance. Some of these are at the authority's headquarters and others are in divisional offices. They too are open to inspection.

Thames Water (Nugent House, Vastern Road, Reading, Berks RG1 8DB). The authority participates in the industrial archaeology working party set up by the Water Authorities Association in order to formulate a policy for the management of its technological and architectural heritage; Thames Water also encourages the preservation of documents, plans, books and photographs illustrating the history of the water industry and makes them available to interested parties. Some records, particularly those of the Thames Conservancy, are in the Berkshire Record Office. Others are in the safekeeping of the authority.

Wessex Water (Wessex House, Passage Street, Bristol BS2 0JQ). This authority is also interested in conserving archaeological material and is exploring the possibility of a water supply museum for the region. Details of industrial artefacts have been prepared for each of the three divisions. As regards documents and maps, it is the authority's policy to deposit records with the appropriate county archivist in the case of more important material, with other items retained by the authority. Access to the latter is normally possible, either directly or through searches by staff, although very few requests are received.

Yorkshire Water Authority (38 Southgate, Wakefield, W. Yorkshire WF1 1TF). All documents of historical interest are passed to the library, where they are scrutinised and any required for library stock are retained. Others are then passed to county record offices on permanent loan. The authority's library is accessible to the public on request, although some material is confidential.

Welsh Water (Cambrian Way, Brecon, Powys LD3 7HP). Some records have been deposited with county archivists, others are held by the authority either as hard-copy or microform. There is reasonable public access to non-confidential documents.

NOTES TO TEXT

Chapter 1, pp. 9-21

1 W.B. Stephens, *Sources for English Local History,* Cambridge University Press, 1981; P. Riden, *Local History. A Handbook for Beginners,* Batsford, 1983. In view of the extent of recent changes in the field, few, if any, of the textbooks published during the local history boom of the 1960s retain much practical value.

2 See H. Jenkinson, *A Manual of Archive Administration,* Lund Humphries, 1937, for a classic definition of terms; cf. also L.J. Redstone and F.W. Steer, ed., *Local Records. Their Nature and Care,* Bell, 1953, pp. 1-3, and *Guide to the Public Records Part 1. Introductory,* HMSO, 1949, pp. 1-2. Mr A.A.H. Knightbridge has recently pointed out (see note 10) that there appears to be no parliamentary definition of either 'record' or 'archive'.

3 Riden, op.cit., pp. 54-5.

4 R.H. Ellis, 'The Historical Manuscripts Commission 1869-1969', *Journal of the Society of Archivists,* vol. 2, 1960-4, pp. 233-42, and R.H. Ellis and others, 'The Centenary of the Royal Commission on Historical Manuscripts', ibid., vol. 3, 1965-9, pp. 441-69, of which the latter includes an acount of the NRA. HMSO Sectional List 17 is a catalogue of HMC publications.

5 Riden, op.cit., pp. 67-9; 'The Royal Commission on Historical Manuscripts' Companies Index', *Business History,* vol. 26, 1984, p. 80.

6 Stephens, op.cit., pp. 268-96, which has full references to earlier surveys of the field; a useful article which has appeared since his book was last revised is W. Leary, 'The Methodist Archives', *Archives,* vol. 16, 1983-4, pp. 16-27.

7 J. Druker and R. Storey, 'The Modern Records Centre at Warwick and the Local Historian', *The Local Historian,* vol. 12, 1976-7, pp. 394-400; cf. R. & E. Frow and M. Katanka, *The History of British Trade Unionism. A Select Bibliography,* Historical Association, 1969.

8 Dr Stewart Ball, Dept of History, Leicester University, is currently conducting a survey of local Conservative association archives, to be published by the department as *The Conservative Party: A List of National, Regional and Local Records.* The Labour Party Archives (150 Walworth Road, London SE17 1JT) have some records from local parties and also a survey list of material in local repositories. The Liberal Party failed to reply to an enquiry from me concerning their archive policy.

9 Those engaged in this project were also largely responsible for establishing Llafur, a society devoted to the study of Welsh labour history, whose journal (of the same name) carries articles and news about the Miners' Library and its holdings. See also D. Bevan, *Guide to the South Wales Coalfield Archive,* University College, Swansea, 1980.

10 A.A.H. Knightbridge, *Archive Legislation in the United Kingdom,* Society of Archivists, Winchester, 1985; Mr Knightbridge surveyed the same subject more discursively in 'National Archives Policy', *Journal of the Society of Archivists,* vol. 7, 1982-5, pp. 213-223. Cf. P.D.A. Harvey, 'Archives in Britain: Anarchy or Policy?' *American Archivist,* vol. 46, 1983, pp. 22-30.

11 R.B. Pugh, 'Charles Abbot and the Public Records: the first phase', *Bulletin of the Institute of Historical Research,* vol. 39, 1966, pp. 69-85; P. Walne, 'The Record Commissions, 1800-1837', *Journal of the Society of Archivists,* vol. 2, 1960-4, pp. 8-16; E.M. Smith, 'The Tower of London as a Record Office', *Archives,* vol. 14, 1979-80, pp. 3-10; M.M. Condon and E.M. Hallam, 'Government Printing of the Public Records in the Eighteenth Century', *Journal of the Society of Archivists,* vol. 7, 1982-5, pp. 348-88.

12 Ironically, there is no official (or unofficial) history of the PRO or its contents, although both will be included in the new *Current Guide* (cf. p. 20); see, however, the *Guide to the Public Records. Part 1. Introductory,* HMSO 1949, a pamphlet intended as the first instalment of a new guide, although the scheme was not proceeded with; C. Johnson, 'The Public Record Office', in J.C. Davies, ed., *Studies Presented to Sir Hilary Jenkinson, C.B.E., LL.D., F.S.A.,* Oxford University Press, 1957, pp. 178-95; J. Cantwell, 'The 1838 Public Record Office Act and its Aftermath: a new Perspective', *Journal of the Society of Archivists,* vol. 7, 1982-5, pp. 277-86, and idem, 'The Making of the first Deputy Keeper of the Records', *Archives,* vol. 17, 1985-6, pp. 22-37. R.H. Ellis, 'The British Archivist and his Society', *Journal of the Society of Archivists,* vol. 3, 1965-9, pp. 43-8, is an interesting discussion of the outlook of the pre-war office.

13 H.C. Johnson, 'The Public Record Office and its Problems', *Bulletin of the Institute of Historical Research,* vol. 42, 1969, pp. 86-95, surveys the scene at the end of a miserable decade; H.G. Nicholas, 'The Public Records: the Historian, the National Interest and Official Policy', *Journal of the Society of Archivists,* vol. 3, 1965-9, pp. 1-6, is more bland.

14 For another recent view see M.S. Moss, 'Public Record Office: good or bad?', *Journal of the Society of Archivists,* vol. 7, 1982-5, pp. 156-66. Cf. also L. Bell, 'The new Public Record Office at Kew', ibid., vol. 5, 1974-77, pp. 1-7. Publications on modern records of possible interest to local historians include the three handbooks by B. Swann and M. Turnbull, *Records of Interest to Social Scientists 1919 to 1939,* HMSO, 1971-78, and *The Second World War. A Guide to Documents in the Public Record Office,* HMSO, 1972. On modern records generally see M. Roper, 'Public Records and the Policy Process in the Twentieth Century', *Public Adminisration,* vol. 55, 1977, 253-68. The List & Index Society may be contacted by writing to its secretary at the PRO, Kew.

15 Knightbridge, op. cit., provides a concise, authoritative statement of the present position.

16 Sir D. Wilson, 'Public Records: the Wilson Report and the White Paper', *Historical Journal,* vol. 25, 1982, pp. 985-94.

17 For the development of local offices see J.R. Ede, 'The Record Office: Central and Local. 1. Evolution of a Relationship', *Journal of the Society of Archivists,* vol. 5, 1974-77, pp. 207-14, continued in 'II. The Way Ahead', ibid., pp. 491-99; M.F. Bond, 'Record Offices today: facts for Historians', *Bulletin of the Institute of Historical Research,* vol. 30, 1957, pp. 1-16; W.R. Serjeant, 'The Survey of Local Archive Services, 1968', *Journal of the Society of Archivists,* vol. 4, 1970-73, pp. 301-26; F. Hull, 'Towards a National Archives Policy – the Local Scene', ibid., vol. 7, 1982-5, pp. 224-9. Early issues of *Archives* (1949 onwards) contained interesting articles on the establishment of the service in different counties, while the growth of a new profession can be followed through the pages of the *Journal of the Society of Archivists* from 1955. From time to time the view has been stated that record-keeping should be undertaken on a regional rather than county basis: see, e.g., D. Charman, 'On the Need for a new Local Archives Service for

England', *Journal of the Society of Archivists,* vol. 3, 1965-9, pp. 341-7.

18 Knightbridge, op.cit., sets out the statutory provisions, admitting that they generally merely confirmed what local record offices were already doing.

19 For the situation in two of the West Midlands districts see U. Rayska, 'The Archives Section of Birmingham Reference Library', *Archives,* vol. 12, 1975-6, pp. 59-67, and M. Lewis, 'The Walsall Metropolitan Borough Archives Service', ibid., vol. 14, 1979-80, pp. 225-31.

20 R.I. Jack, *Medieval Wales,* Hodder & Stoughton, 1972, pp. 106-9, also discusses the problems of Welsh record keeping.

21 J. Foster and J. Sheppard, *British Archives. A Guide to Archive Resources in the United Kingdom,* Macmillan, 1984. This has been used extensively in later chapters without further references in every case. J. Gibson and P. Peskett, *Record Offices: How to Find Them,* Federation of Family History Societies, 1985, is a useful guide to the main local authority offices and a number of repositories in central London, including sketch maps of town centres. See also T.M. Aldridge, *Directory of Registers and Records,* Fourth Edition, Oyez, Longman, 1984.

22 For Record Commission and PRO publications see *British National Archives* (Government Publications Sectional List No 24), HMSO, periodically revised, together with A. Morton and G. Donaldson, *British National Archives and the Local Historian. A Guide to Official Record Publications,* Historical Association, 1980. The Sectional List does not include List & Index Society publications, which, at the time of writing, number 212. The Society has recently issued a list of volumes arranged by PRO group letters, which makes it much easier to check whether a particular class has a published list.

23 *Guide to the Contents of the Public Record Office,* HMSO, 1963-8. It is impossible to overstate my indebtedness to these volumes, which have generally not been cited in the later references but form the basis of my descriptions of many of the classes at the PRO mentioned here. Also invaluable for local studies (but not, it should be stressed, completely comprehensive) is *Maps and Plans in the Public Record Office. I. British Isles, c.1410-1860,* HMSO, 1967.

24 E.L.C. Mullins, *Texts and Calendars. An Analytical Guide to Serial Publications,* Royal Historical Society, 1958, and *Texts and Calendars II. An Analytical Guide to Serial Publications, 1957-1982,* RHS, 1983. These volumes join those cited in notes 21, 22 and 23 as ones which I assume the reader will use alongside this book without the need for further references.

25 In view of the inevitable similarity between some of the references given here and in the footnotes to Stephens, op.cit., I would prefer this point to be distinctly understood.

26 See J.D. Marshall, 'Local or Regional History – or Both', *The Local Historian,* vol. 12, 1976-7, pp. 3-10, developed more fully in his later article on 'The Study of Local and Regional "Communities": some Problems and Possibilities', *Northern History,* vol. 17, 1981, pp. 203-30; cf. Stephens, op.cit., p. 1.

Chapter 2, pp. 22-50

1 Cf. Chapter 1, pp. 14-16 on the evolution of record keeping and publication, and the works cited in notes 22 and 24 of that chapter.

2 The best way into this formidable subject is probably S.B. Chrimes, *An Introduction to the Administrative History of Medieval England,* Blackwell, Oxford, 1966, which has a full, if slightly out of date, bibliography. Another standard work, whose usefulness extends beyonds the dates in the title, is J.F. Willard, W.A. Morris and W.H. Dunham, ed., *The English Government at Work, 1327-1336*, Medieval Academy of America, Cambridge, Mass., 1940-50.

3   G.R. Elton, *England 1200-1640*, Hodder & Stoughton, 1969, and J.J. Bagley, *Historical Interpretation. Sources of English Medieval History, 1066-1540*, Penguin, Harmondsworth, 1965, also cover this period on somewhat similar lines to this chapter.

4   In addition to the general works cited above, see H.C. Maxwell-Lyte, *Historical Notes on the use of the Great Seal of England*, HMSO, 1926.

5   M.E. Avery, 'The History of the Equitable Jurisdiction of the Chancery before 1460', *Bulletin of the Institute of Historical Research*, vol. 42, 1969, pp. 129-44.

6   W.G. Hoskins, *Fieldwork in Local History*, Faber & Faber, 1967, pp. 48-50.

7   W.J. Jones, 'An Introduction to Petty Bag Proceedings in the Reign of Elizabeth I', *California Law Review*, vol. 51, 1963, pp. 882-905.

8   J.T. Smith, *English Gilds*, Early English Text Society, vol. 11, 1870, prints extensive extracts from this material.

9   D.R. Bates, *A Bibliography of Domesday Book*, Boydell & Brewer, 1986, will henceforth be an indispensable guide to this subject; another of the more durable products of the novocentenary is P. Sawyer, ed., *Domesday Book: A Reassessment*, Edward Arnold, 1985. The publication by Messrs Phillimore of county volumes combining a facsimile of the edition of 1783 with a rather loose translation is now complete; for many counties the translation in the early volumes of the *Victoria County History* is still to be preferred.

10   H.M. Cam, *The Hundred and the Hundred Rolls. An Outline of Local Government in Medieval England*, Methuen, 1930; idem, *Studies in the Hundred Rolls. Some Aspects of Thirteenth-Century Administration*, Oxford University Press, 1921; D.W. Sutherland, *Quo Warranto Proceedings in the Reign of Edward I 1278-1294*, Clarendon Press, Oxford, 1963.

11   By the Pipe Roll Society, for which see Mullins, *Texts and Calendars* (cf. Chapter 1, note 24).

12   List & Index Society 172 is a list of escheators.

13   Two older studies are still useful: H. Hall, *A History of the Customs Revenue in England*, Elliot Stock, 1895, and N.S.B. Gras, *The Early English Customs System. A Documentary Study of the Institutional and Economic History of the Customs from the Thirteenth to the Sixteenth Century*, Harvard University Press, Cambridge, Mass., 1918. Cf. H.S. Cobb, 'The Medieval Royal Customs and their Records', *Journal of the Society of Archivists*, vol. 6, 1979-81, pp. 227-9, and idem, 'Local Port Customs Accounts prior to 1550', ibid., vol. 1, 1955-9, pp. 213-4.

14   J.F. Hadwin, 'The Medieval Lay Subsidies and Economic History', *Economic History Review*, 2nd series, vol. 36, 1983, pp. 200-217, is a good recent survey; J.F. Willard, *Parliamentary Taxes on Personal Property 1290 to 1334. A Study in Medieval English Financial Administration*, Medieval Academy of America, Cambridge, Mass., 1934, and S.K. Mitchell, ed., *Taxation in Medieval England*, Yale University Press, New Haven, Conn., 1951, are two standard older studies; G.L. Harriss, *King, Parliament and Public Finance in Medieval England to 1369*, Clarendon Press, Oxford, 1975, discusses the evolution of taxation. For the major impost of 1334 see R.E. Glasscock, ed., *The Lay Subsidy of 1334*, Oxford University Press for British Academy, 1975; cf. also R. Virgoe, 'The Parliamentary Subsidy of 1450', *Bulletin of the Institute of Historical Research*, vol. 55, 1982, pp. 125-37.

15 C.R. Young, *The Royal Forests of Medieval England,* Leicester University Press, 1979, has a full bibliography of earlier work on this subject. J.C. Cox, *The Royal Forests of England,* Methuen, 1905, has chapters on each district.

16 H. Jenkinson and B. Fermoy, ed., *Select Cases in the Exchequer of Pleas,* Selden Society, vol. 48, 1931.

17 Besides the PRO *Guide* and standard administrative and legal histories see two good introductions: A. Harding, *The Law Courts of Medieval England,* Allen & Unwin, 1977, and J. Bellamy, *Crime and Public Order in England in the Later Middle Ages,* Routledge, 1973. See also R.B. Pugh, *Imprisonment in Medieval England,* Cambridge University Press, 1968.

18 M. Blatcher, *The Court of King's Bench, 1450-1550. A Study in Self-Help,* Athlone Press, 1978. For pleas from the Curia Regis Rolls see D.M. Stenton, ed., *Pleas before the King or his Justices,* Selden Sociey, vols. 67 (1948), 68 (1949), 83 (1966) and 84 (1967). For King's Bench proceedings see G.O. Sayles, ed., *Select Cases in the Court of King's Bench,* Selden Society, vols. 55 (1936), 57 (1938), 58 (1939), 74 (1955), 76 (1957), 82 (1965) and 88 (1971). See also C. Flower, *Introduction to the Curia Regis Rolls, 1199-1230,* Selden Society, vol. 62, 1943.

19 M. Hastings, *The Court of Common Pleas in Fifteenth-Century England,* Cornell University Press, Ithaca, N.Y., 1947.

20 A.A. Dibben, *Title Deeds 13th-19th Centuries,* Historical Association, 1971, pp. 17-19, provides a simple introduction; see *Texts and Calendars* for details of local editions.

21 D. Crook, *Records of the General Eyre,* HMSO, 1982; idem, 'The Later Eyres', *English Historical Review,* vol. 97, 1982, pp. 241-68; R.B. Pugh, *Itinerant Justices in English History,* University of Exeter, 1967. For eyre and assize rolls in print see Selden Society, vols. 1 (1887), 3 (1889), 30 (1914), 53 (1934), 56 (1937), 59 (1940), 90 (1972-3), 96 (1980) and 97-8 (1981-2). See *Texts and Calendars* for editions published by local societies.

22 G.T. Lapsley, *The County Palatine of Durham. A Study in Constitutional History,* Harvard University Press, New York, 1900, is the classic study; see also J. Scammell, 'The Origin and Limitations of the Liberty of Durham', *English Historical Review,* vol. 81, 1966, pp. 449-73; C.M. Fraser, 'Prerogative and the Bishops of Durham, 1267-1376', ibid., vol. 74, 1959, pp. 467-76.

23 See B.E. Harris, ed., *The History of the County Palatine of Chester: A Short Bibliography and Guide to Sources,* Cheshire Community Council, 1983. The main modern study is G. Barraclough, *The Earldom and County Palatine of Chester,* Oxford University Press, 1953; cf. also P.H.W. Booth, *The Financial Administration of the Lordship and County of Chester, 1272-1377,* Chetham Society, 3rd series, vol. 28, 1981; I am indebted to Mr Booth for these references.

24 R. Somerville, 'The Duchy of Lancaster Records', *Transactions of the Royal Historical Society,* 4th series, vol. 29, 1947, pp. 1-17; idem, 'The Duchy of Lancaster Council and Court of Duchy Chamber', ibid., vol. 23, 1941, pp. 159-77; both were preliminary to Sir Robert's major study, *History of the Duchy of Lancaster,* Vol. I, Duchy of Lancaster, 1953. No further volume appeared but see his more recent work, *Office-Holders in the Duchy and County Palatine of Lancaster from 1603,* Phillimore, Chichester, 1972, which consists of rather more than mere lists.

25 R.I. Jack, *Medieval Wales,* Hodder & Stoughton, 1972, p. 61n.

26 The following is based on R.I. Jack's full-scale study cited in the previous note.

27 H.M. Jewell, *English Local Administration in the Middle Ages,* David &

Charles, Newton Abbot, 1972, provides a reasonable introduction, with short bibliography. See also Willard, Morris and Dunham, op. cit., especially Vol. III, and Cam, op. cit.

28 Besides the works cited in the previous note see R.C. Palmer, *The County Courts of Medieval England 1150-1350,* Princeton University Press, New Jersey, 1982; R.F. Hunnisett, *The Medieval Coroner,* Cambridge University Press, 1961; and the works cited in note 13 on the customs; there is no full-length study of the escheator. For an early study of the sheriff see W.A. Morris, *The Medieval English Sheriff to 1300,* Manchester University Press, 1927.

29 A. Harding, 'The Origins and Early History of the Keeper of the Peace', *Transactions of the Royal Historical Society,* 5th series, vol. 10, 1960, pp. 85-109; B.H. Putnam, 'The Transformation of the Keepers of the Peace into the Justices of the Peace, 1327-80', ibid., 4th series, vol. 12, 1929, pp. 19-48; idem, *Proceedings before the Justices of the Peace in the Fourteenth and Fifteenth Centuries. Edward III to Richard III,* Spottiswoode, Ballantyne, 1938; J.B. Post, 'Some Limitations of the Medieval Peace Rolls', *Journal of the Society of Archivists,* vol. 4, 1970-73, pp. 633-45. Cf. Hunnisett, op.cit., for medieval coroners' records.

30 S. Reynolds, *An Introduction to the History of English Medieval Towns,* Clarendon, Oxford, 1975, and C. Platt, *The English Medieval Town,* Secker & Warburg, 1976, are both useful introductory works.

31 A. Ballard, *British Borough Charters, 1042-1216,* Cambridge University Press, 1913; idem and J. Tait, *British Borough Charters, 1216-1307,* Cambridge University Press, 1923; and M. Weinbaum, *British Borough Charters, 1307-1660,* Cambridge University Press, 1943, are the standard lists.

32 Cf. G.H. Martin, 'The Origins of Borough Records', *Journal of the Society of Archivists,* vol. 2, 1960-64, pp. 147-53; idem, 'The English Borough in the Thirteenth Century', *Transactions of the Royal Historical Society,* 5th series, vol. 13, 1963, pp. 123-44; D. Postles, 'Record-Keeping in the Medieval Borough: Proof of Wills', *Archives,* vol. 16, 1983-4, pp. 12-15.

33 H.F. Westlake, *The Parish Gilds of Medieval England,* SPCK, 1919; K.L. Wood-Legh, *Perpetual Chantries in Britain,* Cambridge University Press, 1965; C. Gross, *The Gild Merchant. A Contribution to British Municipal History,* Clarendon Press, Oxford, 1890; S. Kramer, *The English Craft Gilds. Studies in their Progress and Decline,* Columbia University Press, New York, 1927.

34 P.D.A. Harvey, *Manorial Records,* British Records Association, 1984, is a full and up-to-date survey, with a bibliography of published examples. It forms the basis of the following section.

35 Dibben, op. cit., is a good introduction but a more detailed study would be useful; for the BL collections see M.A.E. Nickson, *The British Library. Guide to the Catalogues and Indexes of the Department of Manuscripts,* British Library, 1978, and *Index of Manuscripts in the British Library,* Chadwyck-Healey, Cambridge, 1984-6. For a case-study see J. Blair and P. Riden, 'Computer-assisted Analysis of Medieval Deeds', *Archives,* vol. 15, 1981-2, pp. 195-208.

36 P.H. Sawyer, *Anglo-Saxon Charters. An Annotated List and Bibliography,* Royal Historical Society, 1968. Prof. Sawyer is also editing the British Academy's series of volumes on each collection of charters.

37 Dibben, op.cit.; B. English and J. Saville, *Strict Settlement. A Guide for Historians,* University of Hull Press, 1983, provides a clear explanation of the complexities of an institution which accounts in part for the obscurities of conveyancing in this period.

38 C. Drew, *Early Parochial Organisation in England. The Origins of the Office of Churchwarden,* Borthwick Institute of Historical Research, York, 1954; cf. also note 22 to Chapter 4.

39 D.M. Owen, *The Records of the Established Church in England excluding Parochial Records,* British Records Association, 1970, remains the standard guide. See also C.R. Cheney, *English Bishops' Chanceries, 1100-1250,* Manchester University Press, 1950.

40 D.M. Smith, *Guide to Bishops' Registers of England and Wales: a Survey from the Middle Ages to the Abolition of Episcopacy in 1646,* Royal Historical Society, 1981.

41 See Chapter 3, pp. 80-83, and notes 40 and 41. The Lambeth Palace wills are indexed in J.C.C. Smith, *Index of Wills recorded in the Archiepiscopal Registers at Lambeth Palace,* Privately Published, 1919. For the early history of the courts of the southern province see N. Adams and C. Donahue, ed., *Select Cases from the Ecclesiastical Courts of the Province of Canterbury, c.1200-1301,* Selden Society, vol. 95, 1978-9; B.L. Woodcock, *Medieval Ecclesiastical Courts in the Diocese of Canterbury,* Oxford University Press, 1952; and M.M. Sheehan, *The Will in Medieval England from the Conversion of the Anglo-Saxons to the end of the Thirteenth Century,* Institute of Pontifical Studies, Toronto, 1963.

42 Besides Owen, op. cit., see S. Bond, 'Chapter Act Books', *History,* vol. 54, 1969, pp. 406-9.

43 D. Knowles and R.N. Hadcock, *Medieval Religious Houses, England and Wales,* 2nd edition, Longman, 1971; G.R.C. Davis, *Medieval Cartularies of Great Britain. A Short Catalogue,* Longman, 1958. See also D. Knowles, C.N.L. Brooke and V.C.M. London, ed., *The Heads of Religious Houses, England and Wales, 940-1216,* Cambridge University Press, 1972. For *VCH* see Riden, *Handbook,* pp. 20-21, or Stephens, *Sources,* pp. 10-11.

Chapter 3, pp. 51-83

1 G.R. Elton, *Reform and Revolution. England 1509-1558,* Edward Arnold, 1977, includes a full bibliography for the period, including Elton's seminal work and subsequent discussion. See also P.H. Williams, *The Tudor Regime,* Clarendon Press, Oxford, 1979.

2 In this chapter I have followed in general the plan laid out by G.E. Aylmer in the opening chapters of his two books on seventeenth-century government, *The King's Servants. The Civil Service of Charles I. 1625-1642,* 2nd edition, Routledge, 1974, and *The State's Servants. The Civil Service of the English Republic 1649-1660,* Routledge, 1973. K. Powell and C. Cook, *English Historical Facts 1485-1603,* Macmillan, 1977, also provides a convenient overview of this period.

3 This and following paragraphs are based on J. Otway-Ruthven, *The King's Secretary and Signet Office in the XV Century,* Cambridge University Press, 1939; F.M.G. Evans, *The Principal Secretary of State. A Survey of the Office from 1558 to 1680,* Manchester University Press, 1923; M.A. Thomson, *The Secretaries of State 1681-1782,* Clarendon Press, Oxford, 1932.

4 E.R. Turner, *The Privy Council of England in the Sixteenth and Seventeenth Centuries 1603-1784,* Johns Hopkins Press, Baltimore 1927, remains the fullest study of the period as a whole. Cf. D.E. Hoak, *The King's Council in the Reign of Edward VI,* Cambridge University Press, 1976, for a more recent view. See also E.R. Adair, *The Sources for the History of the Council in the Sixteenth and Seventeenth Centures,* SPCK, 1924.

5 P.H. Williams, *The Council in the Marches of Wales under Elizabeth I,* University of Wales Press, Cardiff, 1958; idem, 'The Activities of the Council in the Marches under the Early Stuarts', *Welsh History Review,* vol. 1, 1960-3, pp. 133-60; R.R. Reid, *The King's Council in the North,* Longman, 1921; F.W. Brooks, *The Council of the North,* Historical Association, revised edition, 1966; J. Youings, 'The Council of the West', *Transactions of the Royal Historical Society,* 5th series, vol. 10, 1960, pp. 41-59. For a published volume of records see R. Flenley, ed., *A Calendar of the Register of the Queen's Majesty's Council in the Dominions and Principality of Wales and the Marches of the Same* [*1535*] *1569-1591,* Cymmrodorion Society, 1916.

6 See in general for this section, F.C. Dietz, *English Government Finance 1485-1558,* Reprinted, Cass, 1964; idem, *English Public Finance 1558-1641,* Reprinted, Cass, 1964; W.C. Richardson, *Tudor Chamber Administration 1485-1547,* Louisiana State University Press, Baton Rouge, 1952.

7 For the Treasury itself see H. Roseveare, *The Treasury. The Evolution of a British Institution,* Allen Lane The Penguin Press, 1969; S.B. Baxter, *The Development of the Treasury, 1660-1702,* Longman, 1957; and (with examples of documents) Roseveare's more recent work, *The Treasury 1660-1870. The Foundations of Control,* Allen & Unwin, 1973. For the wider history of public finance see C.D. Chandaman, *The English Public Revenue 1660-1688,* Clarendon Press, Oxford, 1975, and J.E.D. Binney, *British Public Finance and Administration 1774-92,* Clarendon Press, Oxford, 1958, of which the latter has a usefulness that extends well beyond the dates in the title. Roseveare, Baxter and Chandaman all discuss the value of W.A. Shaw's introductions to his monumental *Calendar of Treasury Books,* for which see Sectional List 24.

8 PRO, *Descriptive List of Exchequer, Queen's Remembrancer, Port Books. Part 1. 1565 to 1700* (n.d.). D.M. Woodward, 'Port Books', *History,* vol. 58, 1970, pp. 207-10, cites the other principal references on this source.

9 See Chapter 6, p. 170, and note 14.

10 I have recently demonstrated this in 'An English Factor at Stockholm in the 1680's, *Scandinavian Economic History Review,* vol. 35, 1987, making use of the unusual survival of a merchant's own accounts.

11 See R.S. Schofield, 'The Geographical Distribution of Wealth in England, 1334-1649', *Economic History Review,* 2nd series, vol. 18, 1965, pp. 483-510; J. Cornwall, 'English Country Towns in the Fifteen-Twenties', ibid., vol. 15, 1962-3, pp. 52-69; idem, 'The Early Tudor Gentry', ibid., vol. 17, 1964-5, pp. 456-75; idem, 'English Population in the Early Sixteenth Century', ibid., vol. 23, 1970, pp. 32-44. The latter also discusses the muster returns of 1522, as does another article by Cornwall, 'A Tudor Domesday. The Musters of 1522', *Journal of of the Society of Archivists,* vol. 3, 1965-9, pp. 19-24. For a comparison of 1523 and 1543 in a northern county see P. Riden, *Tudor and Stuart Chesterfield,* Chesterfield Borough Council, 1984, pp. 92; for Wales see W.R.B. Robinson, 'The First Subsidy Assessment of the Hundreds of Swansea and Llangyfelach, 1543', *Welsh History Review,* vol. 2, 1964-5, pp. 125-45, and M. Griffiths, 'The Vale of Glamorgan in the 1543 Lay Subsidy Returns', *Bulletin of the Board of Celtic Studies,* vol. 29, 1980-2, pp. 709-48. For later subsidies see S.A. Peyton, 'The Village Population in the Tudor Lay Subsidy Rolls', *English Historical Review,* vol. 30, 1915, pp. 234-50.

12 M.D. Gordon, 'The Collection of Ship-Money in the reign of Charles I', *Transactions of the Royal Historical Society,* 3rd series, vol. 4, 1910, pp. 141-62; R.J.W. Swales, 'The Ship Money Levy of 1628', *Bulletin of the Institute of Historical Research,* vol. 50, 1977, pp. 164-76. For the Excise see E. Hughes, *Studies in Administration and Finance 1558-1825 with special reference to the History of Salt Taxation in England,* Manchester University Press, 1934, pp. 116-66, and Chandaman, op.cit., pp. 37-76; cf. generally, M. Ashley,

Financial and Commercial Policy under the Cromwellian Protectorate, 2nd edition, Cass, 1962.

13 J.S.W. Gibson, *The Hearth Tax and other Later Stuart Tax Lists and the Association Oath Rolls,* Federation of Family History Societies, 1985, surveys all the 1660-88 material; for the tax of 1695 see D.V. Glass, 'Introduction', in *London Inhabitants within the Walls 1695,* London Record Society, vol. 2, 1966; cf. also P.E. Jones, 'Local Assessments for Parliamentary Taxes', *Journal of the Society of Archivists,* vol. 4, 1970-3, pp. 55-9.

14 Chandaman, op.cit., pp. 77-109; L.M. Marshall, 'The levying of the Hearth Tax, 1662-88', *English Historical Review,* vol. 51, 1936, pp. 628-46; R. Howell, 'Hearth Tax Records', *History,* vol. 49, 1964, pp. 42-5; Gibson, op.cit., in note 13 lists the documents in central and local custody and includes a note of published texts; see most recently C.A.F. Meekings, S. Porter and I. Roy, ed., *The Hearth Tax Collectors' Book for Worcester 1678-1680,* Worcestershire Historical Society, new series, vol. 11, 1983.

15 W.R. Ward, *The English Land Tax in the Eighteenth Century,* Oxford University Press, 1953, is the standard administrative history; cf. J.V. Beckett, 'Land Tax or Excise: the Levying of Taxation in Seventeenth- and Eighteenth-Century England', *English Historical Review,* vol. 100, 1985, pp. 285-308.

16 J.S.W. Gibson and D.R. Mills, *Land Tax Assessments c.1690-c.1950,* Federation of Family History Societies, 1983, provides a full list with introductory notes; H.G. Hunt, 'Land Tax Assessments', *History,* vol. 52, 1967, pp. 283-6, includes references to earlier work on this difficult source, beginning with E. Davies, 'The Small Landowner, 1780-1832, in the Light of the Land Tax Assessments', *Economic History Review,* vol. 1, 1927-8, pp. 87-113. See also G.E. Mingay 'The Land Tax Assessments and the Small Landowner', ibid., 2nd series, vol. 17, 1964-5, pp. 381-88, and J.M. Martin, 'Landownership and the Land Tax Returns', *Agricultural History Review,* vol. 14, 1966, pp. 96-103.

17 See note 7 for standard authorities; cf. also W.R. Ward, 'The Administration of the Window and Assessed Taxes, 1696-1798', *English Historical Review,* vol. 67, 1952, pp. 522-42. A. Hope-Jones, *Income Tax in the Napoleonic Wars,* Cambridge University Press, 1939, describes surviving records on pp. 1-4, 126-8; B.E.V. Sabine, *A History of Income Tax,* Allen & Unwin, 1966, revises some of Hope-Jones's judgments; see also A.D. Harvey, 'The Regional Distribution of Incomes in England and Wales, 1803', *The Local Historian,* vol. 14, 1978-9, pp. 332-7. For the tax on shops see I. Mitchell, 'Pitt's Shop Tax in the History of Retailing', *The Local Historian,* vol. 14, 1980-1, pp. 348-51.

18 W.C. Richardson, *History of the Court of Augmentations 1536-1554,* Louisiana State University, Baton Rouge, 1961, is a comprehensive history, which includes (Chapter 14) an account of the court's records. For a more recent survey see C. Kitching, 'The Disposal of Monastic and Chantry Lands', in F. Heal and R. O'Day, ed., *Church and Society in England: Henry VIII to James I,* Macmillan, 1977, pp. 119-36. For Welsh material see E.A. Lewis and J.C. Davies, ed., *Records of the Court of Augmentations relating to Wales and Monmouthshire,* University of Wales Press, Cardiff, 1954.

19 L.S. Snell, 'Chantry Certificates', *History,* vol. 48, 1964, pp. 332-5.

20 S.C. Newton, 'Parliamentary Surveys', *History,* vol. 53, 1968, pp. 51-4.

21 G.F.A. Best, *Temporal Pillars. Queen Anne's Bounty, the Ecclesiastical Commissioners, and the Church of England,* Cambridge University Press, 1964, is a comprehensive administrative history with full bibliography.

22 H.E. Bell, *An Introduction to the History and Records of the Court of Wards &*

Liveries, Cambridge University Press, 1953; J. Hurstfield, *The Queen's Wards. Wardship and Marriage under Elizabeth I,* Longman, 1958.

23 A.A. Dibben, *Title Deeds 13th-19th Centuries,* Historical Association, 1971, pp. 17-21.

24 J.S.Cockburn, *A History of English Assizes 1558-1714,* Cambridge University Press, 1972, forms the basis of this section; cf. also his article 'Early-Modern Assize Records as Historical Evidence', *Journal of the Society of Archivists,* vol. 5, 1974-7, pp. 215-31. See Sectional List 24 for details of the calendars.

25 W. Ll. Williams, 'The King's Court of Great Sessions in Wales', *Y Cymmrodor,* vol. 26, 1916, pp. 1-87; W.R. Williams, *The History of the Great Sessions in Wales 1542-1830,* Printed for the Author, Brecknock, 1899; K.O. Fox, 'The Records of the Courts of Great Sessions', *Journal of the Society of Archivists,* vol. 3, 1965-9, pp. 177-82; idem, 'An Edited Calendar of the first Brecknockshire Plea Roll of the Courts of the King's Great Sessions in Wales, July 1542', *National Library of Wales Journal,* vol. 14, 1965-6, pp. 469-84; and E.J. Sherrington, 'The Plea-Rolls of the Courts of Great Sessions 1541-1575', ibid., vol. 13, 1963-4, pp. 363-73.

26 W.J. Jones, *The Elizabethan Court of Chancery,* Clarendon Press, Oxford, 1967, covers this transitional period in great detail; for earlier years see M.E. Avery, 'The History of the Equitable Jurisdiction of the Chancery before 1460', *Bulletin of the Institute of Historical Research,* vol. 42, 1969, pp. 129-44; for the late seventeenth century see D.E.C. Yale, ed., *Lord Nottingham's Chancery Cases,* Selden Society, vol. 73, 1954, and 79, 1961. See also M.W. Beresford, 'The Decree Rolls of Chancery as a Source for Economic History, 1547-c.1700', *Economic History Review,* 2nd series, vol. 32, 1979, pp. 1-10.

27 *Calendars of the Proceedings in Chancery in the Reign of Queen Elizabeth,* Record Commission, 1827-32; W.P. Baildon, ed., *Select Cases in the Court of Chancery (1364-1471),* Selden Society, vol. 10, 1896.

28 See PRO Leaflet 32 for details of these.

29 There is no modern study of this aspect of the Exchequer, although for examples of the records see E.G. Jones, ed., *Exchequer Proceedings (Equity) concerning Wales. Henry VIII-Elizabeth. Abstracts of Bills and Inventory of Further Proceedings,* University of Wales Press, Cardiff, 1939, and T.I.J. Jones, ed., *Exchequer Proceedings concerning Wales in tempore James I. Abstracts of Bills and Answers and Inventory of Further Proceedings,* University of Wales Press, Cardiff, 1955.

30 I.S. Leadam, ed., *Select Cases in the Court of Requests (1497-1569),* Selden Society, vol. 12, 1898; there is no modern history of the court.

31 C.L. Scofield, *A Study of the Court of Star Chamber largely based on Manuscripts in the British Museum and the Public Record Office,* Chicago University Press, 1900, is an old account; J.A. Guy, *The Cardinal's Court. The Impact of Thomas Wolsey in Star Chamber,* Harvester Press, Hassocks, 1977, is a more recent study of part of the period. See also T.G. Barnes, 'The Archives and Archival Problems of the Elizabethan and Early Stuart Star Chamber', in F. Ranger, ed., *Prisca Munimenta. Studies in Archival and Administrative History presented to Dr A.E.J. Hollaender,* University of London Press, 1973, pp. 130-49. Barnes also edited the *List and Index to the Proceedings in Star Chamber for the Reign of James I (1603-1625) in the Public Record Office, London. Class STAC8,* American Bar Foundation, Chicago, 1975; J.A. Guy has recently described the earlier records in *The Court of Star Chamber and its Records to the Reign of Elizabeth I,* HMSO, 1985. For Wales see I. ab O. Edwards, ed., *A Catalogue of Star Chamber Proceedings relating to Wales,* University of Wales Press, Cardiff, 1929.

32 *Ducatus Lancastriae,* Record Commission, 1823-34.

33 Cf. *The Complete Peerage,* revised edition, St Catherine's Press, 1910-59, vol. 4, pp. 761-7 for the origin of the honour.

34 G.R. Lewis, *The Stannaries. A Study of the English Tin Mines,* Harvard University Press, Cambridge, Mass, 1924; M. Coate, 'The Duchy of Cornwall: its History and Administration 1640 to 1660', *Transactions of the Royal Historical Society,* 4th series, vol. 10, 1927, pp. 135-69.

35 There is no modern study of either the Low Peak court, which still sits, or others which no longer sit but are presumably still in existence; see, however, R.A.H. O'Neal, *Derbyshire Lead and Lead Mining. A Bibliography,* Derbyshire County Library, Matlock, 1960. The records at Chatsworth are accessible (cf. *British Archives,* No 28) and a list, at present in manuscript, has been compiled by R.B. Flindall of the Peak District Mines Historical Society.

36 G.D. Squibb, *The High Court of Chivalry. A Study of the Civil Law in England,* Clarendon Press, Oxford, 1959; cf. A.R. Wagner, *Records and Collections of the College of Arms,* Burke's Peerage, 1974, and G.D. Squibb, *Visitation Pedigrees and the Genealogist,* Pinhorn, 1978.

37 R.G. Marsden, ed., *Select Pleas in the Court of Admiralty,* Selden Society, vol. 6, 1892, and 11, 1897; there is no modern history.

38 G.I.O. Duncan, *The High Court of Delegates,* Cambridge University Press, 1971; P.A. Howell, *The Judicial Committee of the Privy Council 1833-1876. Origins, Structure and Development,* Cambridge University Press, 1979.

39 R.G. Usher, *The Rise and Fall of the High Commission,* 2nd edition with Introduction by P. Tyler, Clarendon Press, Oxford 1968 (the introduction contains important references bringing up-to-date what is otherwise still the standard work). There is no comparable history of the Court of Arches but see M.D. Slatter, 'The Records of the Court of Arches', *Journal of Ecclesiastical History,* vol. 4, 1953, pp. 139-53; idem, 'The Study of the Records of the Court of Arches', *Journal of the Society of Archivists,* vol. 2, 1960-64, pp. 29-31; and J. Houston, ed., *Index of Cases in the Records of the Court of Arches at Lambeth Palace Library,* Index Library, vol. 85, 1972.

40 J. Cox, *The Records of the Prerogative Court of Canterbury and the Death Duty Registers,* PRO, 1980; C.J. Kitching, 'Probate during the Civil War and Interregnum. Part I: The Survival of the Prerogative Court in the 1640's', *Journal of the Society of Archivists,* vol. 5, 1974-77, pp. 283-93, and 'Part II: The Court for Probate, 1653-1660', ibid., pp. 346-56; cf. also Dr Kitching's note on 'The Probate Jurisdiction of Thomas Cromwell as Vicegerent', *Bulletin of the Institute of Historical Research,* vol. 46, 1973, pp. 102-6. For the inventories see J.S.W. Gibson, 'Inventories in the Records of the Prerogative Court of Canterbury', *The Local Historian,* vol. 14, 1980-1, pp. 222-225.

41 See D.M. Smith, *A Guide to the Archive Collections in the Borthwick Institute of Historical Research,* BIHR, York, 1973, and idem, *Supplemental Guide,* 1980; cf. also C.C. Webb, *A Guide to Genealogical Sources in the Borthwick Institute of Historical Research,* BIHR, 1981. The Institute has an extensive range of published calendars, texts and other studies based on its collections. See note 38 to Chapter 4 for guides to probate records generally.

Chapter 4, pp. 84-108

1 Sidney and Beatrice Webb, *English Local Government from the Revolution to the Municipal Corporations Act,* 9 volumes, Longman, 1906-29, reprinted Cass, 1963. Individual volumes are as follows: 1: *The Parish and the County* (1906); 2 & 3: *The Manor and the Borough* (1908); 4: *Statutory Authorities for Special Purposes with a Summary of the Development of the Local Government Structure*

(1922); 5: *The Story of the King's Highway* (1913); 6: *English Prisons under Local Government* (1922); 7: *English Poor Law History, Part 1: The Old Poor Law* (1927); 8 & 9: *English Poor Law History, Part 2: The Last Hundred Years* (1929). The 1963 reprint included (as Volumes 10 and 11) two other works by the Webbs which were not in the original series: *English Poor Law Policy* (1910) and *The History of Liquor Licensing in England principally from 1700 to 1830* (1903). A good short introduction to the later part of this period is B. Keith-Lucas, *The Unreformed Local Government System*, Croom Helm, 1980.

2 F.G. Emmison and I. Gray, *County Records (Quarter Sessions, Petty Sessions, Clerk of the Peace and Lieutenancy)*, Historical Association, revised edition, 1973; PRO, *Lists and Indexes*, 9, corrected reprint, Kraus, New York, 1963; T.E. Hartley, 'Under-sheriffs and bailiffs in some English shrievalties, c.1580 to c.1625', *Bulletin of the Institute of Historical Research*, vol. 47, 1974, pp. 164-85; C.H. Karraker, *The seventeenth-century Sheriff. A Comparative Study of the Sheriff in England and the Chesapeake Colonies 1607-1689*, University of N. Carolina Press, Philadelphia, 1930.

3 Emmison and Gray, op.cit., p. 17; G.S. Thomson, *Lords Lieutenants in the Sixteenth Century: a Study in Tudor Local Administration*, Longman, 1923; idem, 'The origin and growth of the office of deputy-lieutenant', *Transactions of the Royal Historical Society*, 4th series, vol. 5, 1922, pp. 150-66; J.C. Sainty, *Lieutenants of Counties, 1585-1642*, Bulletin of the Institute of Historical Research, Special Supplement, No 8, 1970; idem, *List of Lieutenants of Counties of England and Wales 1660-1974*, List & Index Society, Special Series, vol. 12, 1979. For the militia see L. Boynton, *The Elizabethan Militia 1558-1638*, Routledge, 1967, and J.R. Western, *The English Militia in the Eighteenth Century. The Story of a Political Issue*, Routledge, 1965.

4 The best general modern study is probably E. Moir, *The Justice of the Peace*, Penguin, Harmondsworth, 1969; cf. also B. Osborne, *Justices of the Peace 1361-1848. A History of the Justices of the Peace for the Counties of England*, Sedgehill Press, Shaftesbury, 1960; C.A. Beard, *The Office of Justice of the Peace in England in its Origin and Development*, Columbia University Press, New York, 1904; J.H. Gleason, *The Justices of the Peace in England 1558 to 1640. A Later Eirenarcha*, Clarendon Press, Oxford, 1969; T.G. Barnes and A.H. Smith, 'Justices of the Peace from 1558 to 1688 – a Revised List of Sources', *Bulletin of the Institute of Historical Research*, vol. 32, 1959, pp. 22-42; L.K.J. Glassey and N. Landau, 'The Commission of the Peace in the Eighteenth Century: a new Source', ibid., vol. 45, 1972, pp. 247-65. See also Sir E. Stephens, *The Clerks of the Counties 1360-1960*, Society of Clerks of the Peace of Counties and of Clerks of County Councils, Warwick, 1961, and T.G. Barnes, *The Clerk of the Peace in Caroline Somerset*, Leicester University Press, 1961. For the justices' activities in individual counties see Moir, op. cit. Especially useful studies include T.G. Barnes, *Somerset 1625-1640. A County's Government during the 'Personal Rule'*, Oxford University Press, 1961; E.G. Dowdell, *A Hundred Years of Quarter Sessions. The Government of Middlesex from 1660 to 1760*, Cambridge University Press, 1932; and a pioneer study, which covers other aspects of local administration, W.B. Willcox, *Gloucestershire. A Study in Local Government 1590-1640*, Yale University Press, New Haven, 1940.

5 Keith-Lucas, op.cit., pp. 40-2; V.D. Lipman, *Local Government Areas 1834-1945*, Basil Blackwell, Oxford, 1949, pp. 6-16; Moir, op.cit., pp. 167-81.

6 R.C.K. Ensor, 'The Supersession of County Government', *Politica*, vol. 1, 1934-5, pp. 425-42; J.P.D. Dunbabin, 'The Politics of the Establishment of

County Councils', *Historical Journal,* vol. 6, 1963, pp. 226-52; idem, 'Expectations of the new County Councils, and their Realization', *Historical Journal,* vol. 8, 1965, pp. 353-79.

7   The following is based mainly on Emmison and Gray, op.cit., which includes a list of published calendars. See also J.S.W. Gibson, *Quarter Sessions Records for Family Historians: a Select List,* Federation of Family History Societies, 2nd edition, 1983.

8   R. Hunt, 'Quarter Sessions Order Books', *History,* vol. 55, 1970, pp. 397-400; on the Statute of Artificers (1563) specifically see W.E. Minchinton, ed., *Wage Regulation in Pre-Industrial England,* David & Charles, Newton Abbot, 1972, which has a critical introduction and bibliography; M.G. Davies, *The Enforcement of English Apprenticeship. A Study in Applied Mercantilism 1563-1642,* Harvard University Press, Cambridge, Mass, 1956; and, most recently, D. Woodward, 'The Background to the Statute of Artificers: the Genesis of Labour Policy, 1558-63', *Economic History Review,* 2nd series, vol. 33, 1980, pp. 32-44. For price regulation see T.S. Willan, 'The Justices of the Peace and the Rates of Land Carriage, 1692-1827', *Journal of Transport History,* vol. 5, 1962, pp. 197-204.

9   S. and B. Webb, *The Story of the King's Highway* (see note 1).

10   Idem, *English Prisons under Local Government.*

11   Cf. J.A. Chartres, *Internal Trade in England 1500-1700,* Macmillan, 1977, and D. Hey, Packmen, *Carriers and Packhorse Roads. Trade and Communications in North Derbyshire and South Yorkshire,* Leicester University Press, 1980, pp. 178-86.

12   See in general, J.B. Harley, *Maps for the Local Historian. A Guide to the British Sources,* Standing Conference for Local History, 1972. On enclosure awards see the following works by M.E. Turner, 'Recent Progress in the Study of Parliamentary Enclosure', *The Local Historian,* vol. 12, 1976-7, pp. 18-25; *A Domesday of English Enclosure Acts and Awards [compiled by] W.E. Tate,* Reading University Library, 1978; *English Parliamentary Enclosure: its Historical Geography and Economic History,* Dawson, 1980; and *Enclosures in Britain 1750-1830,* Macmillan, 1984. Cf. also J. Chapman, 'Some Problems in the Interpretation of Enclosure Awards', *Agricultural History Review,* vol. 26 (1978), pp. 108-114. On deposited plans see H.S. Cobb, 'Parliamentary Records relating to Internal Navigation', *Archives,* vol. 9, 1969-70, pp. 73-9.

13   F. Sheppard and V. Belcher, 'The Deeds Registries of Yorkshire and Middlesex', *Journal of the Society of Archivists,* vol. 6 (1978-81), pp. 274-86; I. Darlington, 'The Registration of Land in England and Wales and its effect on Conveyancing Records', ibid., vol. 1, 1955-9, pp. 224-6.

14   Moir, op.cit., p. 46; Keith-Lucas op.cit., pp. 47-8, 141-2; cf. note 18.

15   A.E.B. Owen, 'Records of Commissions of Sewers', *History,* vol. 52, 1967, pp. 35-8; idem, 'Land Drainage Authorities and their Records', *Journal of the Society of Archivists,* vol. 2, 1960-64, pp. 417-23.

16   J. Mather, 'The Parliamentary Committee and the Justices of the Peace, 1642-1661', *American Journal of Legal History,* vol. 23, 1979, pp. 120-43; among local studies an outstanding recent contribution, which deals with administration at all levels and takes the story across the divide of 1660, is S.K. Roberts, *Recovery and Restoration in an English County: Devon Local Administration, 1646-1670,* Exeter University Press, 1985. See also C.B. Phillips, 'County Committees and Local Government in Cumberland and Westmorland, 1642-1660', *Northern History,* vol. 4, 1969, pp. 34-66, and G.C.F. Forster, 'County Government in Yorkshire during the Interregnum', ibid., vol. 12, 1976, pp. 84-104.

17 For the parish and its records generally see the standard work by W.E. Tate, *The Parish Chest. A Study of the Records of Parochial Administration in England,* 3rd edition, Cambridge University Press, 1969, which forms the basis of the following paragraphs. For a view of parish administration from a nineteenth-century practictioner's standpoint see, e.g., H.J. Hodgson, ed., *Steer's Parish Law; being a Digest of the Law relating to the Civil and Ecclesiastical Government of Parishes; Friendly Societies, etc, etc, and the Relief, Settlement and Removal of the Poor,* 3rd edition, Sweet and Maxwell, 1857.

18 Tate, op.cit., pp. 176-87; H.B. Simpson, 'The Office of Constable', *English Historical Review,* vol. 10, 1895, pp. 625-41. P. Riden, *Tudor and Stuart Chesterfield,* Chesterfield Borough Council, 1984, pp. 201-3, is an instance of constablery boundaries reflecting tenurial, rather than parochial, geography; there are presumably others which I am not aware of.

19 PCCs were provided for in the Church of England Assembly Powers Act, 1919 (9 & 10 Geo. V, c.76), and established under the Parochial Church Councils (Powers) Measure, 1921 (11 & 12 Geo. V, No 1): K.M. Macmorran, *A Handbook for Churchwardens and Church Councillors,* Mowbray, 1921.

20 A.G. Veysey, 'Ecclesiastical Parish Records in Wales', *Journal of the Society of Archivists,* vol. 6 (1978-81), pp. 31-3; R.W. McDonald, 'The Parish Registers of Wales', *National Library of Wales Journal,* vol. 19, 1975-6, pp. 399-429. A fine new union list of Welsh registers has recently been produced: C.J. Williams and J. Watts-Williams, *Cofrestri Plwyf Cymru: Parish Registers of Wales,* National Library of Wales and Welsh County Archivists' Group, Aberystwyth, 1986.

21 The comprehensive bibliography in E.A. Wrigley and R.S. Schofield, *The Population History of England 1541-1871: a Reconstruction,* Edward Arnold, 1981, makes it unnecesary to cite earlier work on this subject. For recent conservation measures see A. Henstock, 'The Nottinghamshire Parish Registers Microfilming Project', *Journal of the Society of Archivists,* vol. 7, 1982-5, pp. 443-9. C.R. Humphery-Smith, *Phillimore Atlas and Index of Parish Registers,* Phillimore, Chichester, 1984, is useful for England but for Wales use the catalogue cited in the previous note.

22 J.C. Cox, *Churchwardens' Accounts from the Fourteenth Century to the Close of the Seventeenth Century,* Methuen, 1913, supplements the section in Tate, op. cit., pp. 84-108.

23 D.M. Barratt, 'Glebe Terriers', *History,* vol. 51, 1966, pp. 35-8.

24 J.D. Marshall, *The Old Poor Law, 1795-1834,* Macmillan, 1968, brings the subect up to date from where the Webbs left it; G.W. Oxley, *Poor Relief in England and Wales 1601-1834,* David & Charles, Newton Abbot, 1974, is a good guide to local sources. See also E.M. Leonard, *The Early History of English Poor Relief,* Cambridge University Press, 1900.

25 E.G. Thomas, 'Pauper Apprenticeship', *The Local Historian,* vol. 14, 1980-1, pp. 400-406.

26 P. Grey, 'Parish Workhouses and Poorhouses', *The Local Historian,* vol. 10, 1972-3, pp. 70-75.

27 M. Weinbaum, *The Incorporation of Boroughs,* Manchester University Press, 1937; idem, *British Borough Charters, 1307-1660,* Cambridge University Press, 1943; S. Bond and N. Evans, 'The Process of granting Charters to English Boroughs, 1547-1649', *English Historical Review,* vol. 91, 1976, pp. 102-20; R. Tittler, 'The Incorporation of Boroughs', *History,* vol. 62, 1977, pp. 24-42; R.H. George, 'The Charters granted to English Parliamentary Corporations in 1688', *English Historical Review,* vol. 55, 1940, pp. 47-56; and J. Miller, 'The Crown and the Borough Charters in the Reign of Charles II', ibid., vol. 100, 1985, pp. 53-84. For particular classes of record mentioned here see D.M. Woodward, 'Freemen's Rolls', *The Local Historian,* vol. 9, 1970-1, pp. 89-95, and C. Phythian-Adams, 'Records of the Craft Gilds', ibid., pp. 267-74.

28 For the background to reform see G.B.A.M. Finlayson, 'The Municipal Corporation Commission and Report', *Bulletin of the Institute of Historical Research,* vol. 36, 1963, pp. 36-52.

29 Besides the Webbs, *Statutory Authorities,* and Keith-Lucas, op.cit., see F.H. Spencer, *Municipal Origins. An Account of English Private Bill Legislation relating to Local Government, 1740-1835; with a Chapter on Private Bill Procedure,* Constable, 1911. J. West, *Town Records,* Phillimore, Chichester, 1983, pp. 173-205, is of some value on this topic, although in other ways unreliable.

30 W. Albert, *The Turnpike Road System in England 1663-1840,* Cambridge University Press, 1972, and E. Pawson, *Transport and Economy: the Turnpike Roads of the Eighteenth Century,* Academic Press, 1977, the two standard modern authorities; both have full bibliographies of local studies and post-Webb general work. See also B.F. Duckham, 'Turnpike Records', *History,* vol. 53, 1968, pp. 217-220, and idem, 'Roads in the Eighteenth Century: a Reassessment?', *The Local Historian,* vol. 15, 1982-3, pp. 338-44.

31 Cf. C. Hadfield, *The Canals of the West Midlands,* David & Charles, Newton Abbot, 1969, p. 23.

32 The standard authority for this period, as for the middle ages, is D.M. Owen, *The Records of the Established Church in England excluding Parochial Records,* British Records Association, 1970, on which the following paragraphs are in general based. Cf. also R.A. Marchant, *The Church under the Law. Justice, Administration and Discipline in the Diocese of York 1560-1640,* Cambridge University Press, 1969. J.S. Purvis, *Tudor Parish Documents of the Diocese of York. A Selection with Introduction & Notes,* Cambridge University Press, 1948, is a useful collection of diocesan records relating to parishes.

33 For registration see D.M. Smith, 'The York Institution Act Books: Diocesan Registration in the Sixteenth Century', *Archives,* vol. 13, 1977-8, pp. 171-9; for some of the other material J.S.W. Gibson, *Bishops Transcripts and Marriage Licences, Bonds and Allegations. A Guide to their Location and Indexes,* Federation of Family History Societies, 1981.

34 D.M. Palliser and L.J. Jones, A Neglected Source for English Population History: the Bishops' Returns of 1563 and 1603', *The Local Historian,* vol. 15, 1982-3, pp. 155-6. Dr E.A.O. Whiteman's edition of the Compton Census of 1676 is about to be published by Oxford University Press for the British Academy.

35 W.R. Powell, 'Sources for the History of Protestant Nonformist Churches in England', *Bulletin of the Institute of Historical Research,* vol. 25, 1952, pp. 213-27; E. Welch, 'The Registration of Meeting Houses', *Journal of the Society of Archivists,* vol. 3, 1965-9, pp. 116-20.

36 D.M. Owen, 'Episcopal Visitation Books', *History,* vol. 49, 1964, pp. 185-8.

37 R. Houlbrooke, *Church Courts and the People during the English Reformation 1520-1570,* Oxford University Press, 1979, is the standard study; cf. also A.M. Erskine, 'Ecclesiastical Courts and their Records in the Province of Canterbury', *Archives,* vol. 3, 1957-8, pp. 8-17; local studies include P. Tyler, 'The Church Courts at York and the Witchcraft Prosecutions 1567-1640', *Northern History,* vol 4, 1969, pp. 84-110, and P. Rushton, 'Women, Witchcraft and Slander in Early Modern England: Cases from the Church Courts of Durham, 1560-1675', op.cit., vol. 18, 1982, pp. 116-32.

38 J.S.W. Gibson, *A Simplified Guide to Probate Jurisdictions: Where to Look for Wills,* Federation of Family History Societies, 3rd edition, 1985, is thorough and up-to-date, superseding the two older books, both of which are in any case out of print: A.J. Camp, *Wills and their Whereabouts,* Phillimore, Chichester, 1963, and Gibson's own *Wills and Where to Find Them,* Phillimore, Chichester, 1974.

39 For a recent general survey see the contributions to P. Riden, ed., *Probate Records and the Local Community,* Alan Sutton, Gloucester, 1985; cf. also M.L. Zell, 'Fifteenth- and Sixteenth-Century Wills as Historical Sources', *Archives,* vol. 14, 1979-80, pp. 67-74.

40 S. Bond, 'Chapter Act Books', *History,* vol. 54, 1969, pp. 406-9.

41 K.A. Thompson, *Bureacracy and Reform. The Organizational Response of the Church of England to Social Change 1800-1965,* Clarendon Press, Oxford, 1970, and E.R. Norman, *Church and Society in England, 1770-1970: a Historical Study,* Clarendon Press, Oxford, 1976, both provide an excellent background to the records of this period.

42 G.F.A. Best, *Temporal Pillars. Queen Anne's Bounty, the Ecclesiastical Commissioners, and the Church of England,* Cambridge University Press, 1964.

43 See three articles, all entitled 'The Records of the Church Commissioners', in the *Journal of the Society of Archivists,* vol. 1, 1955-9, pp. 14-16 (by C.E. Welch), in idem, vol. 3, 1965-9, pp. 347-56 (by E.J. Robinson) and in *The Local Historian,* vol. 9, 1970-1, pp. 215-21, also by Robinson. Cf. Foster and Sheppard, *British Archives,* No 325, for access to the records.

43 Lambeth Palace Library has published numerous guides to its collections, of which a list is obtainable on request; for the northern province see, principally, D.M. Smith, *A Guide to the Archives Collections in the Borthwick Institute of Historical Research,* BIHR, York, 1973, with a *Supplemental Guide,* also by Dr Smith, in 1980. They too issue a list of other publications.

45 C.A.H. Green, *The Setting of the Constitution of the Church in Wales,* Sweet & Maxwell, 1937; D. Walker, 'Disestablishment and Independence', in idem, ed., *A History of the Church in Wales,* Church in Wales, Penarth, 1976, pp. 164-87, is more discursive.

46 E.D. Jones, 'The Migration of Probate Records in Wales, 1945-49', *Archives,* vol. 1, 1949-52, pp. 7-12, which includes an early enunciation of the Library's unchanging view that Welsh local records should not be divided between Welsh local record offices.

Chapter 5, pp. 109-161

1 The background to the reform of 1972-4 can be traced in H.V. Wiseman, ed., *Local Government in England 1958-69,* Routledge, 1970 (which in fact begins in 1945); B. Wood, *The Process of Local Government Reform 1966-74,* Allen & Unwin, 1976; P.G. Richards, *The Local Government Act 1972. Problems of Implementation,* PEP and Allen & Unwin, 1975; and the same author's *The Reformed Local Government System,* Allen & Unwin, 1973.

2 B. Keith-Lucas, *English Local Government in the Nineteenth and Twentieth Centuries,* Historical Association, 1977, provides a simple introduction; K.B. Smellie, *A History of Local Government,* Allen & Unwin, 1968, remains a more detailed standard text. B. Keith-Lucas and P.G. Richards, *A History of Local Government in the Twentieth Century,* Allen & Unwin, 1978, is up to date and has an excellent bibliography. For a more reflective approach see J.P.D. Dunbabin, 'British Local Government Reforms: the Nineteenth Century and After', *English Historical Review,* vol. 92, 1977, pp. 777-805.

3 The modern literature on the nineteenth-century poor law is enormous, including many local studies: A. Digby, 'Recent Developments in the Study of the English Poor Law', *The Local Historian*, vol. 12, 1976-7, pp. 206-11. M.E. Rose, *The Relief of Poverty, 1834-1914*, Macmillan, 1972, brings the subject up to date from where the Webbs left it, as do the essays in D. Fraser, ed., *The New Poor Law in the Nineteenth Century*, Macmillan, 1976. The latter's standard text on *The Evolution of the British Welfare State. A History of Social Policy since the Industrial Revolution*, 2nd edition, Macmillan, 1984, sets poor relief in a wider context.

4   R.G. Hodgkinson, *The Origins of the National Health Service. The Medical Services of the New Poor Law, 1834-1871*, Wellcome Historical Medical Library, 1967; R.J. Lambert, 'A Victorian National Health Service: State Vaccination, 1855-71', *Historical Journal*, vol.5, 1962, pp. 1-18.

5   C. Hill and J. Woodcock, *The National Health Service*, Christopher Johnson, 1949, provides a clear explanation of the Act.

6   J.M. Coleman, 'Guardians' Minute Books', *History*, vol. 48, 1963, pp. 181-4.

7   K.H. Baker, 'General Ledgers of Boards of Guardians', *Journal of the Society of Archivists*, vol. 2, 1960-64, pp. 367-9.

8   R.M. Gutchen, 'Paupers in Union Workhouses. Computer Analysis of Admissions and Discharges', *The Local Historian*, vol. 11, 1974-5, pp. 452-6.

9   For the problems now confronting archivists see N.J.M. Kerling, 'Hospital Records', *Journal of the Society of Archivists*, vol. 5, 1974-77, pp. 181-3; for a solution in one area see D.N. Thompson, 'Wirral Hospital Records', ibid., vol. 7, 1982-5, 421-42.

10 There is no full-scale history of the General Register Office, which was not included in either the Whitehall or New Whitehall series; the often cited but elusive title, *The Story of the General Register Office and its Origins from 1538-1937*, HMSO, 1937, is merely an exhibition catalogue compiled by the Registrar General to mark the centenary of civil registration. The only modern study appears to be D.V. Glass, *Numbering the People. The Eighteenth-Century Population Controversy and the Development of Census and Vital Statistics in Britain*, Saxon House, Farnborough, 1973. Guides to civil registration go out of date rapidly: see therefore Eve McLaughlin, *St Catherine's House*, Federation of Family History Societies, 1985, which is frequently reprinted. C.D. Rogers, *The Family Tree Detective. A Manual for analysing and solving Genealogical Problems in England and Wales, 1538 to the Present Day*, Manchester University Press, 1983, claims more in its title than it delivers but is detailed and reliable on civil registration.

11 D.J. Steel, ed., *National Index of Parish Registers*, Society of Genealogists, vols. I-III, 1968-74; R.W. Ambler, 'Non-Parochial Registers and the Local Historian', *The Local Historian*, vol. 10, 1972-3, pp. 59-64. See also Stephens, *Sources*, pp. 275-6, for registration of chapels by the Registrar General.

12 Glass, op.cit.; E.A. Wrigley (ed.), *Nineteenth-Century Society. Essays in the Use of Quantitative Methods for the Study of Social Data*, Cambridge University Press, 1972; and R. Lawton, ed., *The Census and Social Structure. An Interpretative Guide to Nineteenth Century Censuses for England and Wales*, Cass, 1978, are probably the best starting-points for work on the census; see also Office of Population Censuses and Surveys and General Register Office, Edinburgh, *Guide to Census Reports. Great Britain 1801-1966*, HMSO, 1977, and S.A. Royle, 'Clergymen's Returns to the 1831 Census', *The Local Historian*, vol. 14, 1980-1, pp. 79-90.

13 Rogers, op.cit.; J.S.W. Gibson, *Census Returns 1841-1881 on Microfilm. A Directory to Local Holdings*, Federation of Family History Societies, 1983; J.S.W. Gibson and C. Chapman, ed., *Census Indexes and Indexing*, FFHS,

1981; E. McLaughlin, *The Censuses 1841-1881. Their Use and Interpretation*, FFHS, 1985.

14 M. Goldstrom, 'Education in England and Wales in 1851', pp. 224-40 of R. Lawton, ed., op.cit.; D.M. Thompson, 'The Religious Census of 1851', pp. 241-86 of ibid.; B.I. Coleman, *The Church of England in the Mid-Nineteenth Century: a Social Geography,* Historical Association, 1980; I.G. Jones, ed., *The Religious Census of 1851: a Calendar of the Returns relating to Wales,* University of Wales Press, Cardiff, 1976-81. For a short introduction see R.W. Ambler, 'The 1851 Census of Religious Worship', *The Local Historian,* vol. 11, 1974-5, pp. 375-81.

15 K. Jones, *A History of the Mental Health Services,* Routledge, 1972; A.T. Scull, *Museums of Madness. The Social Organisation of Insanity in Nineteenth-Century Britain,* Allen Lane, 1979; J.J. Clarke, *Social Administration including the Poor Laws,* 2nd edition, Pitman, 1935, pp. 249-64.

16 W.Ll. Parry-Jones, *The Trade in Lunacy. A Study of Private Madhouses in England in the Eighteenth and Nineteenth Centuries,* Routledge, 1972; also R.A. Hunter, I. Macalpine and L.M. Payne, 'The Country Register of Houses for the Reception of "Lunatics", 1798-1812', *Journal of Mental Science,* vol. 102, 1956, pp. 856-63, written when the document was still in the custody of the Board of Control.

17 C.F. Brockington, *Public Health in the Nineteenth Century,* Livingstone, Edinburgh, 1965, pp. 3-15, 67-93; R.J. Morris, *Cholera 1832. The Social Response to an Epidemic,* Croom Helm, 1976.

18 R.A. Lewis, *Edwin Chadwick and the Public Health Movement, 1832-1854,* Longman, 1952, and R. Lambert, *Sir John Simon (1816-1904) and English Social Administraton,* MacGibbon and Kee, 1963, remain standard works; see also Lambert's article, 'Central and Local Relations in Mid-Victorian England: the Local Government Act Office, 1858-71', *Victorian Studies,* vol. 6, 1962-3, pp. 121-50.

19 A. Newsholme, *The Ministry of Health,* Putnam, 1925; F. Honigsbaum, *The Struggle for the Ministry of Health 1914-1919,* Bell, 1970; E. Sharp, *The Ministry of Housing and Local Government,* Allen & Unwin, 1969, pp. 11-15; P. Draper, *Creation of the D.O.E.,* HMSO, 1977. There is no full-length published history of the LGB but see R.M. MacLeod, *Treasury Control and Social Administration. A Study of Establishment Growth at the Local Government Board 1871-1905,* Bell, 1968; W.A. Ross, 'Local Government Board and After: Retrospect', *Public Administration,* vol. 34, 1956, pp. 17-25; K.D. Brown, 'John Burns at the Local Government Board: a Reassessment', *Journal of Social Policy,* vol. 6, 1977, pp. 157-70.

20 H. Williams, 'Public Health and Local History', *The Local Historian,* vol. 14, 1980-1, pp. 202-10. Idem, ed., 'Public Health in Mid-Victorian Wales. Correspondence from the Principality to the General Board of Health & the Local Government Act Office 1848-71', Typescript distributed by University of Wales Board of Celtic Studies to copyright libraries, Institute of Historical Research and constituent colleges of the University of Wales, 1983, contains transcripts or summaries of the Welsh correspondence in MH 13. For some of the later material in MH 12 see A. Morton, 'Inland Sanitary Survey 1893-5', *Public Administration,* vol. 62, 1984, pp. 494-6.

21 H.J. Smith, 'Local Reports to the General Board of Health', *History,* vol. 56, 1971, pp. 46-9.

22 See Chapter 4, note 6, for the establishment of the county councils. Their fiftieth anniversary was marked by a series of handbooks with the general title of *The Jubilee of County Councils 1889 to 1939. Fifty Years of Local*

Government, Evans Brother, 1939. Each authority issued a volume consisting partly of a general review common to the whole series and partly of a survey of its own services. J.M. Lee, *Social Leaders and Public Persons. A Study of County Government in Cheshire since 1888,* Clarendon Press, Oxford, 1963, was an early attempt at a history of a county council; the reorganization of 1972-4 stimulated several others: *Monmouthshire County Council 1888-1974,* Monmouthshire County Council, 1974; J.D. Marshall (ed.), *The History of Lancashire County Council,* Martin Robertson, 1977; C.R.V. Bell, *A History of East Sussex County Council,* Phillimore, Chichester, 1975; J. Barber and M. Beresford, *The West Riding County Council, 1889-1974. Historical Studies,* W. Riding CC, 1979; B. Barrows, *A County and its Health: a History of the Development of the West Riding Health Services, 1889-1974;* W. Yorks MCC, 1974; J. Varley, *The Parts of Kesteven. Studies in Law and Local Government,* Kesteven CC, 1975. Kent has been tackled twice: E. Melling, *A History of the Kent County Council, 1889-1974,* Kent CC, 1975, and P. A. Moylan, *The Form and Reform of County Government: Kent, 1889-1914,* Leicester University Press, 1978.

23 Stephens, *Sources,* p. 93, notes various parliamentary papers; cf. F.A. Youngs, *Guide to the Local Administrative Units of England. I. Southern England,* Royal Historical Society, 1979.

24 *Records of District Councils,* British Records Association, 1974; I. Darlington, 'Rate Books', *History,* vol. 47, 1962, pp. 42-5.

25 P.J. Aspinall and J.W.R. Whitehand, 'Building Plans: a major source for urban studies', *Area,* vol. 12, 1980, pp. 199-203.

26 The classic text remains W. Ashworth, *The Genesis of Modern British Town Planning. A Study in Economic and Social History of the Nineteenth and Twentieth Centuries,* Routledge, 1954. See also the historical sections in two books by J.B. Cullingworth, *Town and Country Planning in England and Wales. An Introduction,* Allen & Unwin, 1964, and *Housing and Local Government in England and Wales,* Allen & Unwin, 1966. See also J. Burnett, *A Social History of Housing 1815-1970,* David & Charles, Newton Abbot, 1978; M.J. Daunton, *House and Home in the Victorian City: Working-Class Housing 1850-1914,* Edward Arnold, 1983.

27 M. Bowley, *Housing and the State 1919-1944,* Allen & Unwin, 1944; M. Swenarton, *Homes fit for Heroes. The Politics and Architecture of early State Housing in Britain,* Heinemann, 1981. See most recently, M.J. Daunton, ed., *Councillors and Tenants. Local Authority Housing in English Cities, 1919-1939,* Leicester University Press, 1984.

28 J.M. Imray, 'Town and Country Planning Records and the County Archivist', *Journal of the Society of Archivists,* vol. 1, 1955-9, pp. 43-6.

29 I. Gowan, 'The Administration of the National Parks', *Public Administration,* vol. 33, 1955, pp. 425-38.

30 M. Aldridge, *The British New Towns. A Programme without a Policy,* Routledge, 1979, is polemical but has a good bibliography.

31 Sharp, op.cit., provides both an historical introduction and an account of her former department's more recent activities.

32 P.J. Randall, 'Wales in the Structure of Central Government', and E. Rowlands, 'The Politics of Regional Administration: the Establishment of the Welsh Office', *Public Administration,* vol. 50, 1972, pp. 333-72; I.C. Thomas, *The Creation of the Welsh Office: conflicting purposes in institutional change,* Strathclyde University, Glasgow, 1981.

33 S. and B. Webb, *The Story of the King's Highway,* Longman, 1913, repr. Cass, 1963, remains the best account of highway administration in this period.

34 D. Williams, *The Rebecca Riots. A Study in Agrarian Discontent,* University of Wales Press, Cardiff, 1955; B.F. Duckham, 'Road Administration in South Wales: the Carmarthenshire Roads Board, 1845-89', *Journal of Transport History,* 3rd series, vol. 5, 1984, pp. 45-65.

35 The literature on the history of education since 1833 is now enormous, with a vast number of local studies. I have simply followed P.H.J.H. Gosden, *The Development of Educational Administration in England and Wales,* Basil Blackwell, Oxford, 1966, for the following section. Stephens, *Sources,* pp. 203-47, supplies numerous other references to secondary works.

36 K. Jeffereys, 'R.A. Butler, the Board of Education and the 1944 Education Act', *History,* vol. 69, 1984, pp. 415-31, provides a good survey of work on this period; Sir W. Pile, *The Department of Education and Science,* Allen & Unwin, 1979, chronicles subsequent developments.

37 G. Sutherland, 'A View of Education Records in the Nineteenth and Twentieth Centuries', *Archives,* vol. 15, 1981-2, pp. 79-85, surveys the field; P.H.J.H. Gosden, 'Twentieth-century Archives of Education as Sources for the Study of Education Policy and Administration', ibid., pp. 86-95, describes the archival background to his study (written jointly with P.R. Sharp) of *The Development of an Education Service: the West Riding 1889-1974,* W. Yorks MCC, 1978. Another local study is P. Keane, 'An English County and Education: Somerset, 1889-1902', *English Historical Review,* vol. 88, 1973, pp. 286-311.

38 Stephens, *Sources,* pp. 208-9.

39 P.M. Jacobs, 'Registers of the Universities, Colleeges and Schools of Great Britain and Ireland', *Bulletin of the Institute of Historical Research,* vol. 37, 1964, pp. 185-232.

40 T.A. Critchley, *A History of Police of England and Wales 900-1966,* Constable, 1967, is a good general account; C. Steedman, *Policing the Victorian Community. The Formation of English Provincial Police Forces, 1856-80,* Routledge, 1984, includes some local case studies and has a full bibliography. See also E.C. Midwinter, *Social Administration in Lancashire 1830-1860. Poor Law, Public Health and Police,* Manchester University Press, 1969, and V. Bailey, ed., *Policing and Punishment in Ninteenth Century Britan,* Croom Helm, 1981.

41 G.V. Blackstone, *A History of the British Fire Service,* Routledge, 1957, is a comprehensive general account.

42 M.E. Falkus, 'The Development of Municipal Trading in the Nineteenth Century', *Business History,* vol. 19, 1977, pp. 134-61; contemporary works includes D. Knoop, *Principles and Methods of Municipal Trading,* Macmillan, 1912, and H. Finer, *Municipal Trading. A Study in Public Administration,* Allen & Unwin, 1941. Falkus has also written on 'The British Gas Industry before 1850', *Economic History Review,* 2nd series, vol. 20, 1967, pp. 494-508, and on 'The Early Development of the British Gas Industry, 1790-1815', ibid., vol. 35, 1982, pp. 217-34. On water see W.M. Stern, 'Water Supply in Britain: the Development of a Public Service', *Royal Sanitary Institute Journal,* vol. 77, 1954, pp. 998-1004, and F.W. Robins, *The Story of Water Supply,* Oxford University Press, 1946, pp. 191-201: both are thin but there seems to be no other study. See also Appendix 3. L. Hannah, *Electricity before Nationalisation. A Study of the Development of the Electricity Supply Industry in Britain,* Macmillan, 1979, pp. 357-61, includes a note on sources and their accessibility; the story is continued by Hannah in *Engineers, Managers and Politicians. The First Fifteen Years of Nationalised Electricity Supply in Britain,* Macmillan, 1982, which depends more on closed industry and ministry records. See also L. Symons, 'Archives and Records of the Institution of Electrical Engineers', *Archives,* vol. 16, 1983-4, pp. 54-60.

43 L. Ellison, 'Petty Sessions Records and Social Deprivation', *The Local Historian,* vol. 15, 1982-3, 74-9, appears to be one of the few published references on the historical use of modern petty sessions records. R.M. Jackson, *The Machinery of Justice in England,* Cambridge University Press, 1940 (and later editions), is a good general guide to the modern system.

44 T. Snagge, *The Evolution of the County Court,* William Clowes, 1904; H. Smith, 'The Resurgent County Court in Victorian Britain', *American Journal of Legal History,* vol. 13, 1969, pp. 126-38; G.R. Rubin. 'The County Courts and the Tally Trade, 1846-1914', pp. 321-48, and P.W.J. Bartrip, 'County Court and Superior Court Registrars, 1820-1875: the Making of a Judicial Office', pp. 349-79, in G.R. Rubin and D. Sugarman, ed., *Law, Economy and Society, 1750-1914: Essays in the History of English Law,* Professional Books, Abingdon, 1984.

45 R.G.A. Chesterman, *Laughter in the House. Local Taxation and the Motor Car in Cheshire 1888-1978,* Cheshire Record Office, Chester, 1978, is of considerable general value on this subject. See also R. Storey, 'Motor Vehicle Registers', *Archives,* vol. 8, 1965-6, pp. 91-2.

46 There does not appear to be a history of the modern coroner to complement Dr Hunnisett's work on the middle ages (Chapter 2, note 28).

Chapter 6, pp. 162-81

1 For the general development of the department see R.R. Nelson, *The Home Office, 1782-1801,* Duke University Press, Durham, N. Carolina, 1969; A.P. Donajgrodzki, 'New Roles for Old: the Northcote-Trevelyan Report and the Clerks of the Home Office 1822-48', in G. Sutherland, ed., *Studies in the Growth of Nineteenth-Century Government,* Routledge, 1972, pp. 82-109; E. Troup, *The Home Office,* Putnam, 1925; and (most usefully) J. Pellew, *The Home Office 1848-1914. From Clerks to Bureaucrats,* Heinemann, 1982.

2 For a recent survey with good references to earlier work see P.W.J. Bartrip, 'British Government Inspection, 1832-1875: some Observations', *Historical Journal,* vol. 25, 1982, pp. 605-26.

3 Cf. *The Second World War, A Guide to Documents in the Public Record Office,* HMSO, 1972 and S.L. Mayer and W.J. Koenig, ed., *The Two World Wars: a Guide to Manuscript Collections in the United Kingdom,* Bowker, 1976.

4 C.S. Orwin and E.H. Whetham, *History of British Agriculture 1846-1914,* Longman, 1964, pp. 178-202; T.H. Elliott, 'The Organisation and Work of the Board of Agriculture and Fisheries', in G.M. Harris, ed., *Problems of Local Government,* P.S. King, 1911, pp. 419-36; F.L.C. Floud, *The Ministry of Agriculture and Fisheries,* Putnam, 1927; J. Winnifrith, *The Ministry of Agriculture, Fisheries and Food,* Allen & Unwin, 1962.

5 R.J.P. Kain and H.C. Prince, *The Tithe Surveys of England and Wales,* Cambridge University Press, 1985, is so thorough, with such a full bibliography that further references are possibly redundant, although for tithes from a social historian's standpoint see E.J. Evans, *The Contentious Tithe. The Tithe Problem and English Agriculture, 1750-1850,* Routledge, 1976, and his useful booklet, *Tithes and the Tithe Commutation Act 1836,* Standing Conference for Local History, 1978. My own *Local History. A Handbook for Beginners,* Batsford, 1983, pp. 76-86, has some well tried suggestions for local projects based on the surveys.

6 See note 12 to Chapter 4.

7 L.D. Stamp and W.G. Hoskins, *The Common Lands of England and Wales,*

Collins, 1963; cf. J.W. Aitchison and E.J. Hughes, 'The Common Land Registers of England and Wales: a problematic data source', *Area,* vol. 14, 1982, pp. 151-6.

8   W.E. Minchinton, 'Agricultural Returns and the Government during the Napoleonic Wars', *Agricultural History Review,* vol. 1, 1953, pp. 29-43; idem, 'The Agricultural Returns of 1800 for Wales', *Bulletin of the Board of Celtic Studies,* vol. 21, 1964-66, pp. 74-93 (extensive references to publications on England); Ministry of Agriculture, Fisheries and Food and Department of Agriculture and Fisheries for Scotland, *A Century of Agricultural Statistics. Great Britain 1866-1966,* HMSO, 1968; J.T. Coppock, 'The Statistical Assessment of British Agriculture', *Agricultural History Review,* vol. 4, 1956, pp. 4-21 and 66-79; W. Vamplew, 'A Grain of Truth: the Nineteenth-Century Corn Averages', ibid., vol. 28, 1980, pp. 1-17.

9   F.G. Aldsworth, 'Parish Boundaries on Record', *The Local Historian,* vol. 15, 1982-3, pp. 34-40, and M.L. Faull, 'Boundary Records of the Ordnance Survey', ibid., pp. 483-5. Cf. generally W.A. Seymour, ed., *A History of the Ordnance Survey,* Dawson, Folkestone, 1980, and J.R.S. Booth, *Public Boundaries and the Ordnance Survey, 1840-1980,* Ordnance Survey, 1980.

10 C.E. Hart, *The Verderers and Speech-Court of the Forest of Dean,* John Bellows, Gloucester, 1950.

11 R.B. Pugh, *The Crown Estate. An Historical Essay,* HMSO, 1960.

12 H.M. Colvin, ed., *The History of the King's Works,* HMSO, 1963-82, is a monumental account down to 1851; H. Emmerson, *The Ministry of Works,* Allen & Unwin, 1956, is a New Whitehall series volume with the usual historical introduction; P. Draper, *Creation of the D.O.E,* HMSO, 1977, describes recent changes.

13 In the course of my work on the topographical development of Chesterfield, Derbys., I asked if I might see the WORK 50 entries relating to government estate in the town; the request was refused, as was a subsequent request to see deeds relating to the site of the former Employment Exchange in the town prior to 1850. On this occasion, PSA supplied a schedule of the deeds concerned, the oldest of which was dated 1785 but, the current law relating to titles in real property notwithstanding, even this could apparently not be produced for study, although no reason, beyond immunity from the Public Records Act, 1958, was offered.

14 E.E. Hoon, *The Organization of the English Customs System, 1696-1786,* reprinted with new introduction by R.C. Jarvis, David & Charles, Newton Abbot, 1968; G.N. Clark, *Guide to English Commercial Statistics, 1696-1782,* Royal Historical Society, 1938; E.B. Schumpeter, *English Overseas Trade Statistics 1697-1808,* Clarendon Press, Oxford, 1960; R. Davis, *The Industrial Revolution and British Overseas Trade,* Leicester University Press, 1979; E.A. Carson, 'Sources for Maritime History (I): Customs Bills of Entry', *Maritime History,* vol. 1, 1971, pp. 176-89.

15 For an example of out-port records as they were being surveyed prior to transfer to the PRO see E.A. Carson, 'The Customs Records of the Kent Ports – A Survey', *Journal of the Society of Archivists,* vol. 4, 1970-73, pp. 31-44.

16 For the general history of the department see H. Ll. Smith, *The Board of Trade,* Putnam, 1928; R. Prouty, *The Transformation of the Board of Trade 1830-1855. A Study of Administrative Reorganization in the Heyday of Laissez Faire,* Heinemann, 1957.

17 Cf. Carson, art. cit.; for the material now at Memorial see K. Matthews, 'Crew Lists, Agreements, and Official Logs of the British Empire 1863-1913',

Business History, vol. 16, 1974; pp. 78-80; D. Alexander, 'A Description of Indexing Procedures for the "Agreement on Account of Crew"', *Archives,* vol. 11, 1973-4, pp. 86-93; L.R. Fischer and E.W. Sager, 'An Approach to the Quantitative Analysis of British Shipping Records', *Business History,* vol. 22, 1980, pp. 135-51. The Registrar General has an unpublished list of his department's records and their division between various locations, copies of which are obtainable on request. See also N. Cox, 'Sources for Maritime History (II): the Records of the Registrar General of Shipping and Seamen', *Maritime History,* vol. 2, 1972, pp. 168-88. On registration cf. R.C. Jarvis, 'Ship Registry – 1786', ibid., vol. 4, 1974, pp. 12-30.

18 H.A. Shannon, 'The Coming of General Limited Liability', *Economic History,* vol. 2, 1930-33, pp. 267-91; idem, 'The first five thousand Limited Companies and their Duration', ibid., pp. 396-419; and idem, 'The Limited Liability Companies of 1866-1883', *Economic History Review,* vol. 4, 1932-4, pp. 290-316. See also G. Todd, 'Some Aspects of Joint Stock Companies, 1844-1900', ibid., vol. 4, 1932-4, pp. 46-71; J. Saville, 'Sleeping Partnership and Limited Liability, 1850-1856' *Economic History Review,* 2nd series, vol. 8, 1955-6, pp. 418-33. For company records themselves see L. Richmond and B. Stockford, *Company Archives. The Survey of the Records of 1000 of the first Registered Companies in England and Wales,* Gower, Aldershot, 1986. For particular classes of record see L.S. Pressnell and John Orbell, *A Guide to the Historical Records of British Banking,* Gower, Aldershot, 1985; H.A.L. Cockerell and E. Green, *The British Insurance Business, 1547-1970. An Introduction and Guide to Historical Records in the United Kingdom,* Heinemann, 1976; and P. Mathias and A.W.H. Pearsall, ed., *Shipping. A Survey of Historical Records,* David & Charles, Newton Abbot, 1971. The Companies Registration Office issues a Guide to Public Search and a General Brief on request.

19 G. McCrone, *Regional Policy in Britain,* Allen & Unwin, 1969, pp. 106-19. The older standard work is S.R. Dennison, *The Location of Industry and the Depressed Areas,* Oxford University Press, 1939.

20 A.E. Horton, 'Records and the National Coal Board', *Archives,* vol. 1, 1949-52, pp. 28-31. A new history of the industry, sponsored by British Coal, is in process of publication through the Clarendon Press, Oxford, but as yet only the volumes covering the period 1700-1914 have appeared, which make limited use of NCB predecessor archives.

21 i.e. at Shotton Works, Deeside, Clwyd CH5 2NH; Unit F2, Commerce Way, Skippers Lane Industrial Estate, South Bank, Middlesbrough, Cleveland TS6 6UT; and By-Pass Road, Irthlingborough, Wellingborough, Northants NN9 5QH (see *British Archives,* Nos 140, 530 and 687). The record centres formerly at Glasgow and Cardiff have now shut, with material transferred from the former to Irthlingborough and the latter to Deeside. I am indebted to Mr Peter Emmerson of BSC for this information; cf. J. Armstrong, *A Directory of Corporate Archives,* Business Archives Council, 1985.

22 This is well illustrated by T. Rath's useful article, 'Business Records in the Public Record Office in the Age of the Industrial Revolution', *Business History,* vol. 17, 1975, pp. 189-200, since most of the classes described by him are not strictly business records.

23 H. Parris, *Government and the Railways in Nineteenth-Century* Britain, Routledge, 1965.

24 J. Heath, 'Private 'bus services before 1930', *The Local Historian,* vol. 15, 1982-3, pp. 221-4.

25 L.C. Johnson, 'Historical Records of the British Transport Commission', *Journal of the Society of Archivists*, vol. 1, 1955-9, pp. 94-100; idem, 'British Transport Historical Records Department: the first decade', *Archives*, vol. 6, 1963-4, pp. 163-71; and E.H. Fowkes, 'Sources of History in Railway Records of British Transport Historical Records', *Journal of the Society of Archivists*, vol. 3, 1965-9, pp. 476-88. For legal and departmental material see D.B. Wardle, 'Sources for the History of Railways at the Public Record Office', *Journal of Transport History*, vol. 2, 1955-6, pp. 214-34.

26 H.S. Cobb, 'Parliamentary Records relating to Internal Navigation', *Archives*, vol. 9, 1969-70, pp. 73-9.

27 P.H.J.H. Gosden, *The Friendly Societies in England, 1815-1875*, Manchester University Press, 1961; idem, *Self-Help. Voluntary Associations in the 19th Century*, Batsford, 1973. Cf also R.G. Garnett, 'The Records of Early Co-operation with particular reference to pre-Rochdale Consumer Co-operation', *The Local Historian*, vol. 9, 1970-1, pp. 163-71, and R.L.M. James, 'The Records of Friendly Societies', ibid., vol. 6, 1963-4, pp. 223-4. On trade union records see E.J. Hobsbawm, 'Records of the Trade Union Movement', *Archives*, vol. 4, 1959-60, pp. 129-37; also useful is A. Marsh and V. Ryan, *Historical Directory of Trade Unions*, Gower, Aldershot, 1980-84.

28 R. Tompson, *The Charity Commission and the Age of Reform*, Routledge, 1979.

29 M. Brasnett, *Voluntary Social Action. A History of the National Council of Social Service 1919-1969*, NCSS, 1969. Cf. *British Archives*, No 421.

30 J.S.W. Gibson, *A Simplified Guide to Probate Jurisdictions: Where to look for wills*, Federation of Family History Societies, 3rd edition, 1985; idem, 'Printed Indexes to Probate Records after 1850', *The Local Historian*, vol. 15, 1982-3, pp. 218-220; E. McLaughlin, *Somerset House Wills from 1858*, Federation of Family History Societies, 1985. See also W.D. Rubinstein and D.H. Duman, 'Probate Valuations. A Tool for the Historian', *The Local Historian*, vol. 11, 1974-5, pp. 68-71.

31 S. Marriner, 'English Bankruptcy Records and Statistics before 1850', *Economic History Review*, 2nd series, vol. 33, 1980, pp. 351-66; I.P.H. Duffy, 'English Bankrupts, 1571-1861', *American Journal of Legal History*, vol. 24, 1980, pp. 283-306.

BIBLIOGRAPHY

This is simply a list of works cited in the text notes, arranged alphabetically by author. It does not include titles found in HMSO Sectional List 24 or the publications of the List and Index Society (cf. p. 198, note 22).

Adair, E.R., *The Sources for the History of the Council in the Sixteenth and Seventeenth Centuries*, SPCK, 1924.

Adams, N., and Donahue, C., ed., *Select Cases from the Ecclesiastical Courts of the Province of Canterbury, c.1200–1301*, Selden Society, vol. 95, 1978–9.

Ministry of Agriculture, Fisheries and Food and Department of Agriculture and Fisheries for Scotland, *A Century of Agricultural Statistics. Great Britain 1866–1966*, HMSO, 1968.

Aitchison, J.W., and Hughes, E.J., 'The Common Land Registers of England and Wales: a Problematic Data Source', *Area*, vol. 14, 1982, pp. 151–6.

Albert, W., *The Turnpike Road System in England 1663–1840*, Cambridge University Press, 1972.

Aldridge, M., *The British New Towns. A Programme without a Policy*, Routledge, 1979.

Aldridge, T.M., *Directory of Registers and Records*, 4th edition, Oyez Longman, 1984.

Aldsworth, F.G., 'Parish Boundaries on Record', *The Local Historian* vol. 15, 1982–3, pp. 34–40.

Alexander, D., 'A Description of Indexing Procedures for the "Agreement on Account of Crew"', *Archives*, vol. 11, 1973–4, pp. 86–93.

Ambler, R.W., 'Non-Parochial Registers and the Local Historian', *The Local Historian*, vol. 10, 1972–3, pp. 59–64.

Ambler, R.W., 'The 1851 Census of Religious Worship', *The Local Historian*, vol. 11, 1974–5, pp. 375–81.

Armstrong, J., *A Directory of Corporate Archives*, Business Archives Council, 1985.

Ashley, M, *Financial and Commercial Policy under the Cromwellian Protectorate*, 2nd edition, Cass, 1962.

Ashworth, W., *The Genesis of Modern British Town Planning. A Study in Economic and Social History of the Nineteenth and Twentieth Centuries*, Routledge, 1954.

Aspinall, P.J., and Whitehand, J.W.R., 'Building Plans: a major source for Urban Studies', *Area*, vol. 12, 1980, pp. 199–203.

Avery, M.E., 'The History of the Equitable Jurisdiction of the Chancery before 1460', *Bulletin of the Institute of Historical Research*, vol. 42, 1969, pp. 129–44.

Aylmer, G.E., *The State's Servants. The Civil Service of the English Republic 1649–1660*, Routledge, 1973.

Aylmer, G.E, *The King's Servants. The Civil Service of Charles I 1625–1642*, 2nd edition, Routledge, 1974.

Bagley, J.J., *Historical Interpretation. Sources of English Medieval History, 1066–1540*, Penguin, Harmondsworth, 1965.

Baildon, W.P., ed., *Select Cases in the Court of Chancery (1364–1471)*, Selden Society, vol. 10, 1896.

Bailey, V., ed., *Policing and Punishment in Nineteenth Century Britain*, Croom Helm, 1981.

Baker, K.H., 'General Ledgers of Boards of Guardians', *Journal of the Society of Archivists*, vol. 2, 1960–64, pp. 367–9.

Ball, S., *The Conservative Party: a List of National, Regional and Local Records*, Dept of History, University of Leicester, forthcoming.

Ballard, A., *British Borough Charters, 1042–1216*, Cambridge University Press, 1913.

Ballard, A., and Tait, J., *British Borough Charters, 1216–1307*, Cambridge University Press, 1923.

Barber, J., and Beresford, M., *The West Riding County Council, 1889–1974. Historical Studies*. W. Yorkshire MCC, 1979.

Barnes, T.G., *Somerset 1625–1640. A County's Government during the 'Personal Rule'*, Oxford University Press, 1961.

Barnes, T.G., *The Clerk of the Peace in Caroline Somerset*, Leicester University Press, 1961.

Barnes, T.G., 'The Archives and Archival Problems of the Elizabethan and Early Stuart Star Chamber', in Ranger, F., ed., *Prisca Munimenta. Studies in Archival and Administrative History presented to Dr A.E.J. Hollaender*, University of London Press, 1973, pp. 130–49.

Barnes, T.G., ed., *List and Index to the Proceedings in Star Chamber for the Reign of James I (1603–1625) in the Public Record Office, London, Class STAC8*, American Bar Foundation, Chicago, 1975.

Barnes, T.G., and Smith, A.H., 'Justices of the Peace from 1558 to 1688 – a Revised List of Sources', *Bulletin of the Institute of Historical Research*, vol. 32, 1959, pp. 221–42.

Barraclough, G., *The Earldon and County Palatine of Chester*, Oxford University Press, 1953.

Barratt, D.M., 'Glebe Terriers', *History*, vol. 51, 1966, pp. 35–38.

Barrows, B., *A County and its Health: a History of the Development of the West Riding Health Services, 1889–1974*, W. Riding CC, 1974.

Bartrip, P.W.J., 'British Government Inspection, 1832–1875: some observations', *Historical Journal*, vol. 25, 1982, pp. 605–26.

Bartrip, P.W.J., 'County Court and Superior Court Registrars, 1820–1875: the Making of a Judicial Office', in Rubin, G.R., and Sugarman, D., ed., *Law, Economy and Society, 1750–1914: Essays in the History of English Law*, Professional Books, Abingdon, 1984, pp. 349–79.

Bates, D.R., *A Bibliography of Domesday Book*, Boydell & Brewer, 1986.

Baxter, S.B., *The Development of the Treasury, 1660–1702*, Longman, 1957.

Beard, C.A., *The Office of Justice of the Peace in England in its Origin and Development*, Columbia University Press, New York, 1904.

Beckett, J.V., 'Land Tax or Excise: the Levying of Taxation in Seventeenth- and Eighteenth-Century England', *English Historical Review*, vol. 100, 1985, pp. 285–308.

Belcher, V., see Sheppard, F.

Bell, C.R.V., *A History of East Sussex County Council*, Phillimore, Chichester, 1975.

Bell, H.E., *An Introduction to the History and Records of the Court of Wards & Liveries*, Cambridge University Press, 1953.

Bell, L., 'The new Public Record Office at Kew', *Journal of the Society of Archivists*, vol. 5, 1974–7, pp. 1–7.

Bellamy, J., *Crime and Public Order in England in the Later Middle Ages*, Routledge, 1973.

Beresford, M.W., 'The Decree Rolls of Chancery as a Source for Economic History, 1547–c.1700', *Economic History Review*, 2nd series, vol. 32, 1979, pp. 1–10.

Beresford, M.W., see also Barber, J.

Best, G.F.A., *Temporal Pillars. Queen Anne's Bounty, the Ecclesiastical Commissioners, and the Church of England*, Cambridge University Press, 1964.

Bevan, D., *Guide to the South Wales Coalfield Archive*, University College, Swansea, 1980.

Binney, J.E.D., *British Public Finance and Administration, 1774–92*, Clarendon Press, Oxford, 1958.

Blackstone, G.V., *A History of the British Fire Service*, Routledge, 1957.

Blair, J., and Riden, P., 'Computer-assisted analysis of Medieval Deeds', *Archives*, vol. 15. 1981–2, pp. 195–208.

Blatcher, M., *The Court of King's Bench 1450–1550. A Study in Self-Help*, University of London Press, 1978.

Bond, M.F., 'Record Offices today: facts for Historians', *Bulletin of the Institute of Historical Research*, vol. 30, 1957, pp. 1–16.

Bond, S., 'Chapter Act Books', *History*, vol. 54, 1969, pp. 406–9.

Bond, S., and Evans, N., 'The Process of Granting Charters to English Boroughs, 1547–1649', *English Historical Review*, vol. 91, 1976, pp. 102–20.

Booth, J.R.S., *Public Boundaries and the Ordnance Survey, 1840–1980*, Ordnance Survey, 1980.

Booth, P.H.W., *The Financial Administration of the Lordship and County of Chester, 1272–1377*, Chetham Society, 3rd series, vol. 28, 1981.

Bowley, M., *Housing and the State 1919–1944*, Allen & Unwin, 1944.

Boynton, L., *The Elizabethan Militia 1558–1638*, Routledge, 1967.

Brasnett, M., *Voluntary Social Action. A History of the National Council of Social Service 1919–1969*, National Council of Social Service, 1969.

British Library, *Index of Manuscripts in the British Library*, Chadwyck-Healey, Cambridge, 1984–6.

British Records Association, *Records of District Councils*, BRA, 1974.

Brockington, C.F, *Public Health in the Nineteenth Century*, Livingstone, Edinburgh, 1965.

Brooke, C.N.L., see Knowles, D.

Brooks, F.W., *The Council of the North*, Revised Edition, Historical Association, 1966.

Brown, K.D., 'John Burns at the Local Government Board: a Reassessment', *Journal of Social Policy*, vol. 6, 1977, pp. 157–70.

Burnett, J., *A Social History of Housing 1815–1970*, David & Charles, Newton Abbot, 1978.

Cam, H.M., *Studies in the Hundred Rolls. Some Aspects of Thirteenth-Century Administration*, Oxford University Press, 1921.

Cam, H.M., *The Hundred and the Hundred Rolls. An Outline of Local Government in Medieval England*, Methuen, 1930.

Camp, A.J., *Wills and their Whereabouts*, Phillimore, Chichester, 1963.

Cantwell, J., 'The 1838 Public Record Office Act and its Aftermath: a new Perspective', *Journal of the Society of Archivists*, vol. 7, 1982–5, pp. 277–86.

Cantwell, J., 'The Making of the first Deputy Keeper of the Records', *Archives*, vol. 17, 1985–6, pp. 22–37.

Carson, E.A., 'Sources for Maritime History (I): Customs Bills of Entry', *Maritime History*, vol. 1, 1971, pp. 176–89.

Carson, E.A., 'The Customs Records of the Kent Ports – a Survey', *Journal of the Society of Archivists*, vol. 4, 1970–73, pp. 31–44.

Chandaman, C.D., *The English Public Revenue 1660–1688*, Clarendon Press, Oxford, 1975.

Chapman, C., see Gibson, J.S.W.

Chapman, J., 'Some Problems in the Interpretation of Enclosure Awards', *Agricultural History Review*, vol. 26, 1978, pp. 108–114.

Charman, D., 'On the need for a new Local Archives Service for England', *Journal of the Society of Archivists*, vol. 3, 1965–9, pp. 341–7.

Chartres, J.A., *Internal Trade in England 1500–1700*, Macmillan, 1977.

Cheney, C.R., *English Bishops' Chanceries, 1100–1250*, Manchester University Press, 1950.

Chesterman, R.G.A., *Laughter in the House. Local Taxation and the Motor Car in Cheshire 1888–1978*, Cheshire Record Office, Chester, 1978.

Chrimes, S.B., *An Introduction to the Administrative History of Medieval England*, Blackwell, Oxford, 1966.

Clark, G.N., *Guide to English Commercial Statistics, 1696–1782*, Royal Historical Society, 1938.

Clarke, J.J., *Social Administration including the Poor Laws*, 2nd edition, Pitman, 1935.

Coate, M, 'The Duchy of Cornwall: its History and Administration 1640 to 1660', *Transactions of the Royal Historical Society*, 4th series, vol. 10, 1927, pp. 135–69.

Cobb, H.S., 'Local Port Customs Accounts prior to 1550', *Journal of the Society of Archivists*, vol. 1, 1955–9, pp. 213–24.

Cobb, H.S., 'Parliamentary Records relating to Internal Navigation', *Archives*, vol. 9, 1969–70, pp. 73–79.

Cobb, H.S., 'The Medieval Royal Customs and their Records', *Journal of the Society of Archivists*, vol. 6, 1978–81, pp. 227–9.

Cockburn, J.S., *A History of English Assizes 1558–1714*, Cambridge University Press, 1972.

Cockburn, J.S., 'Early-Modern Assize Records as Historical Evidence', *Journal of the Society of Archivists*, vol. 5, 1974–77, pp. 215–31.

Cockerell, H.A.L., and Green, E., *The British Insurance Business, 1547–1970. An Introduction and Guide to Historical Records in the United Kingdom*, Heinemann, 1976.

Coleman, B.I., *The Church of England in the Mid-Nineteenth Century: a Social Geography*, Historical Association, 1980.

Coleman, J.M., 'Guardians' Minute Books', *History*, vol. 48, 1963, pp. 181–4.

Colvin, H.M., ed., *The History of the King's Works*, HMSO, 1963–82.

The Complete Peerage, revised edition, St Catherine's Press, 1910–59.

Condon, M.M., and Hallam, E.M., 'Government Printing of the Public Records in the Eighteenth Century', *Journal of the Society of Archivists*, vol. 7, 1982–5, pp. 348–88.

Cook, C., see Powell, K.

Coppock, J.T., 'The Statistical Assessment of British Agriculture', *Agricultural History Review*, vol. 4, 1956, pp. 4–21, 66–79.

Cornwall, J., 'English Country Towns in the Fifteen-Twenties', *Economic*

History Review, 2nd series, vol. 15, 1962–3, pp. 529–69.

Cornwall, J., 'The Early Tudor Gentry', *Economic History Review*, 2nd series, vol. 17, 1964–5, pp. 456–75.

Cornwall, J., 'A Tudor Domesday. The Musters of 1522', *Journal of the Society of Archivists*, vol. 3, 1965–9, pp. 19–24.

Cornwall, J., 'English Population in the Early Sixteenth Century', *Economic History Review*, 2nd series, vol. 23, 1970, pp. 32–44.

Cox, J., *The Records of the Prerogative Court of Canterbury and the Death Duty Registers*, Public Record Office, 1980.

Cox, J.C., *The Royal Forests of England*, Methuen, 1905.

Cox, J.C., *Churchwardens' Accounts from the Fourteenth Century to the close of the Seventeenth Century*, Methuen, 1913.

Cox, N., 'Sources for Maritime History (II): the Records of the Registrar General of Shipping and Seamen', *Maritime History*, vol. 2, 1972, pp. 168–88.

Critchley, T.A., *A History of Police in England and Wales 900–1966*, Constable, 1967.

Crook, D., *Records of the General Eyre*, HMSO, 1982.

Crook, D., 'The Later Eyres', *English Historical Review*, vol. 97, 1982, pp. 241–68.

Cullingworth, J.B., *Town and Country Planning in England and Wales. An Introduction*, Allen & Unwin, 1964.

Cullingworth, J.B., *Housing and Local Government in England and Wales*, Allen & Unwin, 1966.

Darlington, I., 'The Registration of Land in England and Wales and its effect on Conveyancing Records', *Journal of the Society of Archivists*, vol. 1, 1955–9, pp. 224–6.

Darlington, I., 'Rate Books', *History*, vol. 47, 1962, pp. 42–5.

Daunton, M.J., *House and Home in the Victorian City: Working-Class Housing 1850–1914*, Edward Arnold, 1983.

Daunton, M.J., ed., *Councillors and Tenants. Local Authority Housing in English Cities, 1919–1939*, Leicester University Press, 1984.

Davies, E., 'The Small Landowner, 1780–1832, in the Light of the Land Tax Assessments', *Economic History Review*, 2nd series, 1927–8, pp. 87–113.

Davies, J.C., see Lewis, E.A.

Davies, MG., *The enforcement of English Apprenticeship. A Study in Applied Mercantilism 1563–1642*, Harvard University Press, Cambridge, Mass., 1956.

Davis, G.R.C., *Medieval Cartularies of Great Britain, A Short Catalogue*, Longman, 1958.

Davis, R., *The Industrial Revolution and British Overseas Trade*, Leicester University Press, 1979.

Dennison, S.R., *The Location of Industry and the Depressed Areas*, Oxford University Press, 1939.

Dibben, A.A., *Title Deeds 13th–19th Centuries*, Historical Association, 1971.

Dietz, F.C., *English Government Finance 1485–1558*, Cass, 1964.

Dietz, F.C., *English Public Finance 1558–1641*, Cass, 1964.

Digby, A., 'Recent Developments in the Study of the English Poor Law', *The Local Historian*, vol. 12, 1976–7, pp. 206–11.

Donahue, C., see Adams, N.

Donajgrodzki, A.P., 'New Roles for Old: the Northcote-Trevelyan Report and the Clerks of the Home Office 1822–48', in Sutherland, G., ed., *Studies in the Growth of Nineteenth-Century Government*, Routledge, 1972, pp. 82–109.

Donaldson, G., see Morton, A.

Dowdell, E.G., *A Hundred Years of Quarter Sessions, The Government of Middlesex from 1660 to 1760*, Cambridge University Press, 1932.

Draper, P., *Creation of the D.O.E.*, HMSO, 1977.

Drew, C., *Early Parochial Organisation in England. The Origins of the Office of Churchwarden*, Borthwick Institute of Historical Research, York, 1954.

Druker, J., and Storey, R., 'The Modern Records Centre at Warwick and the Local Historian', *The Local Historian*, vol. 12, 1976–7, pp. 394–400.

Duckham, B.F., 'Turnpike Records', *History*, vol. 53, 1968, pp. 217–220.

Duckham, B.F., 'Roads in the Eighteenth Century: a Reassessment', *The Local Historian*, vol. 15, 1982–3, pp. 338–44.

Duckham, B.F., 'Road Administration in South Wales: the Carmarthenshire Roads Board, 1845–89', *Journal of Transport History*, 3rd series, vol. 5, 1984, pp. 45–65.

Duffy, I.P.H., 'English Bankrupts, 1571–1861', *American Journal of Legal History*, vol. 24, 1980, pp. 283–306.

Duman, D.H., see Rubinstein, W.D.

Dunbabin, J.P.D., 'The Politics of the Establishment of County Councils', *Historical Journal*, vol. 6, 1963, pp. 226–52.

Dunbabin, J.P.D., 'Expectations of the new County Councils, and their Realization', *Historical Journal*, vol. 8, 1965, pp. 353–79.

Dunbabin, J.P.D., 'British Local Government Reforms: the Nineteenth Century and After', *English Historical Review*, vol. 92, 1977, pp. 777–805.

Duncan, G.I.O., *The High Court of Delegates*, Cambridge University Press, 1971.

Dunham, W.H., see Willard, J.F.

Ede, J.R., 'The Record Office: Central and Local. I. Evolution of a Relationship; II. The Way Ahead', *Journal of the Society of Archivists*, vol. 5, 1974–77, pp. 207–14, 491–99.

Edwards, I. ab O., ed., *A Catalogue of Star Chamber Proceedings relating to Wales*, University of Wales Press, Cardiff, 1929.

Elliott, T.H., 'The Organisation and Work of the Board of Agriculture and Fisheries', in Harris, G.M., ed., *Problems of Local Government*, King, 1911, pp. 419–36.

Ellis, R.H., 'The Historical Manuscripts Commission 1869–1969', *Journal of the Society of Archivists*, vol. 2, 1960–64, pp. 233–42.

Ellis, R.H., and others, 'The Centenary of the Royal Commission on Historical Manuscripts', *Journal of the Society of Archivists*, vol. 3., 1965–9, pp. 441–69.

Ellis, R.H., 'The British Archivist and his Society', *Journal of the Society of Archivists*, vol. 3, 1965–9, pp. 43–8.

Ellison, L., 'Petty Sessions Records and Social Deprivation', *The Local Historian*, vol. 15, 1982–3, pp. 74–9.

Elton, G.R., *England 1200–1640*, Hodder & Stoughton, 1969.

Elton, G.R., *Reform and Reformation. England 1509–1558*, Edward Arnold, 1977.

Emmerson, H., *The Ministry of Works*, Allen & Unwin, 1956.

Emmerson, H., *The Ministry of Works*, Allen & Unwin, 1956.

Emmison, F.G., and Gray, I., *County Records (Quarter Sessions, Petty Sessions, Clerk of the Peace and Lieutenancy)*, revised edition, Historical Association, 1973.

English, B., and Saville, J., *Strict Settlement. A Guide for Historians*, University of Hull Press, 1983.

Ensor, R.C.K., 'The Supersession of County Government', *Politica*, vol. 1, 1934–5, pp. 425–42.

Erksine, A.M., 'Ecclesiastical Courts and their Records in the Province of Canterbury', *Archives*, vol. 3, 1957–8, pp. 8–17.

Evans, E.J., *The Contentious Tithe. The Tithe Problem and English Agriculture, 1750–1850*, Routledge, 1976.

Evans, E.J., *Tithes and the Tithe Commutation Act 1836*, Standing Conference for Local History, 1978.

Evans, F.M.G., *The Principal Secretary of State. A Survey of the Office from 1558 to 1680*, Manchester University Press, 1923.

Evans, N., see Bond, S.

Falkus, M.E., 'The British Gas Industry before 1850', *Economic History Review*, 2nd series, vol. 20, 1967, pp. 494–508.

Falkus, M.E., 'The Development of Municipal Trading in the Nineteenth Century', *Business History*, vol. 19, 1977, pp. 134–61.

Falkus, M.E., 'The Early Development of the British Gas Industry, 1790–1815', *Economic History Review*, 2nd series, vol. 35, 1982, pp. 217–34.

Faull, M.L., 'Boundary Records of the Ordnance Survey', *The Local Historian*, vol. 15, 1982–3, pp. 483–5.

Fermoy, B., see Jenkinson, H.

Finer, H., *Municipal Trading. A Study in Public Administration*, Allen & Unwin, 1941.

Finlayson, G.B.A.M., 'The Municipal Corporation Commission and Report', *Bulletin of the Institute of Historical Research*, vol. 36, 1963, pp. 36–52.

Fischer, L.R., and Sager, E.W., 'An Approach to the Quantitative Analysis of British Shipping Records', *Business History*, vol. 22, 1980, pp. 135–51.

Flenley, R., *A Calendar of the Register of the Queen's Majesty's Council in the Dominions and Principality of Wales and the Marches of the Same [1535] 1569–1591*, Cymmrodorion Society, 1916.

Floud, F.L.C., *The Ministry of Agriculture and Fisheries*, Putnam, 1927.

Flower, C., *Introduction to the Curia Regis Rolls, 1199–1230*, Selden Society, vol. 62, 1943.

Forster, G.C.F., 'County Government in Yorkshire during the Interregnum', *Northern History*, vol. 12, 1976, pp. 84–104.

Foster, J., and Sheppard, J., *British Archives. A Guide to Archive Resources in the United Kingdom*, Macmillan, 1984.

Fowkes, E.H., 'Sources of History in Railway Records of British Transport Historical Records', *Journal of the Society of Archivists*, vol. 3, 1965–9, pp. 476–88.

Fox, K.O., 'An Edited Calendar of the first Brecknockshire Plea Roll of the Courts of the King's Great Sessions in Wales, July 1542', *National Library of Wales Journal*, vol. 14, 1965–6, pp. 469–84.

Fox, K.O., 'The Records of the Courts of Great Sessions', *Journal of the Society of Archivists*, vol. 3, 1965–9, pp. 177–82.

Fraser, C.M., 'Prerogative and the Bishops of Durham, 1267–1376', *English Historical Review*, vol. 74, 1959, pp. 467–76.

Fraser, D., ed., *The New Poor Law in the Nineteenth Century*, Macmillan, 1976.

Fraser, D., *The Evolution of the British Welfare State. A History of Social Policy since the Industrial Revolution*, 2nd edition, Macmillan, 1984.

Frow, R. and E., and Katanka, M., *The History of British Trade Unionism. A Select Bibliography*, Historical Association, 1969.

Garnett, R.G., 'The Records of Early Co-operation with particular reference to pre-Rochdale Consumer Co-operation', *The Local Historian*, vol. 9, 1970–1, pp. 163–71.

George, R.H., 'The Charters granted to English Parliamentary Corporations in 1688', *English Historical Review*, vol. 55, 1940, pp. 47–56.

Gibson, J.S.W., *Wills and Where to Find Them*, Phillimore, Chichester, 1974.

Gibson, J.S.W., 'Inventories in the Records of the Prerogative Court of Canterbury', *The Local Historian*, vol. 14, 1980–1, pp. 222–225.

Gibson, J.S.W., *Bishops Transcripts and Marriage Licences, Bonds and Allegations. A Guide to their Location and Indexes*, Federation of Family History Societies, 1981.

Gibson, J.S.W., 'Printed Indexes to Probate Records after 1850', *The Local Historian*, vol. 15, 1982–3, pp. 218–220.

Gibson, J.S.W., *Census Returns 1841–1881 on Microfilm. A Directory to Local Holdings*, Federation of Family History Societies, 1983.

Gibson, J.S.W., *Quarter Sessions Records for Family Historians: a Select List*, 2nd edition, Federation of Family History Societies, 1983.

Gibson, J.S.W., *The Hearth Tax and other Later Stuart Tax Lists and the Association Oath Rolls*, Federation of Family History Societies, 1985.

Gibson, J.S.W., *A Simplified Guide to Probate Jurisdictions: Where to Look for Wills*, 3rd edition, Federation of Family History Societies, 1985.

Gibson, J.S.W., and Chapman, C., ed., *Census Indexes and Indexing*, Federation of Family History Societies, 1981.

Gibson, J.S.W., and Mills, D.R., *Land Tax Assessments c.1690–c.1950*, Federation of Family History Societies, 1983.

Gibson, J.S.W., and Peskett, P., *Record Offices: How to Find Them*, Federation of Family History Societies, 1985.

Glass, D.V., 'Introduction' in *London Inhabitants within the Walls 1695*, London Record Society, vol. 2, 1966.

Glass, D.V., *Numbering the People. The Eighteenth-Century Population Controversy and the Development of Census and Vital Statistics in Britain*, Saxon House, Farnborough, 1973.

Glassock, R.E., ed., *The Lay Subsidy of 1334*, Oxford University Press for the British Academy, 1975.

Glassey, L.K.J., and Landau, N., 'The Commission of the Peace in the Eighteenth Century: a New Source', *Bulletin of the Institute of Historical Research*, vol. 45, 1972 pp. 247–65.

Gleason, J.H., *The Justices of the Peace in England 1558 to 1640. A Later Eirenarcha*, Clarendon Press, Oxford, 1969.

Goldstrom, M., 'Education in England and Wales in 1851', in Lawton, R., ed., *The Census and Social Structure. An Interpretative Guide to Nineteenth Century Censuses for England and Wales*, Cass, 1978, pp 224–40.

Gordon, M.D., 'The Collection of Ship-Money in the Reign of Charles I', *Transactions of the Royal Historical Society*, 3rd series, vol. 4, 1910, pp. 141–62.

Gosden, P.H.J.H., *The Friendly Societies in England, 1815–1875*, Manchester University Press, 1961.

Gosden, P.H.J.H., *The Development of Educational Administration in England and Wales*, Basil Blackwell, Oxford, 1966.

Gosden, P.H.J.H., *Self-Help. Voluntary Associations in the 19th Century*, Batsford, 1973.

Gosden, P.H.J.H., and Sharp, P.R., *The Development of an Education Service: the West Riding 1889–1974*, West Yorkshire MCC, 1978.

Gosden, P.H.J.H., 'Twentieth-Century Archives of Education as Sources for the Study of Education Policy and Administration', *Archives*, vol. 15, 1981–2, pp. 86–95.

Gowan, I., 'The Administration of the National Parks', *Public Administration*, vol. 33, 1955, pp. 425–38.

Gras, N.S.B., *The Early English Customs System. A Documentary Study of the Institutional and Economic History of the Customs from the Thirteenth to the Sixteenth Century*, Harvard University Press, Cambridge, Mass., 1918.

Gray, I., see Emmison, F.G.

Green, E., see Cockerell, H.A.L.

Green, C.A.H., *The Setting of the Constitution of the Church in Wales*, Sweet & Maxwell, 1937.

Griffiths, M., 'The Vale of Glamorgan in the 1543 Lay Subsidy Returns', *Bulletin of the Board of Celtic Studies*, vol. 29, 1980–2, pp.709–48.

Grey, P., 'Parish Workhouses and Poorhouses', *The Local Historian*, vol. 10, 1972–3, pp. 70–75.

Gross, C., *The Gild Merchant. A Contribution to British Municipal History*, Clarendon Press, Oxford, 1890.

Gutchen, R.M., 'Paupers in Union Workhouses. Computer Analysis of Admissions and Discharges', *The Local Historian*, vol. 11, 1974–5, pp. 452–6.

Guy, J.A., *The Cardinal's Court. The Impact of Thomas Wolsey in Star Chamber*, Harvester, Hassocks, 1977.

Guy, J.A., *The Court of Star Chamber and its Records to the Reign of Elizabeth I*, HMSO, 1985.

Hadcock, R.N., see Knowles, D.

Hadfield, C., *The Canals of the West Midlands*, David & Charles, Newton Abbot, 1969.

Hadwin, 'The Medieval Lay Subsidies and Economic History', *Economic History Review*, 2nd series, vol. 36, 1983, pp. 200–217.

Hall, H., *A History of the Customs Revenue in England*, Elliot Stock, 1895.

Hallam, E.M., see Condon, M.M., and Smith, E.M.

Hannah, L., *Electricity before Nationalisation. A Study of the Development of the Electricity Supply Industry in Britain*, Macmillan, 1979.

Hannah, L., *Engineers, Managers and Politicians. The first fifteen years of Nationalised Electricity Supply in Britain*, Macmillan, 1982.

Harding, A., 'The Origins and Early History of the Keeper of the Peace', *Transactions of the Royal Historical Society*, 5th series, vol. 10, 1960, pp. 85–109.

Harding, A., *The Law Courts of Medieval England*, Allen & Unwin, 1977.

Harley, J.B., *Maps for the Local Historian. A Guide to the British Sources*, Standing Conference for Local History, 1972.

Harris, B.E., ed., *The History of the County Palatine of Chester: a Short Bibliography and Guide to Sources*, Cheshire Community Council, 1983.

Harris, G.M., ed., *Problems of Local Government*, King, 1911.

Harriss, G.L., *King, Parliament, and Public Finance in Medieval England to 1369*, Clarendon Press, Oxford, 1975.

Hart, C.E., *The Verderers and Speech-Court of the Forest of Dean*, John Bellows, Gloucester, 1950.

Hartley, T.E., 'Under-Sheriffs and Bailiffs in some English Shrievalties, c.1580 to c.1625', *Bulletin of the Institute of Historical Research*, vol. 47, 1974, pp. 164–85.

Harvey, A.D., 'The Regional Distribution of Incomes in England and Wales, 1803', *The Local Historian*, vol. 13, 1978–9, pp. 332–7.

Harvey, P.D.A., 'Archives in Britain: Anarchy or Policy', *American Archivist*, vol. 46, 1983, pp. 22–30.

Harvey, P.D.A. *Manorial Records*, British Records Association, 1984.

Hastings, M., *The Court of Common Pleas in Fifteenth-Century England*, Cornell University Press, Ithaca, N.Y., 1947.

Heath, J., 'Private Bus Services before 1930', *The Local Historian*, vol. 15, 1982–3, pp. 221–4.

Henstock, A., 'The Nottinghamshire Parish Registers Microfilming Project', *Journal of the Society of Archivists*, vol. 7, 1982–5, pp. 443–9.

Hey, D., *Packmen, Carriers and Packhorse Roads. Trade and Communications in North Derbyshire and South Yorkshire*, Leicester University Press, 1980.

Hill, C., and Woodstock, J., *The National Health Service*, Christopher Johnson, 1949.

Hoak, D.E., *The King's Council in the Reign of Edward VI*, Cambridge University Press, 1976.

Hobsbawm, E.J., 'Records of the Trade Union Movement', *Archives*, vol. 4, 1959–60, pp. 129–37.

Hodgkinson, R.G., *The Origins of the National Health Service. The Medical Services of the New Poor Law, 1834–1871*, Wellcome Historical Medical Library, 1967.

Hodgson, H.J., ed., *Steer's Parish Law; being a Digest of the Law relating to the Civil and Ecclesiastical Government of Parishes; Friendly Societies, etc, etc, and the Relief, Settlement and Removal of the Poor*, 3rd edition, Steven & Norton, Sweet & Maxwell, 1857.

Honingsbaum, F., *The Struggle for the Ministry of Health 1914–1919*, Bell, 1970.

Hoon, E.E., *The Organization of the English Customs System, 1696–1786*, repr. with a new intro. by Jarvis, R.C., David & Charles, Newton Abbot, 1968.

Hope-Jones, A., *Income Tax in the Napoleonic Wars*, Cambridge University Press, 1939.

Horton, A.E., 'Records and the National Coal Board', *Archives*, vol. 1, 1949–52, pp. 28–31.

Hoskins, W.G., *Fieldwork in Local History*, Faber & Faber, 1967.

Hoskins, W.G., see also Stamp, L.D.

Houghton, J., ed., *Index of Cases in the Records of the Court of Arches at Lambeth Palace Library*, Index Library, vol. 85, 1972.

Houlbrooke, R., *Church Courts and the People during the English Revolution 1520–1570*, Oxford University Press, 1979.

Howell, P.A., *The Judicial Committee of the Privy Council 1833–1876. Origins, Structure and Development*, Cambridge University Press, 1979.

Howell, R., 'Hearth Tax Records', *History*, vol. 49, 1964, pp. 42–5.

Hughes, E., *Studies in Administration and Finance 1558–1825 with special reference to the History of Salt Taxation in England*, Manchester University Press, 1934.

Hughes, E.J., see Aitchison, J.W.

Hull, F., 'Towards a National Archives Policy – the Local Scene', *Journal of the Society of Archivists*, vol. 7, 1982–5, pp. 224–9.

Humphery-Smith, C.R., *Phillimore Atlas and Index of Parish Registers*, Phillimore, Chichester, 1984.

Hunnisett, R.F., *The Medieval Coroner*, Cambridge University Press, 1961.

Hunt, H.G., 'Land Tax Assessments', *History*, vol. 52, 1967, pp. 283–6.

Hunt, R., 'Quarter Sessions Order Books', *History*, vol. 55, 1970, pp. 397–400.

Hunter, R.A. MacAlpine, I., and Payne, L.M., 'The Country Register of House for the Reception of "Lunatics", 1798–1812', *Journal of Mental Science*, vol. 102, 1956, pp. 856–63.

Hurstfield, J., *The Queen's Wards. Wardship and Marriage under Elizabeth I*, Longman, 1958.

Imray, J., 'Town and Country Planning Records and the County Archivist', *Journal of the Society of Archivists*, vol. 1, 1955–9, pp. 43–6.

Jack, R.I., *Medieval Wales*, Hodder & Stoughton, 1972.

Jackson, R.M., *The Machinery of Justice in England*, Cambridge University Press, 1940.

Jacobs, P.M., 'Registers of the Universities, Colleges and Schools of Great Britain and Ireland', *Bulletin of the Institute of Historical Research*, vol. 37, 1964, pp. 185–232.

James, R.L.M., 'The Records of Friendly Societies', *Archives*, vol. 6, 1963–4, pp. 223–4.

Jarvis, R.C., 'Ship Registry – 1786', *Maritime History*, vol. 4, 1974, pp. 12–30.

Jarvis, R.C., see also Hoon, E.E.

Jeffereys, K., 'R.A. Butler, the Board of Education and the 1944 Education Act', *History*, vol. 69, 1984, pp. 415–31.

Jenkinson, H., *A Manual of Archive Administration*, Lund, Humphries, 1937.

Jenkinson, H., and Fermoy, B., ed., *Select Cases in the Exchequer of Pleas*, Selden Society, vol. 48, 1931.

Jewell, H.M., *English Local Administration in the Middle Ages*, David & Charles, Newton Abbot, 1972.

Johnson, C., 'The Public Record Office', in Davies, J.C., ed., *Studies Presented to Sir Hilary Jenkinson, C.B.E., LL.D., F.S.A.*, Oxford University Press, 1957, pp. 178–95.

Johnson, H.C., 'The Public Record Office and its Problems', *Bulletin of the Institute of Historical Research*, vol. 42, 1969, pp. 86–95.

Johnson, L.C., 'Historical Records of the British Transport Commission', *Journal of the Society of Archivists*, vol. 1, 1955–9, pp. 94–100.

Johnson, L.C., 'British Transport Historical Records Department: the first decade', *Archives*, vol. 6, 1963–4, pp. 163–71.

Jones, E.D., 'The Migration of Probate Records in Wales, 1945–49', *Archives*, vol. 1, 1949–52, pp. 7–12.

Jones, E.G., ed., *Exchequer Proceedings (Equity) concerning Wales. Henry VIII-Elizabeth. Abstracts of Bills and Inventory of Further Proceedings*, University of Wales Press, Cardiff, 1939.

Jones, I.G., ed., *The Religious Census of 1851: a Calendar of the Returns relating to Wales*, University of Wales Press, Cardiff, 1976–81.

Jones, K., *A History of the Mental Health Services*, Routledge, 1972.

Jones, L.J., see Palliser, D.M.

Jones, P.E., 'Local Assessments for Parliamentary Taxes', *Journal of the Society of Archivists*, vol. 4, 1970–73, pp. 55–9.

Jones, T.I.J., ed., *Exchequer Proceedings concerning Wales in tempore James I. Abstracts of Bills and Answers and Inventory of Further Proceedings*, University of Wales Press, Cardiff, 1955.

Jones, W.J., 'An Introduction to Petty Bag Proceedings in the Reign of Elizabeth I', *California Law Review*, vol. 51, 1963, pp. 882–905.

Jones, W.J., *The Elizabethan Court of Chancery*, Clarendon Press, Oxford, 1967.

The Jubilee of County Councils 1889 to 1939. Fifty Years of Local Government, Evans Brothers, 1939.

Kain, R.J.P., and Prince, H.C., *The Tithe Surveys of England and Wales*, Cambridge University Press, 1985.

Karraker, C.H., *The Seventeenth-Century Sheriff. A Comparative Study of the Sheriff of England and the Chesapeake Colonies 1607–1689*, University of North Carolina Press, Chapel Hill, 1930.

Katanka, M., see Frow, R. and E.

Keane, P., 'An English County and Education: Somerset, 1889–1902' *English Historical Review*, vol. 88, 1973, pp. 286–311.

Keith-Lucas, B., *English Local Government in the Nineteenth and Twentieth Centuries*, Historical Association, 1977.

Keith-Lucas, B., *The Unreformed Local Government System*, Croom Helm, 1980.

Keith-Lucas, B., and Richards, P.G., *A History of Local Government in the Twentieth Century*, Allen & Unwin, 1978.

Kerling, N.J.M., 'Hospital Records', *Journal of the Society of Archivists*, vol. 5, 1974–77, pp. 181–3.

Kitching, C.J., 'The Probate Jurisdiction of Thomas Cromwell as Vicegerent', *Bulletin of the Institute of Historical Research*, vol. 46, 1973, pp. 102–6.

Kitching, C.J., 'Probate during the Civil War and Interregnum. Part 1. The Survival of the Prerogative Court in the 1640s; Part 2. The Court for Probate, 1653–1660', *Journal of the Society of Archivists*, vol. 5, 1974–77, pp. 283–93, 346–56.

Kitching, C.J., 'The Disposal of Monastic and Chantry Lands', in Heal, F., and O'Day, R., ed., *Church and Society of England: Henry VIII to James I*, Macmillan, 1977, pp. 119–36.

Knightbridge, A.A.H., 'National Archives Policy', *Journal of the Society of Archivists*, vol. 7, 1982–5, pp. 213–223.

Knightbridge, A.A.H., *Archive Legislation in the United Kingdom*, Society of Archivists, 1985.

Knoop, D., *Principles and Methods of Municipal Trading*, Macmillan, 1912.

Kramer, S., *The English Craft Gilds. Studies in their Progress and Decline*, Columbia University Press, 1927.

Knowles, D., and Hadcock, R.N., *Medieval Religious Houses, England and Wales*, 2nd edition, Longman, 1971.

Knowles, D., Brooke, C.N.L., and London, V.C.M., ed., *The Heads of Religious Houses, England and Wales, 940–1216*, Cambridge University Press, 1972.

Koenig, W.J., see Mayer, S.L.

Lambert, R.J., 'A Victorian National Health Service: State Vaccination, 1855–71', *Historical Journal*, vol. 5, 1962, pp. 1–18.

Lambert, R.J., 'Central and Local Relations in Mid-Victorian England: the Local Government Act Office, 1858–71', *Victorian Studies*, vol. 6, 1962–3, pp. 121–50.

Lambert, R.J., *Sir John Simon (1816–1904) and English Social Administration*, MacGibbon & Kee, 1963.

Landau, N., see Glassey, L.K.J.

Lapsley, G.T., *The County Palatine of Durham. A Study in Constitutional History*, Harva.d University Press, New York, 1900.

Lawton, R., ed., *The Census and Social Structure. An Interpretative Guide to Nineteenth Century Censuses for England and Wales*, Cass, 1978.

Leadam, I.S., ed., *Select Cases in the Court of Requests (1497–1569)*, Selden Society, vol. 12, 1898.

Leary, W., 'The Methodist Archives', *Archives*, vol. 16, 1983–4, pp. 16–27.

Lee, J.M., *Social Leaders and Public Persons. A Study of County Government in Cheshire since 1888*, Clarendon Press, Oxford, 1963.

Leonard, E.M., *The Early History of English Poor Relief*, Cambridge University Press, 1900.

Lewis, E.A., and Davies, J.C., ed., *Records of the Court of Augmentations relating to Wales and Monmouthshire*, University of Wales Press, Cardiff, 1954.

Lewis, G.R., *The Stannaries. A Study of the English Tin Mines*, Harvard University Press, Cambridge, Mass., 1924.

Lewis, M., 'The Walsall Metropolitan Borough Archives Service', *Archives*, vol. 14, 1979–80, pp. 225–31.

Lewis, R.A., *Edwin Chadwick and the Public Health Movement, 1832–1854*, Longman, 1952.

Lipman, V.D., *Local Government Areas 1834–1945*, Blackwell, Oxford, 1949.

London, V.C.M., see Knowles, D.

Marchant, R.A., *The Church under the Law. Justice, Administration and Discipline in the Diocese of York 1560–1640*, Cambridge University Press, 1969.

Marriner, S., 'English Bankruptcy Records and Statistics before 1850', *Economic History Review*, 2nd series, vol. 33, 1980, pp. 351–66.

Marsden, R.G., ed., *Select Pleas in the Court of Admiralty*, Selden Society, vol. 6, 1892 and 11, 1897.

Marsh, A., and Ryan, V., *Historical Directory of Trade Unions*, Gower, Aldershot, 1980–84.

Marshall, J.D., *The Old Poor Law, 1795–1834*, Macmillan, 1968.

Marshall, J.D., 'Local or Regional History – or both', *The Local Historian*, vol. 12, 1976–7, pp. 3–10.

Marshall, J.D., ed., *The History of Lancashire County Council*, Martin Robertson, 1977.

Marshall, J.D., 'The Study of Local and Regional "Communities": some Problems and Possibilities', *Northern History*, vol. 17, 1981, pp. 203–30.

Marshall, L.M., 'The Levying of the Hearth Tax, 1662–88', *English Historical Review*, vol. 51, 1936, pp. 628–46.

Martin, G.H., 'The Origins of Borough Records', *Journal of the Society of Archivists*, vol. 2, 1960–64, pp. 147–53.

Martin, G.H., 'The English Borough in the Thirteenth Century', *Transactions of the Royal Historical Society*, 5th series, vol. 13, 1963, pp. 123–44.

Martin, J.M., 'Landownership and the Lax Tax Returns', *Agricultural History Review*, vol. 14, 1966, pp. 96–103.

Mather, J., 'The Parliamentary Committee and the Justices of the Peace, 1642–1661', *American Journal of the Legal History*, vol. 23, 1979, pp. 120–43.

Mathias, P., and Pearsall, A.W.H., ed., *Shipping: a Survey of Historical Records*, David & Charles, Newton Abbot, 1971.

Matthews, K., 'Crew Lists, Agreements and Official Logs of the British Empire 1863–1913', *Business History*, vol. 16, 1974, pp. 78–80

Maxwell-Lyte, H.C., *Historical Notes on the use of the Great Seal of England*, HMSO, 1926.

Mayer, S.L., and Koenig, W.J., ed., *The Two World Wars: a Guide to Manuscript Collections in the United Kingdom*, Bowker, 1976.

Meekings, C.A.F., Porter, S., and Roy, I., ed., *The Hearth Tax Collectors' Book for Worcester 1678–1680*, Worcestershire Historical Society, new series, vol. 11, 1983.

Melling, E., *A History of the Kent County Council, 1889–1974*, Kent CC, 1975.

Midwinter, E.C., *Social Administration in Lancashire 1830–1860. Poor Law, Public Health and Police*, Manchester University Press, 1969.

Miller, J., 'The Crown and the Borough Charters in the Reign of Charles II', *English Historical Review*, vol. 100, 1985, pp. 53–84.

Mills, D.R., see Gibson, J.S.W.

Minchinton, W.E., 'Agricultural Returns and the Government during the Napoleonic Wars', *Agricultural History Review*, vol. 1, 1953, pp. 29–43.

Minchinton, W.E., 'The Agricultural Returns of 1800 for Wales', *Bulletin of the Board of Celtic Studies*, vol. 21, 1964–66, pp. 74–93.

Minchinton, W.E., ed., *Wage Regulation in Pre-Industrial England*, David & Charles, Newton Abbot, 1972.

Mingay, G.E., 'The Land Tax Assessments and the Small Landowner', *Economic History Review*, 2nd series, vol. 17, 1964–65, pp. 381–88.

Mitchell, I., 'Pitt's Shop Tax in the History of Retailing', *The Local Historian*, vol. 14, 1980–1, pp. 348–51.

Mitchell, S.K., ed., *Taxation in Medieval England*, Yale University Press, New Haven, Conn., 1951.

Moir, E., *The Justice of the Peace*, Penguin, Harmondsworth, 1969.

Monmouthshire County Council, *Monmouthshire County Council 1889–1974*, Monmouthshire CC, 1974.

Morris, R.J., *Cholera 1832. The Social Response to an Epidemic*, Croom Helm, 1976.

Morris, W.A., *The Medieval English Sheriff to 1300*, Manchester University Press, 1927.

Morris, W.A., see also Willard, J.F.

Morton, A., 'Inland Sanitary Surveys 1893–5', *Public Administration*, vol. 62, 1984, pp. 494–6.

Morton, A., and Donaldson, G., *British National Archives and the Local*

Historian. A Guide to Official Record Publications, Historical Association, 1980.

Moss, M.S., 'Public Record Office: good or bad?', *Journal of the Society of Archivists*, vol. 7, 1982–5, pp. 156–66.

Moylan, P.A., *The Form and Reform of County Government: Kent, 1889–1914*, Leicester University Press, 1978.

Mullins, E.L.C., *Texts and Calendars. An Analytical Guide to Serial Publications*, Royal Historical Society, 1958.

Mullins, E.L.C., *Texts and Calendars II. An Analytical Guide to Serial Publications, 1957–1982*, Royal Historical Society, 1983.

MacAlpine, I., see Hunter, R.A.

McCrone, G., *Regional Policy in Britain*, Allen & Unwin, 1969.

McDonald, R.W., 'The Parish Registers of Wales', *National Library of Wales Journal*, vol. 19, 1975–6, pp. 399–429.

McLaughlin, E., *St Catherine's House*, Federation of Family History Societies, 1985.

McLaughin, E., *Somerset House Wills from 1858*, Federation of Family History Societies, 1985.

McLaughlin, E., *The Censuses 1841–1881. Their Use and Interpretation*, Federation of Family History Societies, 1985.

MacLeod, R.M., *Treasury Control and Social Administration. A Study of Establishment Growth at the Local Government Board 1871–1905*, Bell, 1968.

MacMorran, K.M., *A Handbook for Churchwardens and Church Councillors*, Mowbray 1921.

Nelson, R.R., *The Home Office, 1782–1801*, Duke University Press, Durham, N.C., 1969.

Newsholme, A., *The Ministry of Health*, Putnam, 1925.

Newton, S.C., 'Parliamentary Surveys', *History*, vol. 53, 1968, pp. 51–4.

Nicholas, H.G., 'The Public Records: the Historian, the National Interest and Official Policy', *Journal of the Society of Archivists*, vol. 3, 1965–9, pp. 1–6.

Nickson, M.A.E., *The British Library, Guide to the Catalogues and Indexes of the Department of Manuscripts*, British Library, 1978.

Norman, E.R., *Church and Society in England, 1770–1970: a Historical Study*, Clarendon Press, Oxford, 1976.

Office of Population Censuses and Surveys and General Register Office, Edinburgh, *Guide to Census Reports. Great Britain 1801–1966*, HMSO, 1977.

O'Neal, R.A.H., *Derbyshire Lead and Lead Mining. A Bibliography*, Derbyshire County Library, 1960.

Orbell, J., see Pressnell, L.S.

Orwin, C.S., and Whetham, E.H., *History of British Agriculture 1846–1914*, Longman, 1964.

Osborne, B., *Justices of the Peace 1361–1848. A History of the Justices of the Peace for the Counties of England*, Sedgehill Press, Shaftesbury, 1960.

Otway-Ruthven, J., *The King's Secretary and the Signet Office in the XV Century*, Cambridge University Press, 1939.

Owen, A.E.B., 'Land Drainage Authorities and their Records', *Journal of the Society of Archivists*, vol. 2, 1960–64, pp. 417–23.

Owen, A.E.B., 'Records of Commissions of Sewers', *History*, vol. 52, 1967, pp. 35–8.

Owen, D.M., *The Records of the Established Church in England excluding Parochial Records*, British Records Association, 1970.

Owen, D.M., 'Episcopal Visitation Books', *History*, vol. 49, 1964, pp. 185–8.

Oxley, G.W., *Poor Relief in England and Wales 1601–1834*, David & Charles, Newton Abbot, 1974.

Palliser, D.M., and Jones, L.J., 'A Neglected Source for English Population History: the Bishops' Returns of 1563 and 1603', *The Local Historian*, vol. 15, 1982–3, pp. 155–6.

Palmer, R.C., *The County Courts of Medieval England 1150–1350*, Princeton University Press, New Jersey, 1982.

Parris, H., *Government and the Railways in Nineteenth-Century Britain*, Routledge, 1965.

Parry-Jones, W. Ll., *The Trade in Lunacy. A Study of Private Madhouses in England in the Eighteenth and Nineteenth Centuries*, Routledge, 1972.

Pawson, E., *Transport and Economy: the Turnpike Roads of Eighteenth Century Britain*, Academic Press, 1977.

Payne, L.M., see Hunter, R.A.

Pearsall, A.W.H., see Mathias, P.

Pellew, J., *The Home Office 1848–1914. From Clerks to Bureaucrats*, Heinemann, 1982.

Peskett, P., see Gibson, J.S.W.

Peyton, S.A., 'The Village Population in the Tudor Lay Subsidy Rolls', *English Historical Review*, vol. 30, 1915, pp. 234–50.

Phillips, C.B., 'County Committees and Local Government in Cumberland and Westmorland, 1642–1660', *Northern History*, vol. 4, 1969, pp. 34–66.

Phythian-Adams, C., 'Records of the Craft Gilds', *The Local Historian*, vol. 9, 1970–1, pp. 267–74.

Pile, W., *The Department of Education and Science*, Allen & Unwin, 1979.

Platt, C., *The English Medieval Town*, Secker & Warburg, 1976.

Porter, S., see Meekings, C.A.F.

Post, J.B., 'Some Limitations of the Medieval Peace Rolls', *Journal of the Society of Archivists*, vol. 4, 1970–73, pp. 633–45.

Postles, D., 'Record-keeping in the Medieval Borough: Proof of Wills', *Archives*, vol. 16, 1983–4, pp. 12–15.

Powell, K., and Cook, C., *English Historical Facts 1485–1603*, Macmillan, 1977.

Powell, W.R., 'Sources for the History of Protestant Nonconformist Churches in England', *Bulletin of the Institute of Historical Research*, vol. 25, 1952, pp. 213–227.

Pressnell, L.S., and Orbell, J., *A Guide to the Historical Records of British Banking*, Gower, Aldershot, 1985.

Prouty, R., *The Transformation of the Board of Trade 1830–1855. A Study of Administrative Reorganisation in the Heyday of Laissez Faire*, Heinemann, 1957.

Public Record Office, *Guide to the Public Records. Part 1. Introductory*, HMSO, 1949.

Public Record Office, *Guide to the Contents of the Public Record Office*, HMSO, 1963–8.

Public Record Office, *Maps and Plans in the Public Record Office. I. British Isles, c.1410–1860*, HMSO, 1967.

Public Record Office, *The Second World War. A Guide to Documents in the Public Record Office*, HMSO, 1972.

Public Record Office, *Descriptive List of Exchequer, Queen's Remembrancer, Port Books. Part 1. 1565 to 1700*, PRO, n.d.

Pugh, R.B., *The Crown Estate. An Historical Essay*, HMSO, 1960.

Pugh, R.B., 'Charles Abbot and the Public Records: the first phase', *Bulletin of the Institute of Historical Research*, 1966, pp. 69–85.

Pugh, R.B., *Itinerant Justices in English History*, University of Exeter, 1967.

Pugh, R.B., *Imprisonment in Medieval England*, Cambridge University Press, 1981.

Purvis, J.S., *Tudor Parish Documents of the Diocese of York. A Selection with Introduction & Notes*, Cambridge University Press, 1948.

Putnam, B.H., 'The Transformation of the Keepers of the Peace into the Justices of the Peace, 1327–80', *Transactions of the Royal Historical Society*, 4th series, vol. 12, 1929, pp. 19–48.

Putnam, B.H., *Proceedings before the Justices of the Peace in the Fourteenth and Fifteenth Centuries. Edward III to Richard III*, Spottiswoode, Ballantyne, 1938.

Randall, P.J., 'Wales in the Structure of Central Government', *Public Administration*, vol. 50, 1972, pp. 353–72.

Rath, T., 'Business Records in the Public Record Office in the Age of the Industrial Revolution', *Business History*, vol. 17, 1975, pp. 189–200.

Rayska, U., 'The Archives Section of Birmingham Reference Library', *Archives*, vol. 12, 1975–6, pp. 59–67.

Redstone, L.J., and Steer, F.W., ed., *Local Records. Their Nature and Care*, Bell, 1953.

Registrar General, *The Story of the General Register Office and its Origins from 1538 to 1937*, HMSO, 1937.

Reid, R.R., *The King's Council in the North*, Longman, 1921.

Reynolds, S., *An Introduction to the History of English Medieval Towns*, Clarendon Press, Oxford, 1975.

Richards, P.G., *The Reformed Local Government System*, Allen & Unwin, 1973.

Richards, P.G., *The Local Government Act 1972. Problems of Implementation*, PEP and Allen & Unwin, 1975.

Richards, P.G., see also Keith–Lucas, B.

Richardson, W.C., *Tudor Chamber Administration 1485–1547*, Louisiana State University Press, Baton Rouge, La., 1952.

Richardson, W.C., *History of the Court of Augmentations 1536–1554*, Louisiana State University Press, Baton Rouge, La., 1961.

Richmond, L., and Stockford, B., *Company Archives. The Survey of the Records of 1000 of the first Registered Companies in England and Wales*, Gower, Aldershot, 1986.

Riden, P., *Local History. A Handbook for Beginners*, Batsford, 1983.

Riden, P., *Tudor and Stuart Chesterfield*, Chesterfield Borough Council, 1984.

Riden, P., ed., *Probate Records and the Local Community*, Alan Sutton, Gloucester, 1985.

Riden, P., 'An English Factor at Stockholm in the 1680's', *Scandinavian Economic History Review*, vol. 35, 1987 (forthcoming).

Riden, P., see also Blair, J.

Roberts, S.K., *Recovery and Restoration in an English County: Devon Local Administration, 1646–1670*, Exeter University Press, 1985.

Robins, F.W., *The Story of Water Supply*, Oxford University Press, 1946.

Robinson, E.J., 'The Records of the Church Commissioners', *Journal of the Society of Archivists*, vol. 3., 1965–9, pp. 347–56.

Robinson, E.J., 'The Records of the Church Commissioners', *The Local Historian*, vol. 9, 1970–1, pp. 215–221.

Robinson, W.R.B., 'The First Subsidy Assessment of the Hundreds of Swansea and Llangyfelach, 1543', *Welsh History Review*, vol. 2, 1964–5, pp. 125–45.

Rogers, C.D., *The Family Tree Detective. A Manual for Analysing and Solving Genealogical Problems in England and Wales, 1538 to the Present Day*, Manchester University Press, 1983.

Roper, M., 'Public Records and the Policy Process in the Twentieth Century', *Public Administration*, vol. 55, 1977, pp. 253–68.

Rose, M.E., *The Relief of Poverty, 1834–1914*, Macmillan, 1972.

Roseveare, H., *The Treasury. The Evolution of a British Institution*, Allen Lane: The Penguin Press, 1969.

Roseveare, H., *The Treasury 1660–1870. The Foundations of Control*, Allen & Unwin, 1973.

Ross, W.A., 'Local Government Board and After: Retrospect', *Public Administration*, vol. 34, 1956, pp. 17–25.

Rowlands, E., 'The Politics of Regional Administration: the Establishment of the Welsh Office', *Public Administration*, vol. 50, 1972, pp. 333–52.

Roy, I., see Meekings, C.A.F.

'The Royal Commission on Historical Manuscripts' Companies Index', *Business History*, vol. 26, 1984, p. 80.

Royle, S.A., 'Clergymen's Returns to the 1831 Census', *The Local Historian*, vol. 14, 1980–1, pp. 79–90.

Rubin, G.R., 'The County Courts and the Tally Trade, 1846–1914', in Rubin, G.R., and Sugarman, D., ed., *Law, Economy and Society, 1750–1914: Essays in the History of English Law*, Professional Books, Abingdon, 1984, pp. 321–48.

Rubinstein, W.D., and Duman, D.H., 'Probate Valuations. A Tool for the Historian', *The Local Historian*, vol. 11, 1974–5, pp. 68–71.

Rushton, P., 'Women, Witchcraft, and Slander in Early Modern England: Cases from the Church Courts of Durham, 1560–1675', *Northern History*, vol. 18, 1982, pp. 116–132.

Ryan, V., see Marsh, A.

Sabine, B.E.V., *A History of Income Tax*, Allen & Unwin, 1966.

Sager, E.W., see Fischer, L.R.

Sainty, J.C., *Lieutenants of Counties, 1585–1642*, Bulletin of the Institute of Historical Research Special Supplement No 8, 1970.

Sainty, J.C., *List of Lieutenants of Counties of England and Wales 1660–1974*, List & Index Society Special Series, vol. 12, 1979.

Saville, J., 'Sleeping Partnership and Limited Liability, 1850–1856', *Economic History Review*, 2nd series, vol. 8, 1955–6, pp. 418–33.

Saville, J., see also English, B.

Sawyer, P.H., *Anglo-Saxon Charters. An Annotated List and Bibliography*, Royal Historical Society, 1968.

Sayles, G.O., ed., *Select Cases in the Court of King's Bench*, Selden Society, vols. 55, 1936, 57, 1938, 58, 1939, 76, 1957, 82, 1965, 88, 1971.

Sawyer, P.H., *Domesday Book: a Reassessment*, Edward Arnold, 1985.

Scammell, J., 'The Origins and Limitations of the Liberty of Durham', *English Historical Review*, vol. 81, 1966, pp. 449–73.

Scofield, R.S., 'The Geographical Distribution of Wealth in England, 1334–1649', *Economic History Review*, 2nd series, vol. 18, 1965, pp. 483–510.

Schofield, R.S., see also Wrigley, E.A.

Schumpeter, E.B., *English Overseas Trade Statistics 1697–1808*, Clarendon Press, Oxford, 1960.

Schofield, C.L., *A Study of the Court of Star Chamber largely based on Manuscripts in the British Museum and the Public Record Office*, Chicago University Press, 1900.

Scull, A.T., *Museums of Madness. The Social Organization of Insanity in Nineteenth-Century England*, Allen Lane, 1979.

Serjeant, W.R., 'The Survey of Local Archive Services, 1968', *Journal of the Society of Archivists*, vol. 4, 1970–73, pp. 301–26.

Seymour, W.A., ed., *A History of the Ordnance Survey*, Dawsons, Folkestone, 1980.

Shannon, H.A., 'The Coming of General Limited Liability', *Economic History*, vol. 2, 1930–33, pp. 267–91.

Shannon, H.A., 'The First Five Thousand Companies and their Duration', *Economic History*, vol. 2, 1930–33, pp. 396–419.

Shannon, H.A., 'The Limited Liability Companies of 1866–1883', *Economic History Review*, vol. 4, 1932–4, pp. 290–316.

Sharp, E., *The Ministry of Housing and Local Government*, Allen & Unwin, 1969.

Sharp, P.R., see Gosden, P.H.J.H.

Sheehan, M.M., *The Will in Medieval England from the Conversion of the Anglo-Saxons to the end of the Thirteenth Century*, Pontifical Institute of Mediaeval Studies, Toronto, 1963.

Sheppard, F., and Belcher, V., 'The Deeds Registries of Yorkshire and Middlesex', *Journal of the Society of Archivists*, vol. 6, 1978–81, pp. 274–86.

Sheppard, J., see Foster, J.

Sherrington, E.J., 'The Plea-Rolls of the Courts of Great Sessions 1541–1575', *National Library of Wales Journal*, vol. 13, 1963–4, pp. 363–73.

Simpson, H.B., 'The Office of Constable', *English Historical Review*, vol. 10, 1895, pp. 625–41.

Slatter, M.D., 'The Records of the Court of Arches', *Journal of Ecclesiastical History*, vol. 4, 1953, pp. 139–53.

Slatter, M.D., 'The Study of the Records of the Court of Arches', *Journal of the Society of Archivists*, vol. 2, 1960–64, pp. 29–31.

Smellie, K.B., *A History of Local Government*, Allen & Unwin, 1968.

Smith, A.H., see Barnes, T.G.

Smith, D.M., *A Guide to the Archive Collections in the Borthwick Institute of Historical Research*, Borthwick Institute of Historical Research, 1973.

Smith, D.M., 'The York Institution Act Books: Diocesan Registration in the Sixteenth Century', *Archives*, vol. 13, 1977–8, pp. 171–9.

Smith, D.M., *A Supplemental Guide to the Archive Collections in the Borthwick Institute of Historical Research*, Borthwick Institute of Historical Research, 1980.

Smith, D.M., *Guide to Bishops' Registers of England and Wales: a Survey from the Middle Ages to the Abolition of Episcopacy in 1646*, Royal Historical Society, 1981.

Smith, E.M., 'The Tower of London as a Record Office', *Archives*, vol. 14, 1979–80, pp. 3–10.

Smith, E.M., see also Condon, M.M.

Smith, H., 'The Resurgent County Court in Victorian Britain', *American Journal of Legal History*, vol. 13, 1969, pp. 126–38.

Smith, H.J., 'Local Reports to the General Board of Health', *History*, 56, 1971, pp. 46–9.

Smith, H.Ll., *The Board of Trade*, Putnam, 1928.

Smith, J.C.C., ed., *Index of Wills Recorded in the Archiepiscopal Registers at Lambeth Palace*, Privately Published, 1919.

Smith, J.T., *English Gilds*, Early English Text Society, vol. 11, 1870.

Snagge, T., *The Evolution of the County Court*, William Clowes, 1904.

Snell, L.S., 'Chantry Certificates', *History*, vol. 48, 1964, pp. 332–5.

Somerville, R., 'The Duchy of Lancaster Council and Court of Duchy Chamber', *Transactions of the Royal Historical Society*, 4th series, vol. 23, 1941, pp. 159–77.

Somerville, R., 'The Duchy of Lancaster Records', *Transactions of the Royal Historical Society*, 4th series, vol. 29, 1947, pp. 1–17.

Somerville, R., *History of the Duchy of Lancaster*, vol. I, Duchy of Lancaster, 1953.

Somerville, R., *Office-Holders in the Duchy and County Palatine of Lancaster from 1603*, Phillimore, Chichester, 1972.

Spencer, F.H., *Municipal Origins. An Account of English Private Bill Legislation relating to Local Government, 1740–1835; with a Chapter on Private Bill Procedure*, Constable, 1911.

Squibb, G.D., *The High Court of Chivalry. A Study of the Civil Law in England*, Clarendon Press, Oxford, 1959.

Squibb, G.D., *Visitation Pedigrees and the Genealogist*, Pinhorns, 1978.

Stamp, L.D., and Hoskins, W.G., *The Common Lands of England and Wales*, Collin, 1963.

Steedman, C., *Policing the Victorian Community. The Formation of English Provincial Police Forces, 1856–80*, Routledge, 1984.

Steel, D.J., ed., *National Index of Parish Registers*, Society of Genealogists, 1966–.

Steer, F.W., see Redstone, L.J.

Stenton, D.M., ed., *Pleas before the King or his Justices*, Selden Society, vols. 67, 1948, 68, 1949, 83, 1966, 84, 1967.

Stephens, E., *The Clerks of the Counties 1360–1960*, Society of Clerks of the Peace of Counties and of Clerks of County Councils, 1961.

Stephens, W.B., *Sources for English Local History*, Cambridge University Press, 1981.

Stern, W.M., 'Water Supply in Britain: the Development of a Public Service', *Royal Sanitary Institute Journal*, vol. 77, 1954, pp. 998–1004.

Stockford, B., see Richmond, L.

Storey, R., 'Motor Vehicle Registers', *Archives*, vol. 8, 1965–6, pp. 91–2.

Storey, R., see also Druker, J.

Sugarman, D., see Rubin, G.R.

Sutherland, D.W., *Quo Warranto Proceedings in the Reign of Edward I, 1278–1294*, Clarendon Press, Oxford, 1963.

Sutherland, G., ed., *Studies in the Growth of Nineteenth-Century Government*, Routledge, 1972.

Sutherland, G., 'A View of Education Records in the Nineteenth and Twentieth Centuries', *Archives*, vol. 15, 1981–2, pp. 79–85.

Swales, R.J.W., 'The Ship Money Levy of 1628', *Bulletin of the Institute of Historical Research*, vol. 50, 1977, pp. 164–76.

Swann, B., and Turnbull, M., *Records of Interest to Social Scientists 1919 to 1939*, HMSO, 1971–8.

Swenarton, M., *Homes fit for Heroes. The Politics and Architecture of Early State Housing in Britain*, Heinemann, 1981.

Symons, L., 'Archives and Records of the Institution of Electrical Engineers', *Archives*, vol. 16, 1983–4, pp. 54–60.

Tait, J., see Ballard, A.

Tate, W.E., *The Parish Chest. A Study of the Records of Parochial Administration in England*, 3rd edition, Cambridge University Press, 1969.

Thomas, E.G., 'Pauper Apprenticeship', *The Local Historian*, vol. 14, 1980–1, pp. 400–406.

Thomas, I.C., *The Creation of the Welsh Office: conflicting purposes in institutional change*, Strathclyde University, Glasgow, 1981.

Thompson, D.M., 'The Religious Census of 1851', in Lawton, R., ed., *The Census and Social Structure. An Interpretative Guide to Nineteenth Century Censuses for England and Wales*, Cass, 1978, pp. 241–86.

Thompson, D.N., 'Wirral Hospital Records', *Journal of the Society of Archivists*, vol. 7, 1982–5, pp. 421–42.

Thompson, K.A., *Bureaucracy and Reform. The Organizational Response of the Church of England to Social Change 1800–1965*, Clarendon Press, Oxford, 1970.

Thomson, G.S., 'The Origin and Growth of the Office of Deputy-Lieutenant', *Transactions of the Royal Historical Society*, 4th series, vol. 5, 1922, pp. 150–66.

Thomson, G.S., *Lords Lieutenants in the Sixteenth Century. A Study in Tudor Local Administration*, Longman, 1923.

Thomson, M.A., *The Secretaries of State 1681–1782*, Cass, 1968.

Tittler, R., 'The Incorporation of Boroughs, 1540–1558', *History*, vol. 62, 1977, pp. 24–42.

Todd, G., 'Some Aspects of Joint Stock Companies, 1844–1900', *Economic History Review*, vol. 4, 1932–4, pp. 46–71.

Tompson, R., *The Charity Commission and the Age of Reform*, Routledge, 1979.

Troup, E., *The Home Office*, Putnam, 1925.

Turnbull, M., see Swann, B.

Turner, E.R., *The Privy Council of England in the Sixteenth and Seventeenth Centuries 1603–1784*, Johns Hopkins Press, Baltimore, 1927.

Turner, M.E., ed., *A Domesday of English Enclosure Acts and Awards by W.E. Tate*, Reading University Library, 1978.

Turner, M.E., 'Recent Progress in the Study of Parliamentary Enclosure', *The Local Historian*, vol. 12, 1976–7, pp. 18–25.

Turner, M.E., *English Parliamentary Enclosure: its Historical Geography and Economic History*, Dawson, Folkestone, 1980.

Turner, M.E., *Enclosure in Britain 1750–1830*, Macmillan, 1984.

Tyler, P., 'The Church Courts at York and the Witchcraft Persecutions 1567–1640', *Northern History*, vol. 4, 1969, pp. 84–110.

Tyler, P., see also Usher, R.G.

Usher, R.G., *The Rise and Fall of the High Commission*, 2nd ed. with intro. by Tyler, P., Clarendon Press, Oxford, 1968.

Vamplew, W., 'A Grain of Truth: the Nineteenth-Century Corn Averages', *Agricultural History Review*, vol. 28, 1980, pp. 1–17.

Varley, J., *The Parts of Kesteven. Studies in Law and Local Government*, Kesteven CC, 1974.

Veysey, A.G., 'Ecclesiastical Parish Records in Wales', *Journal of the Society of Archivists*, vol. 7, 1978–81, pp. 31–33.

Virgoe, R., 'The Parliamentary Subsidy of 1450', *Bulletin of the Institute of Historical Research*, vol. 55, 1982, pp. 125–37.

Wagner, A.R., *Records and Collections of the College of Arms*, Burke's Peerage, 1974.

Walker, D., 'Disestablishment and Independence', in Walker, D., ed., *A History of the Church in Wales*, Church in Wales, Penarth, 1976.

Walne, P., 'The Record Commissions, 1800–1830', *Journal of the Society of Archivists*, vol. 2, 1960–64, pp. 8–16.

Ward, J.R., 'The Administration of the Window and Assessed Taxes, 1696–1718', *English Historical Review*, vol. 67, 1952, pp. 522–42.

Ward, W.R., *The English Land Tax* in the Eighteenth Century, Oxford University Press, 1953.

Wardle, D.B., 'Sources for the History of Railways at the Public Record Office', *Journal of Transport History*, vol. 2, 1955–6, pp. 214–34.

Watts-Williams, J., see Williams, C.J.

Webb, C.C., *A Guide to Genealogical Sources in the Borthwick Institute of Historical Research*, Borthwick Institute of Historical Research, 1981.

Webb, S. and B., *The History of Liquor Licensing in England principally from 1700 to 1830*, Longman, 1903.

Webb, S. and B., *English Local Government from the Revolution to the Municipal Corporations Act*, Longman, 1906–29.

Webb, S. and B., *English Poor Law Policy*, Longman, 1910.

Weinbaum, M., *The Incorporation of Boroughs*, Manchester University Press, 1937.

Weinbaum, M., *British Borough Charters, 1307–1660*, Cambridge University Press, 1943.

Welch, C.E., 'The Records of the Church Commissioners', *Journal of the Society of Archivists*, vol. 1, 1955–9, pp. 14–16.

Welch, E., 'The Registration of Meeting Houses', *Journal of the Society of Archivists*, vol. 3, 1965–9, pp. 116–120.

West, J., *Town Records*, Phillimore, Chichester, 1983.

Western, J.R., *The English Militia in the Eighteenth Century. The Story of a Political Issue 1600–1832*, Routledge, 1965.

Westlake, H.F., *The Parish Gilds of Medieval England*, SPCK, 1919.

Whetham, E.H., see Orwin, C.S.

Whitehand, J.W.R., see Aspinall, P.J.

Willcox, W.B., *Gloucestershire. A Study in Local Government 1590–1640*, Yale University Press, New Haven, Conn., 1940.

Willan, T.S., 'The Justices of the Peace and the Rates of Land Carriage, 1692–1827', *Journal of Transport History*, vol. 5, 1962, pp. 197–204.

Willard, J.F., *Parliamentary Taxes on Personal Property 1290 to 1334. A Study in Medieval English Financial Administration*, Medieval Academy of America, Cambridge, Mass., 1934.

Willard, J.F., Morris, W.A., and Dunham, W.H., ed., *The English Government at Work, 1327–1336*, Medieval Academy of America, Cambridge, Mass., 1940–50.

Williams, A.H., 'Public Health and Local History', *The Local Historian*, vol. 14, 1980–1, pp. 202–10.

Williams, A.H., ed., 'Public Health in Mid-Victorian Wales. Correspondence from the Principality to the General Board of Health & the Local Government Act Office 1848–71', Unpublished typescript issued by the University of Wales Board of Celtic Studies, 1983.

Williams, C.J., and Watts-Williams, J., *Cofrestri Plwyf Cymru: Parish Registers of Wales*, National Library of Wales and Welsh County Archivists' Group, 1986.

Williams, D., *The Rebecca Riots. A Study in Agrarian Discontent*, University of Wales Press, Cardiff, 1955.

Williams, P.H., *The Council in the Marches of Wales under Elizabeth I*, University of Wales Press, Cardiff, 1958.

Williams, P.H., 'The Activities of the Council in the Marches under the Early Stuarts', *Welsh History Review*, vol. 1, 1960–63, pp. 133–60.

Williams, P.H., *The Tudor Regime*, Clarendon Press, Oxford, 1979.

Williams, W.Ll., 'The King's Court of Great Sessions in Wales', *Y Cymmrodor*, vol. 26, 1916, pp. 1–87.

Williams, W.R., *The History of the Great Sessions in Wales 1542–1830, together with the Lives of the Welsh Judges, and Annotated Lists of the Chamberlains and Chancellors, Attorney Generals, and Prothonotaries of the four Circuits of Chester and Wales; the Lord Presidents of Wales, and the Attorney Generals and Solicitor Generals of the Marches, compiled from the Patent Rolls and Welsh Records in the Record Office*, Brecknock, the Author, 1899.

Wilson, D., 'Public Records: the Wilson Report and the White Paper', *Historical Journal*, vol. 25, 1982, pp. 985–94.

Winnifrith, J., *The Ministry of Agriculture, Fisheries and Food*, Allen & Unwin, 1962.

Wiseman, H.V., ed., *Local Government in England 1958–69*, Routledge, 1970.

Wood, B., *The Process of Local Government Reform 1966–74*, Allen & Unwin, 1976.

Woodcock, B.L., *Medieval Ecclesiastical Courts in the Diocese of Canterbury*, Oxford University Press, 1952.

Woodcock, J., see Hill, C.

Wood-Legh, K.L., *Perpetual Chantries in Britain*, Cambridge University Press, 1965.

Woodward, D.M., 'Port Books', *History*, vol. 55, 1970, pp. 207–10.

Woodward, D.M., 'Freemen's Rolls', *The Local Historian*, vol. 9, 1970–1, pp. 89–95.

Woodward, D.M., 'The Background to the Statute of Artificers: the Genesis of Labour Policy, 1558–63', *Economic History Review*, 2nd series, vol. 33, 1980, pp. 32–44.

Wrigley, E.A., ed., *Nineteenth-Century Society. Essays in the Use of Quantitative Methods for the Study of Social Data*, Cambridge University Press, 1972.

Wrigley, E.A., and Schofield, R.S., *The Population History of England 1541–1871: A Reconstruction*, Edward Arnold, 1981.

Yale, D.E.C., *Lord Nottingham's Chancery Cases*, Selden Society, vols. 73, 1954 and 79, 1961.

Youings, J., 'The Council of the West', *Transactions of the Royal Historical Society*, 5th series, vol. 10, 1960, pp. 41–59.

Young, C.R., *The Royal Forests of Medieval England*, Leicester University Press, 1979.

Youngs, F.A., *Guide to the Local Administrative Units of England. I. Southern England*, Royal Historical Society, 1979.

Zell, M.L., 'Fifteenth- and Sixteenth-Century Wills as Historical Sources', *Archives*, vol. 14, 1979–80, pp. 67–74.

INDEX